CW00969850

MUSIC AS AN ART

MUSIC AS
AN ART

ROGER SCRUTON

BLOOMSBURY CONTINUUM
LONDON • NEW YORK • OXFORD • NEW DELHI • SYDNEY

BLOOMSBURY CONTINUUM
Bloomsbury Publishing Plc
50 Bedford Square, London, WC1B 3DP, UK

BLOOMSBURY, BLOOMSBURY CONTINUUM and the Diana logo are trademarks of
Bloomsbury Publishing Plc

First published in Great Britain 2018

The extract on p. 25 from Alexander Goehr's *Romanza* op. 24 for cello and orchestra is
reproduced by permission of Schott Music Ltd., London.

The extract on p. 26 from Sir James MacMillan's *Seven Last Words from the Cross* is
reproduced by permission of Boosey and Hawkes Music Publishers Ltd.

Lines on p. 155 from 'Funeral Music' by Geoffrey Hill in *Broken Hierarchies:
Poems 1952–2012* (2015), by permission of Oxford University Press.

A catalogue record for this book is available from the British Library

Library of Congress Cataloguing-in-Publication data has been applied for.

ISBN: HB: 978-1-4729-5571-5; EPDF: 978-1-4729-5570-8; EPUB: 978-1-4729-5572-2

2 4 6 8 10 9 7 5 3 1

Typeset by Newgen KnowledgeWorks Pvt. Ltd., Chennai, India
Printed and bound in Great Britain by CPI Group (UK) Ltd, Croydon CR0 4YY

MIX
Paper from
responsible sources
FSC® C020471

To find out more about our authors and books visit www.bloomsbury.com
and sign up for our newsletters.

CONTENTS

INTRODUCTION

This book pursues further the lines of enquiry that I launched in *The Aesthetics of Music* (Oxford University Press, 1997) and took up again in *Understanding Music* (Bloomsbury, 2009). Some of the chapters are new; some have been adapted from articles and discussions in journals, and I am grateful for the permission to reuse already published material. Some chapters derive from articles published on the website of the Future Symphony Institute, and it has been the inspiration provided by that admirable organization and its founder and director, Andy Balio, that has prompted me to bring my thoughts together in the present volume. We live at a critical time for classical music, and it is my hope that this book will contribute to the debate, of which we stand in need, concerning the place of music in Western civilization.

In earlier times our musical culture had secure foundations in the church, in the concert hall and in the home. The common practice of tonal harmony united composers, performers and listeners in a shared language, and people played instruments at home with an intimate sense of belonging to the music that they made, just as the music belonged to them. The repertoire was neither controversial nor especially challenging, and music took its place in the ceremonies and celebrations of ordinary life alongside the rituals of everyday religion and the forms of good manners.

We no longer live in that world. Music at home largely emerges from digital machines, controlled by buttons that require no musical culture to be pressed. For many people, the young especially, music is a form of largely solitary enjoyment, to be absorbed without judgement and stored without effort in the brain. The circumstances of music-making have therefore changed radically, and this is reflected not only in the melodic and harmonic content of popular music but also in the radical *avoidance* of tonal melody and harmony in the 'modern classical' repertoire.

In these new circumstances we can no longer assume that our musical tradition can be passed on merely by encouraging young people to listen to the works that we value. We have to teach them to make discriminations, to recognize that there is both good taste and bad taste in music, that there really are musical values, as well as musical pleasures. Twenty-five years ago, when I took up a position as University Professor at Boston University, I was asked to teach a graduate seminar on the philosophy of music – a request that I welcomed, since it gave me the opportunity to work on themes that had interested me for many years. The seminar was heavily subscribed, and it was immediately clear on entering the classroom that the students were all on my side. This is, or was, the normal experience in an American university. The students wanted me to succeed, since my success was theirs. But it was soon also clear that we had entirely conflicting conceptions of the subject. I assumed that we would be discussing the classical tradition, as a repository of meaning and a fundamental part of our civilization. I assumed that the students would be ardent listeners, maybe also performers, who had been moved to ask, in the wake of some intense experience, what does this music mean? Why does it affect me so deeply, and why has my world been so radically changed by hearing it?

It was only after I had introduced the topic with a recording of Mendelssohn's 'Hebrides' overture that I realized what a difficult position I was in. Of the 30 or so students in the classroom, only 2 had heard the work before – this work that I and my classmates at our local English grammar school had known by heart at the age of 16! Of the remaining students only half could say that they had heard much classical music, and almost all had assumed that I was going to get a discussion going around Hip-Hop, Heavy Metal and the pop groups of the day, such as U2, Guns N' Roses and AC/DC.

Two things soon became clear, however. First, students encountering classical music in the context of study quickly understood that it is serious, in a way that much popular music is not. Secondly, all of them became aware that, when music is properly listened to, judgement of some kind is unavoidable. Listening is a time-consuming and intellect-involving process. It is not the same as hearing something in the background. Listening means singling something out for special attention: you are absorbing, interrogating and evaluating what you hear. Whether the music is worth this kind of attention is a question that arises spontaneously in all who listen seriously.

Taste in music is not like taste in ice-cream: it is not a brute fact, beyond the reach of rational argument. It is based in comparisons, and in experiences that have had a special significance. However impoverished a student's experience, I discovered, it will not, under examination, remain at the level of 'that's what I like'. The question 'why?' pushes itself to the foreground, and the idea that there is a distinction between right and wrong very soon gets purchase.

Those schooled in jazz improvisation understood free improvisation as a discipline, in which chord sequences encode elaborate instructions for voicing and rhythmical emphasis, as well as for the notes of each chord. They knew that one and the same sequence will sound natural and harmonious or jumbled and awkward, depending on the movement of the voices from one place to the next. With a little bit of attention all my students could begin to hear that the voice-leading in U2's 'Street with No Name' is a mess, with the bass guitar drifting for bar after bar.

Jazz improvisation lays great stress on melody, and on the punctuation of melody by semi-closures and ornaments around a note. Pop, however, is increasingly devoid of melody, or based on repeated notes and fragments of the scale, kept together by the drum kit, as it drives the bar-lines into the chords like nails into a coffin. Students would quickly recognize the difference between the standard entry of a pop song, over a relentless four-in-a-bar from the drummer, and the flexible and syncopated melody introduced without any background beat by the solo voice in Elvis's 'Heartbreak Hotel'. In the one case the rhythm is as though added to the music, coming into it from outside, and without respect for the melodic line. In the other case the rhythm arises internally, as it were, being precipitated out from the melody.

3

Pointing out those purely formal differences among pieces of popular music, I discovered, took students a long way towards recognizing what is at stake in the art of listening – namely, the ability to absorb many things at once, and to understand the contribution of each part to the whole. Almost all my students had come to the class with a desire to understand why so much of the music they heard elicited the 'yuk' feeling, while every now and then a song touched them in a way that really mattered – a way they would want to share with someone close to them. So they were ready for the distinction between music that is put together from ready-made effects and music that grows from its own melodic inspiration. Gradually they became aware that songs can have a moral character, not by virtue of their words only, but by virtue of their musical setting. Even in the world of pop there is a clear distinction between kitsch like Toni Braxton's 'Un-break my Heart', immensely popular at the time, and straightforward sentiment, as in the Beatles' most memorable numbers from a quarter of a century before.

Teaching students to make those judgements opened the way to an interesting dialogue between us. I was particularly struck by the Heavy Metal fans, of which my class contained a few. Metal was just beginning to gain a following. It was conceived from the outset as an assault on popular music from a position within it – a kind of subversive rebellion against the norms of weepy sentimentality and gross seductiveness, a reaffirmation of the masculine in a feminized culture. The often psychedelic words, croaked with ape-like *Sprechgesang* over hectic drumming, the improvised melodies in the virtuoso riffs, often on two guitars in heterophonic conjunction, the irregular bar-lines and asymmetrical phrases – all this was like a great 'No' shouted on to the dance-floor from the dark jungle that surrounded it. True Metal fans could talk about its merits for hours, and it amazed me that they had such a precise knowledge of the chords required at every moment, and of the importance of the bass line in maintaining the tension behind the voice. The words, it seemed to me, were pseudo-poetry: but it was nevertheless as poetry that they were judged, since the gasping and croaking that produced them were expressly meant to neutralize all expectations of a melodic kind. In the realm of pop they were the modernists, undergoing in their own way that revulsion again kitsch and cliché that had set Schoenberg and Adorno on the path towards 12-tone serialism.

Encouraging students to judge meant teaching them to listen, and it was never long before their listening extended to the classical repertoire. Jazz enthusiasts had no difficulty in making the transition, but almost all of my students had a problem with the attention span demanded by classical music. Both jazz and pop are largely cyclical in structure – the same tune, chord sequence, riff or chorus comes round again and again until it comes to a stop or fades out. Classical music is rarely cyclical in that way. It consists of thematic and harmonic material that is developed, so that the music moves constantly onwards, extracting more and more significance from the original musical impulse. Should it return to the beginning, as in the recapitulation of a sonata-form movement or the returning first subject of a rondo, it will usually be in order to present the material in a new way, or with new harmonic implications. Moreover, rhythmic organization in classical music is seldom of the ostinato form familiar from pop. Divisions within the bar-lines, syncopations and ties reflect the ongoing melodic process, and cannot be easily anticipated.

Such features, I discovered, are for many young people the real obstacle presented by the classical idiom. Classical music demands an extended act of attention. No detail can be easily anticipated or passed over, and there is no 'backing' – that is to say, no beat to carry you through the difficult bits. (We are familiar with the attempts to rectify this – Tchaikovsky's Fifth with drum-kit backing, which is perhaps the most painful of all musical experiences for the lover of the classical repertoire.) Among modern composers there are several – Steve Reich and John Adams, for example – who cultivate ostinato rhythms in order to reach through all the obstacles to the pop-trained ear. When my students finally opened the door into the realm of symphonic music, Adams's 'A Short Ride in a Fast Machine' was soon added to their list of favourites, precisely because it is sustained throughout by ostinato rhythms, and sounds like a sprinkle of intriguing ornaments on a sturdy rhythmical Christmas tree.

My students showed me what it was that drew me to classical music, and why the search for that thing is worthwhile. They made me conscious of the thing that my music possessed and theirs for the most part seemed to lack, namely *argument*. Music in the classical tradition embodies meaning in the form of melody and harmony and, instead of repeating what it has found, *works* on it, extracting its implications, building a life story around it and, in doing so, exploring emotional possibilities that we might not otherwise have guessed at. Musical arguments of this kind invite judgement: they place themselves in the centre of our lives and invite us to sympathize, to find a resolution for our own conflicts in the resolutions that they work for.

Eventually most of my students came to appreciate this. But it was the Metal fans who saw the point most clearly, since their music had been for them exactly what Mozart had been for me, namely a door out of banality and ordinariness into a world where you, the listener, become caught up in a process of shared emotional development. And I took comfort from the thought that, at my age, when they had put Metal aside as a dead end, they would still be listening to Mozart.

In the chapters that follow I explore some of the conceptual issues suggested by those attempts to justify our musical inheritance and the culture of listening. My aim is not to put ideas in the place where music should be, but to use ideas as a path into music.

Malmesbury, October 2017

Part I

Philosophical Investigations

1

When is a Tune?

The English word 'tune' does not have any simple equivalent in other European languages. The German *Ton* means sound or tone, while *Weise* has the primary meaning of manner, style or custom, and features as a borrowed term in the description of music. 'Melody', from Greek *melos*, has its equivalent in other languages – German *Melodie*, French *mélodie*, Italian *melodia* etc. – but in all languages the implication is of something more extended, and more integrated into a musical argument than the artless 'tune'. Italian has the term *aria*, followed by French and English *air*, whose more central meaning reminds us of the way in which tunes were originally produced. The term occurs in 'Londonderry Air', the name of a paradigm popular tune, half folk-tune, collected by Jane Ross in County Derry in the nineteenth century and published in 1855 (the words of 'Danny Boy' added later by Fred Weatherly). German borrows the term too, but in the *Aria mit verschiedenen Veränderungen* that Bach allegedly composed for Count Kaiserling and his resident harpsichordist, Johann Gottlieb Goldberg, it denotes a piece of melodic and harmonic thinking that is very far from what the English know as a tune.

'Song', *Lied*, *chant* and *canto* denote an entire musical episode, and there are tuneless songs, just as there are tunes that cannot easily be sung, such as the first subject of Rachmaninov's second piano concerto – tuneful though it certainly is – or which contain leaps that can be managed only by the trained voice – like the first subject of Strauss's *Don Juan*. And by using the term 'subject' to describe those examples I have implied something about their inner nature – as the starting points of musical arguments. The Greek word 'theme', which has been adopted into French, English, German and Italian, expresses a similar idea, and the tradition of Western classical music abounds in themes which, for all their intrinsic interest as musical units, are far from being tunes – the theme that opens Beethoven's Fifth Symphony, for example (more gesture than tune), the theme of the Passacaglia from Brahms's Fourth or the opening subject of Mozart's D minor piano concerto, K. 466. A theme can comprise many tunes or tuneful fragments – like the opening theme of Bruckner's Seventh Symphony or that of Elgar's Second. And a tune can govern works, such as the movements of a Tchaikovsky ballet, which have nothing deserving the name of a theme.

The distinctions here are in the first instance verbal, and may have little bearing on the underlying musical reality. Nevertheless, the questions that they naturally provoke tell us something important about music, and in particular about the idea of a musical *individual*, which we can know and love as a whole. Tunes illustrate the way in which repeatable musical individuals have arisen from the human need to sing and dance. Not every musical culture lays stress on the tune, but all – or almost all – have some form of melody, and regard melody as essential to the musical individual that contains it. (The most important exception to that generalization is African drum music, which reproduces in the dimension of rhythm some of the complexities that we know from melodic voice-leading.[1])

The shapes, lengths and intervals of melodies vary wildly from culture to culture, and it is difficult to give a general account that distinguishes genuine melody from a mere sequence of pitches. Melody is something that we hear *in* a sequence of pitched sounds, and which is not a material property of the sound sequence itself. We can therefore hear melody in birdsong, even though this melody is something that birds, which lack imagination and the grouping experiences that

[1] See Gunther Schuller, *Early Jazz: Its Roots and Musical Development* (Oxford, 1968).

Ex. 1

derive from it, cannot hear.[2] With certain qualifications, a melody is a single line in musical space, in which each tone is joined to its neighbours in a sequence, the whole extending an invitation to sing along, or to move in sympathy.

So understood, we can divide melodies roughly into the melismatic, the thematic, the cellular and those that are also tunes. The class of melismatic melodies includes plainchant, raga and certain kinds of Rock – idioms in which the momentum pushes easily through harmonic and rhythmic boundaries, and often has no full closure. Thematic melodies include the themes and 'subjects' of our own classical tradition, in which elements develop in new directions and move towards closures not contained within the original statement. Cellular melodies include the 'motivic cells' of much modern music – little phrases that can be repeated and developed without losing their recognizable contour, as in Ex. 1, from the Schoenberg violin concerto, dividing a 12-tone series into two hexachords arranged as a repeated pitch-pattern. Such phrases capture the attention of the listener largely because of their repeatable *Gestalt*. The rise of the motivic cell preceded the decline of the tune, with Beethoven and Wagner using motivic cells both standing alone and also wrapped into melodies, as in the famous first subject of the Fifth Symphony.

The fourth kind of melody, the tune, which is my topic here, is bounded, usually at each end, contains a distinctive and recognizable internal order and is regarded as a complete individual, to be memorized as a whole. And among tunes we can make a further division, between those associated with word-setting (the logogenic), those that are invitations to the dance (the orchegenic) and those that arise from and express the harmonic relations of the tones that they

---

[2] See the argument of Roger Scruton, *Art and Imagination* (London, 1974), Part 1.

contain (the harmonegenic). Folk music contains tunes of all three kinds, though the harmonegenic are more typical of 'art music', or music influenced by art music, like Blues and Ragtime.

Plainchants are often instantly recognizable and thrilling to the ear – like the *Dies Irae*, the *Hodie Christus natus est* or the *Veni Creator Spiritus*. They are melodious, but are they tunes? Berlioz turns the *Dies Irae* into a tune, but only by squeezing it into diatonic harmony and destroying its modal character. A plainsong chant exhibits another kind of order from the tune – it is a fragment of eternity, which has neither beginning nor end in the scheme of things. It flows endlessly, and that which we know as the beginning is simply the point where the voices enter. We hear the movement of the chant as preceding the entry of the voices, which are 'taking up' a melody that flows in the cosmos unendingly and for the most part silently. Plainsong presents us with another idea of the melodic individual, one that seems not to belong to *us* but to exist eternally in another realm – to exist, indeed, not as a concrete individual but as an unending chant, only segments of which can be captured by finite beings. And, of course, that is part of its meaning, and one reason why these melodies and the performance tradition that protects them, and which has been many times lost and recovered, are important to us.

Two features serve to characterize melody in all its forms. First there is the internal constraint exerted by every note on every other. A melody is a sequence in which no note can be altered without changing the character of the whole. This feature was pointed out by Edmund Gurney: the 'wrong note' phenomenon causes us to cry out in protest at every departure from the known musical line.[3] A non-melodic sequence of tones can be chopped and changed without eliciting protests. But all changes in a melody are noticed, and most condemned as wrong. If a composer is able to change a melody and take it in a new direction – for example, so as to end in another key – this is regarded as an achievement, like that of Berg in incorporating the whole-tone melody of Bach's *Es ist genug* into the last movement of the violin concerto.

[3] Edmund Gurney, *The Power of Sound* (London, 1880), pp. 92–4.

Ex. 2

The second feature that characterizes melody is that of the boundary. Melodies have a beginning and (usually) an end, and often half-endings along the way – though the ending may be postponed until the close of a section or a movement, as in the last movement of Bach's Third Brandenburg Concerto and much other baroque music. Hearing a melody begin is one of the fundamental musical experiences, and it is very difficult to describe what exactly it is that you hear when this happens.

The boundary experience and the 'wrong note' experience are familiar at the phenomenological level, but they do not correspond to any fixed features of the sound sequence. A melody can pass through any note on the diatonic scale, tonic included, without generating the sense of an ending; and it can also end on any note, even a note that does not belong to the scale, as in Ex. 2, from Debussy's *Prélude à l'après-midi d'un faune*. The experience of hearing a melody begin and end is, in other words, *sui generis*, and not reducible to the recognition of any definable pattern in a sound sequence. A melody is a purely *intentional* object of musical perception, something we hear in a sequence when we respond to its musical potential.

Individuality, like the individuality revealed in a face, clings to a tune as to few other musical units. A tune is a melodic whole; it has an expression. It has a beginning, a middle and (in most cases) an end. It may also begin with an upbeat, which both is and is not a part of the tune, and the question whether a tone or a phrase is an upbeat is one on which much may hang and which does not yield an easy answer.

Consider the first three notes of the 'Londonderry Air' – to describe them as an upbeat is to misrepresent the significance they assume as the song proceeds, with just such three-note entrance figures repeated four times, and three-note exit figures occasionally matching them: Ex. 3. I give the tune in full, since this 'air' is such an instructive example. The tune advances towards closure

Ex. 3

through a sequence of half-closures, each pausing on an implied harmony from the basic triads of the key, and one (the G in bar 24) suggesting a brief modulation from tonic to dominant, in preparation for the triumphant return: virtually all the techniques of tune craft are here.

A tune may be diatonically tonal, like 'The Sweet Nightingale', modal, like the English folksong 'Scarborough Fair', pentatonic, like the Scottish folk song 'Skye Boat Song', or even atonal, like the tune that opens Schoenberg's violin concerto. But it must have a beginning, and it should work its way forward, even if, like the tune from Rachmaninov mentioned earlier, it peters out, rather than settling on some final full stop. One of the complaints made by Adorno against the American music industry is that it highlights the tune in place of the theme, and so curtails all possibility of extended musical thinking.[4] His point is that the American popular song has opted for melodic statement against thematic development – in other words,

---

[4] See Theodor Adorno, 'The Musical Fetish and the Regression of Listening', in *The Essential Frankfurt School Reader*, ed. Andrew Arato and Eike Gephardt (New York, 1997), and also 'Popular Song', in *An Introduction to the Sociology of Music*, tr. E. B. Ashton (New York, 1976). See my account of Adorno's thinking in 'Why Read Adorno', in *Understanding Music* (London, 2009).

that it belongs to the tradition of strophic singing rather than patient listening. And its tunes, moreover, come from a fixed repertoire, assembled from familiar phrases, and present no challenge to the ear. Pick up the songbook from any year between 1920 and 1970 and you will find a selection of 32-bar 'numbers': strophic songs consisting of two internally related tunes, the one reserved for the verse, the other for the chorus. This format speaks of the social meaning of the songbook, which consists of so many dialogues between narrator and audience, between the interesting outsider with a story to tell and the community to which he or she appeals. But the American songbook consists only of tunes – alone or paired with a chorus – and tunes which seem so firmly encased in their own unified movement as to stand alone, refusing the very idea of development.

The baroque 'air' is frequently the subject of variation, in which the underlying harmonic progression provides the anchor (as in the Goldberg Variations); the classical theme is the subject of development, which may involve breaking down the theme into its elements, diminishing and augmenting its rhythmical order, elaborating particular phrases and so on. The American song cannot easily be treated in that way: it bursts through any attempt to vary it, wearing the same sociable expression, and demanding the same harmonic sofa on which to sit. It refuses to be discomposed into thematic fragments, and is intrinsically resistant to the classical forms of development. Performers will 'improvise around a tune', without really varying or developing it, and even if it is the harmonic sequence, rather than the melodic line, that is taken as the subject, the improvisations will preserve the outline of the tune and seldom work towards a tune of their own.

The American songbook is only one example of a tradition of popular music centred on the tune. The folksong traditions of Europe and America are similar, and so are many liturgical traditions. The hymnbook is a particularly interesting case, since it shows in all clarity just why tunes are needed. The strophic tune is the companion of the strophic verse form. And whether the verse tells a story or simply praises God, it can be easily memorized only if it has a repeatable pattern: and this pattern is most easily memorized when sung.

This gives a clue to the nature of tunes. The paradigm use of a tune is in a song, with or without chorus. Its beginning, middle and end mirror the beginning, middle and end of verse stanzas. It has a form analogous to a sentence – a clear statement of *where we have got to* in a narrative, which advances by rhythmic and sentential repetition. A tune can bear being many times repeated without variation; and if it is so rarely varied, this is in part because of its solid and bounded character, which resists the attempt to dissolve it in a narrative larger than itself.

Folk songs in the European tradition are also strophic, and this form survives in the verses long after the music has been lost – as in so many of the border ballads and other relics collected in the eighteenth century. (The term 'ballad' is cognate with 'ballet', Italian *ballata* – not something sung, but something danced. Again we are seeing through etymology into the social origins of music in all its popular forms.) Tunes appeal to us because they return us to the strophic order of the hymn and the ballad – the memorable melody that carries a burden of meaning bestowed by words. But their order is a musical order: their devices are those whereby one phrase answers, continues or concludes another. And in all forms they exemplify the way in which tones organize themselves in musical units, so as to create boundaries at both ends of a sequence, and an intelligible contour between them.

It is this experience of the boundary that is most mysterious and most fundamental to the evolution of melody in Western music. It has an evident relation to a phenomenon that we know from our experience of language. Sentences in a language begin and end, and the words that occur in the middle are heard as embedded in the whole. We can explain this experience in terms of the cognitive processes whereby we recuperate from the surface structure the deep structure that generates it, and theories of deep structure will eventually be semantically grounded. The very process whereby we create meanings in words imposes the boundaries and continuities that we hear in language. Music, however, is not semantically organized, and the boundary experience cannot be explained in that way.

There are places where melodies typically start, and (in the Western tradition) places where they typically end. One explanation of the 'upbeat' experience is that the melody is being led to its starting point, both rhythmically, by a 'left-over' beat, and melodically, by an entry on the dominant, as in many British, German and American folk songs. Often the upbeat is required by the verse, when it opens (as in so many English and German examples) with a definite or indefinite article. Thus in 'Lovely Joan' (Chapter 5, Ex. 1, below), which begins, 'A fair young man it was indeed', the article is given to the upbeat. Many folk tunes start *beyond* the boundary, but on the downbeat, as though preceded by a kind of musical glottal stop. A spoken language may place the accent on the first syllable of a word, as in Czech or Hungarian; and there are languages, such as those two, in which articles, whether definite or indefinite, are not routinely used. Hence Czech and Hungarian folk songs tend to begin on the downbeat, preceded by a pronounced but inaudible boundary (Ex. 4, *Kvíti milodějné*).

When we listen to a song, we cross a boundary *into* the tune, either after a few measures or at the very outset: and we know that we have crossed that boundary immediately, by recognizing that each note that occurs thereafter is linked to its predecessor as a note in a tune. What are we hearing when we hear this? The first thing that we hear is *direction*: each note leads *to* its successor. This is a distinctively musical experience and not one that is easily replicated in language, where the position of words is determined by their meaning, rather than by any heard motion from word to word along the time-dimension.

We also hear that the tune is moving to a goal: a place where it comes to an end, so that anything occurring after that point does not belong to the tune, unless the tune has begun again. Scales, modes

Ex. 4

Cho di ła po ro-li' tr-ha-ła kú-ko-lí, aj tú do-bro-my-sel, co by šo-haj při-šél.

and harmonic relations will make it more natural for a tune to end on certain notes – usually on the tonic, if there is one. But not every tonic is heard as a conclusion, and even when a tune comes back to the tonic by scale degrees from the dominant, we may not hear it as having come to an end. Instructive in this respect is 'Baa, baa, Black Sheep', which returns to the tonic and then, continuing an impulse that has not been concluded, goes back to the dominant to try again. And after the second occurrence of the tonic there is no conceivable way in which this tune could be prolonged: any attempt to prolong it will produce another musical individual, and not an expanded form of this one.

That last feature is in part definitive of the tune, as opposed to the theme. Bach's fugal subjects in the *Forty-Eight* are melodious, often catchy, as in 17 of Book I or 7 of Book II, and they have very definite beginnings, rarely with upbeats, since their entry is integral to their dramatic and structural purpose. But they are open at the other end, can be continued *ad lib.*, and also concluded, should the need arise. Something similar can be said of the great themes of the classical repertoire, such as the opening theme of Beethoven's Ninth or the equally great but far more seductive theme that opens Schubert's A minor quartet (the 'Rosamunde'; Ex. 5).

This last theme is a model, since it is so near, in its lyrical melodiousness, to being a tune, and yet so far from it. The theme begins with a phrase that leads naturally to a semi-closure on the tonic. But this is at once repeated with an interpolated phrase, making an asymmetrical variant that now refuses to come to a close: gradually the theme moves on, throwing out phrases that invite (and in due course receive) separate elaboration, and ceasing only when the music has moved into the major key before returning to the minor on a sturdy and slightly menacing downbeat.

By contrast with such themes, a tune is boxed in at both ends, and it is because of this, indeed, that tunes are so easy to remember. Adorno's lament over the 'pre-digested' nature of the melodies that figured in the popular songs of his time[5] seems unpersuasive to us today, partly

---

[5] Adorno, 'Popular Song'.

Ex. 5

because we recognize what has been lost by a society that has no memory bank of song. Pop has become so dependent on the backing for its musical movement that it cannot really be retained as melody, and young people who wish to sing their favourite songs very often cannot sing them at work or while walking, but must wait for Karaoke Night at the pub, when they have the benefit of an external musical movement. In a very real sense they may have no internal repertoire of songs, even though they can recognize hundreds of them.

By contrast, it is interesting to consider a musical culture in which the tune retained a central place – a culture that endured into my lifetime, and which can still be encountered here and there in Wales and in North America – the culture of the English hymnal. During the eighteenth century the hymn became the symbol and triumph of the non-conformist churches, providing to the ordinary congregation the means to memorize holy words and theological doctrines while rehearsing their membership through uplifting song. The Church of England meanwhile kept close to the metrical psalter, which retains the open-ended flow of plainsong, without the melodic seduction. The metrical psalter emphasizes the venerable and untouchable nature of the psalms, sung above and behind the service, as though in some antique realm where the dead mutter endlessly among themselves while we gather to listen, hoping to catch some fragment of their wisdom. No wonder, however, that the people began to drift away.

It was not until 1769 that the first church hymnbook for general use was published in England – though the idea of a hymnbook was far from new. In 1589 Palestrina had published a Latin hymnal – the *Hymni totius anni* – in which the old plainsong chants are measured out in bar-lines and developed polyphonically for the daily use of church choirs: but those gorgeous settings had fallen under the same puritan interdiction as plainsong itself. The English hymnbook expressed a late and reluctant recognition that music is not a distraction from the religious message but a way of communicating it – more, a way of memorizing it and integrating that memory into social life.

Wesleyanism was intimately bound up from the beginning with our native tradition of choral music-making. Hymns passed freely from the non-conformist to the established Church and back again, so that by the middle of the nineteenth century the hymn was the living symbol of the English churches, and of the unity in diversity that made these churches into a single and singular social force. The Church revival brought back many of the old Latin hymns, along with the more dignified products of the German Reformation. Operatic dross was discarded in favour of solid, psalm-like melodies, and these were again the common property of the English churches.

Hymns Ancient and Modern first appeared in 1861. It has no liturgical authority, and was quickly followed by scores of non-conformist songbooks, as well as *Church Hymns* and *The Hymnal Companion to the Book of Common Prayer*. The *English Hymnal* was published in 1906, edited by the young Ralph Vaughan Williams, who added to it some of the most popular of modern hymn tunes, including 'Sine Nomine' ('For All the Saints') and 'Down Ampney' ('Come Down O Love Divine'). The first of those tunes is remarkable for its descending upbeat, reminiscent of the opening of Tchaikovsky's first piano concerto. This upbeat can equally be heard as a downbeat, and pushes the melody forward to the glorious 'Hallelujah', which is such a fitting conclusion even though rhythmically and melodically a completely new departure (Ex. 6).

Look back over this wealth of musical and poetic material, and you will be struck not only by its vitality but also by its extraordinary continuity: except for periods of puritanical zeal, the hymn has grown organically with the Church. The hymnal, like the Bible, has been common property of the established and non-conformist churches, even though hymn-singing was originally forbidden by the Anglican episcopate. The Book of Common Prayer, by contrast, is a specifically Anglican text, although its language permeates the liturgy of all English-speaking churches. The hymns have been shaped by the liturgy; but they in turn have shaped the services of the churches. They have provided the important moments of participation, in which God is praised and worshipped in song, and the drama of the service is momentarily interrupted by the chorus. They have replaced the psalms as vehicles of collective sentiment, and the psalms in their turn have become part of the liturgy. The hymns emancipated themselves from orthodoxy by virtue of their musical power, becoming the foundation of a popular musical culture centred on non-conformist worship. The Labour movement would not have been the peaceful thing it was without the repertoire of hymns that gathered people in congregations, rather than in armies, behind the brass bands of the collieries.

Ex. 6

The very language of English Romanticism, from Parry and Stanford through Elgar and Holst to Vaughan Williams, Ireland and Bax, is saturated with the idiom of the hymnal. Song and collective worship form the background to their music; and it is hardly surprising to discover that some of our most memorable hymns come from their pens. I have already mentioned two of Vaughan Williams's contributions; and everybody knows Parry's 'Jerusalem', adopted by the brass-band movement as its signature tune, and John Ireland's popular setting from 1925 of 'Love Unknown'.

As composers felt the influence, first of folk song and then of Debussy, the harmonization of the hymns changed. Significant in this respect is the *Oxford Book of Carols*, produced in 1928 by Percy Dearmer, Ralph Vaughan Williams and Martin Shaw, as part of a conscious return to a more folk-inspired musical tradition. Vaughan Williams's harmonizations lean over backwards to avoid accidentals, delight in parallel fourths and in general make no concessions to the diatonic scale when a modal harmony seems to be implied by the melodic line. (Witness his harmonization of 'Away in a Manger', which succeeds in de-kitschifying a carol that has been responsible for more puking over the years than all the excesses of Christmas dinner.)

Hymns Ancient and Modern has more or less disappeared from our churches; the *Anglican Hymn Book*, from which many of the Victorian classics have been dropped, is itself being replaced by *Mission Praise*, which, while retaining many of the old hymns in their original settings, shows a marked preference for the happy-clappy over the solemn and the patriotic. Tunes, unlike themes, can enter the market place of popular taste. Those solid borders become flabby and permeable, and those compelling sequences somehow lose their strength. The voice of a living community is no longer heard in the old tunes, but only the echo of a community that was, while the kitsch that has replaced them reminds us of the very thing that kitsch always lacks – the firm foundation in belief that enables people to sing out strongly and rejoice in sincere emotion.

In the decline of the hymn tune, therefore, we witness in poignant form the phenomenon to which Adorno devoted his most acerbic criticism, and which he believed to be indicative of the collapse not of the tune or the song only but of tonality itself. To put it in Adorno's way: that which was once the free expression of a sincere faith has entered the world of commodities, there to be deprived of its aura. It has become a consumer product, addressed to the addictive ear, part of the 'regression of listening' which refuses true creativity in favour of the predictable, the effortless and the banal.[6] And this raises the question of whether tunes have a future, not in pop music only but also in the concert hall. In particular, can we loosen the hold of tonality, shake ourselves free from the lure of keys and modulations and still write recognizable tunes that listeners can keep in their hearts as they keep the melodies of Mozart, Verdi or Bach? I shall conclude with a few thoughts, some of which will be elaborated in the chapters that follow.

There is a distinction between the little tune, which may be less than a tune, and the big tune. The big tunes of Tchaikovsky, Rachmaninov, Sibelius, Elgar and others belong to another age, in which composers did not step back from their work in order to ask themselves 'Do I really mean this, and can I mean it sincerely?' It is true that, even in the hyper-critical atmosphere of the Second Viennese School, the big tune occasionally appears, as in the tune below, in which the dying Countess Geschwitz sings out her undying love for Berg's Lulu (Ex. 7). For the most part, however, melodic thinking in modern music is devoted to motivic cells, which can be combined into melodious sequences but do not have that ineffable 'invitation' with which a tune begins, or the closure, the QED with which it normally ends. Tunes give way to short flutters that separate and coalesce, pursuing each other through the surface of the music, as in the tightly composed chamber works of Alexander Goehr, as though to remind the listener that it is not the surface but the deep organization that counts. Maybe tunes were a passing feature of the concert-hall tradition, a relic of the folk songs and hymn tunes that belonged to a

---

[6] See especially Adorno's essay on 'Jazz', in *Night Music: Essays on Music 1928–1962*, ed. Rolf Tiedemann, tr. Wieland Hoban (London and New York, 2009).

Ex. 7

world of spontaneous music-making. Maybe our ears are becoming used to shorter and tighter musical *Gestalten*, and turning away from big tunes as things too heavy for the new kind of gossamer musical fabric.

The absence of a tune does not mean the absence of melody. Melodic organization exists wherever notes flow from each other, gathering into phrases and promoting in the listener the sense of a continuous movement within a temporal boundary. Moreover melodies can make musical sense without making tonal sense. Even without tonality there may be the rhythmic and spatial organization that enables us to hear one note as an appropriate successor to the note before. The distinction between 'right' and 'wrong' notes may be weakened in modernist compositions; but the result is not for that reason arbitrary. The 'plink selon plonk' of Boulez and Stockhausen was part of a sustained assault on the audience: the punishment administered by visiting angels to the mortals who had spoiled the world with their kitsch emotions. Released from those dominating egos, composers have reconnected with the ordinary ear, acknowledging that melodic movement is the *sine qua non* of the musical invitation. This invitation to 'move with' the music is, to take just one illustrative example, vividly present in the opening melisma of Goehr's *Romanza* for cello

Ex. 8

and orchestra, in which phrases establish themselves by repetition and imitation (Ex. 8). This piece offers a paradigm of what can be done with atonal melody, when the intervals are conceived as invitations from one note to the next, and harmonic implications are not denied but exploited.

The invitation to move is extended in an even more original way by Britten in *Curlew River*, in which voices hover around a shared sequence of pitches, creating close harmonies without being led by them, and listeners move as it were in the wake of the music, fitting their footsteps to sounds that are dwindling just ahead of them. A similar kind of heterophony occurs in James MacMillan's *Seven Last Words from the Cross*, in the beautiful meditation that closes the work ('Father, into thy hands I commend my spirit'). Here the two violin parts weave a melody that neither of them plays and which cannot be heard as a single line. It is a single melody, but woven from two elements, like two hands wrung in grief (Ex. 9). It is a melody that cannot be sung by a single voice, but which is heard nevertheless as a distinct melodic individual.

There is, in such melodic writing, a move back from the static heritage of the Second Viennese School, in which notes stand against each other charged with negative electricity, towards a new spirit of co-operation, in which notes join together, whether in joy or in grief. Such examples suggest new forms of genuinely melodic thinking.

Ex. 9

Tunes (and big tunes especially) may be out. So too are the mathematically conceived structures of late serialism, in which the treatment of each note as a meticulously polished individual creates a fabric in which, paradoxically, everything sounds the same. Motivic cells, and melodies woven from several lines, extend once again an invitation to the listener. Here is your soul, they say, captured in music.

2

Music and Cognitive Science

Many animals have the capacity to hear music, but only humans, I suspect, hear music as music. What is involved in this capacity, and what do we gain from its exercise? Why and how might it have arisen, and what evolutionary function does it serve?

Books and articles on the cognitive neuroscience of music have proliferated in recent years, and there is a great need, it seems to me, to get clear as to what they are about. Here is a definition of music taken from a recent article by Ian Cross, appearing in a collection devoted to *The Cognitive Neuroscience of Music*:

> Musics are cultural particularisations of the human capacity to form multiply-intentional representations through integrating information across different functional domains of temporally extended or sequenced human experience and behaviour, generally expressed in sound.[7]

I think ordinary music lovers would be bewildered by that way of describing the art of Mozart. And they would want to know by what theoretical path the author could have arrived at such a definition: in the service of what intellectual agenda, and on the strength of what experience of the thing itself?

---

[7] Ian Cross, 'Music, Cognition, Culture and Evolution', in Isabelle Peretz and Robert Zatorre, *The Cognitive Neuroscience of Music* (Oxford, 2003), p. 52.

First, there is a certain picture of the human condition that motivates much of the recent research in this area. According to this picture, human beings are evolved organisms, whose distinctive capacities are to be explained as adaptations acquired in the course of a long but ever-accelerating trajectory from the ape-like condition of their ancestors. There are many puzzling features of human beings; but they will cease to be puzzling, once we see how they emerged through the process of adaptation.

Secondly, there is a picture of the human brain that is associated with the 'adaptation' model of the human psyche. According to this picture, the brain is a digitally organized network of synapses, which process information received through the senses and which produce responses that, on the whole, and in normal conditions, contribute to the organism's survival. The brain works by carrying out 'computations', and this is how we should understand such features as perception, emotion and belief – namely, as aspects of the computational process that generates appropriate responses from given inputs.

If we accept all that, then of course we immediately confront important scientific questions about music. For example: is music an adaptation? Are there dedicated neural networks involved in 'processing' musical input? Does music have a cognitive significance like that of language, or is it *sui generis*, and disconnected from the process of gathering information about the world?

Consider the question whether music is an adaptation. There are two broad ways you might set about answering this: one is to speculate about the possible *functions* of music in the lives of humans; the other is to look at the extent and variety of musical behaviour, with a view to discovering whether it emerges widely and spontaneously in human infants. Either way you find yourself looking at musical behaviour in an altogether new light. Nothing is stranger, from the evolutionary point of view, than the silent audience in a concert hall, listening with rapt attention to a sequence of intensely organized sounds, and then departing for a quiet supper. How on earth could this behaviour have an adaptive function? But when you see concert-going and the classical tradition as a kind of attenuated version of collective singing and dancing, and set collective singing and dancing in the context of military and religious affirmations of the community spirit, it might begin to look a little different. And when you study mother–infant vocalizing, and the emergence in all cultures of the lullaby and the spontaneous infant song, you will begin to think that music must be an adaptation after all.

There is no settled view among evolutionary psychologists concerning the origin and function of music. Some, such as Steven Pinker, consider music to be 'evolutionary cheese-cake', whose attractions are a by-product of other and more important adaptations; others believe, with Geoffrey Miller, that musicality confers an independent reproductive advantage on the genes that produce it. But the fact is that either way such theories have little or no bearing on the nature and meaning of music.[8] The case is like that of mathematics. It could be that mathematical competence is a by-product of other and more useful adaptations, or it could be that it is an adaptation in its own right. But neither theory tells us what mathematics is, what numbers are, what makes a mathematical theorem true or what mathematics really means. All the philosophical questions remain when the evolutionary account is called in. And the same is true of most of the problems that concern philosophers of music.

Matters are otherwise with the computational theory of the brain. There is no doubt that this has cast light on the understanding of language. And it is not implausible to suggest that, if the computational theory goes some way towards explaining language, it might go some way towards explaining music too. For it reminds us that music is not sound, but sound organized 'in the brain of the hearer'. Musical organization is something that we 'latch on to', as we latch on to language. And once the first steps in musical comprehension have been taken we advance rapidly to the point where each of us can immediately absorb and take pleasure in an indefinite number of new musical experiences. This recalls a fundamental feature of language, and

---

[8] Steven Pinker, *How the Mind Works* (New York, 1997), p. 534. Geoffrey Miller, 'Evolution of Human Music through Sexual Selection', in Nils L. Wallin, Björn Merker and Steven Brown, eds, *The Origins of Music* (Cambridge, MA, 2000).

not surprisingly results from linguistics have been transferred and adapted to the analysis of musical structure in the hope of showing just how it is that musical order is generated and perceived, and just what it is that explains the grip that music exerts over its devotees.

We should recognize here that music is not just an art of sound. We might combine sounds in sequence as we combine colours on an abstract canvas or flowers in a flowerbed. But the result will not yet be music. It becomes music only if it also makes *musical sense*. Leaving modernist experiments aside, there is an audible distinction between music and mere sequences of sounds, and it is not just a distinction between *types* of sound (e.g., pitched and un-pitched, regular and random). Sounds become music as a result of organization, and this organization is something that we perceive and whose absence we immediately notice, regardless of whether we take pleasure in the result. This organization is not just an aesthetic matter – it is not simply a *style*. It is more like a grammar, in being the precondition of our response to the result *as music*. We must therefore acknowledge that music (or at any rate, tonal music of the kind familiar to the Western listener) has something like a syntax – a rule-guided process linking each episode to its neighbours – which we grasp in the act of hearing, and the absence of which leads to a sense of discomfort or incongruity.

Of course, there are things called music which do not share this syntax – modernist experiments, African drum music, music employing scales that defy harmonic ordering and so on. But from medieval plainsong to modern jazz we observe a remarkable constancy, in rhythmical, melodic and harmonic organization: so much so that one extended part of this tradition has been singled out as 'the common practice' whose principles are taught as a matter of course in classes of music appreciation. This phenomenon demands an explanation.

Leonard B. Meyer, in an influential book (*Emotion and Meaning in Music*, Chicago, 1956), argued that we understand music by a kind of probabilistic reasoning, which endows musical events with varying degrees of redundancy. The common practice has emerged from a steady accumulation of conventions and expectations, which enable listeners to predict what follows from what, and which give rise to the distinctive 'wrong note' experience when things go noticeably astray. This suggestion was taken forward by Eugene Narmour, to produce what he called the 'implication-realization model' of musical structure.[9] And more recently David Temperley has applied Bayesian probability theory to standard rhythms and melodies in order to 'model' the way in which listeners assign meter and tonality to sequences.[10]

Temperley's work raises three questions: What is a 'model'? When is a model 'adequate' to the data? And what might the discovery of an adequate model show, concerning our understanding and appreciation of music? A model that can be rewritten as an algorithm could program a computer to assign metrical order and key to any piece. Such a model can be tested against human performance, and if it successfully predicts our preferences and decisions, it offers the beginning of a theory of musical cognition. It suggests an account of what goes on in the brain when listeners identify the metrical and tonal structure of the piece they are listening to. And that seems to be the aim of Temperley's reflections, especially in his earlier work, in which he develops a computational system for the analysis of music and uses that system to represent patterns and sequences that are 'preferred' by habituated listeners.[11]

However, others use the term 'model' more loosely, to mean any way of representing the musical surface that displays the perceived connections among its parts, and which suggests a way in which we grasp those connections, whether consciously or not. In this sense the circle of fifths, chord-sequence analysis and the old charts of key relations are all partial 'models' of our musical experience. They enable us to predict, up to a point, how people will respond to changes of key and to accidentals in a melody, and they also suggest musical

---

[9] *The Analysis and Cognition of Basic Melodic Structures* (Chicago, 1990).
[10] *Music and Probability* (Cambridge, MA, 2007).
[11] See David Temperley, *The Cognition of Basic Musical Structures* (Cambridge, MA, 2001), and also Temperley's website, which offers access to the Melisma Music Analyzer, a program developed by Temperley and Daniel Sleator.

'constants' on which a composer can lean when constructing the harmonic framework of a piece. But they do not aim to reduce musical understanding to a computational algorithm, nor do they offer anything like a complete theory of musical cognition that will explain how we assemble a coherent musical surface from our experience of its parts. Rather, they describe the surface, by identifying the salient features and the perceived relations between them.

Things would look a little different, however, if we could take the idea of a musical 'syntax' literally. Linguistics attempts to model language use and comprehension in ways that lend themselves to computational analysis. If we could extend to the realm of musicology the advances made in psycholinguistics, therefore, we might be nearer to explaining what goes on when people assemble the notes that they hear into coherent structures. Inconclusive research by the neuroscientists suggests that 'although musical and linguistic syntax have distinct and domain-specific syntactic representations, there is overlap in the neural resources that serve to activate these representations during syntactic processing'.[12] This – 'the shared syntactic integration resource hypothesis' – would be of considerable interest not only to evolutionary psychology but also to musicology if it could be shown that the syntactic processes involved in the two cases work in a similar way. The neurological research does not show this. But there is a kind of speculative cognitive science that suggests that it might nevertheless be true, and that a 'grammar' of tonal music could be developed which both resembles the grammar of language and can also be rewritten as a computational algorithm.

One goal of Chomsky's generative grammar has been to explain how speakers can understand indefinitely many new utterances, despite receiving only finite information from their surroundings. Formal languages like the predicate calculus provide a useful clue, showing how infinitely many well-formed formulae can be derived by recursion. If natural languages are organized in the same way, then from a finite number of basic structures, using a finite number of

---

[12] Aniruddh D. Patel, *Music, Language and the Brain* (Oxford, 2008), p. 297.

transformation rules, an infinite number of well-formed sentences could be extracted. Understanding a new sentence would not be a mystery if speakers were able to recuperate from the string of uttered words the rule-governed process that produced it. Likewise the widespread capacity to latch on to new music without any guidance other than that already absorbed through the ear could be explained if musical surfaces were the rule-governed products of a finite number of basic structures, which might be partly innate and partly acquired during the early years of acculturation.

Certain aspects of music have been modelled in ways that suggest such a generative grammar. If metrical organization proceeds by division, as in Western musical systems, then surface rhythms can be derived from basic structures by recursion and also understood by recuperating that process. This is made into the basis of a generative grammar of metrical rhythm by Christopher Longuet-Higgins and C. S. Lee.[13] Others have made similar first shots at grammars for pitch organization.[14]

Such small-scale proposals were quickly displaced by the far more ambitious theory presented by Fred Lerdahl and Ray Jackendoff in their ground-breaking book *A Generative Theory of Tonal Music* (1983). Their argument is bold, ambitious and detailed, and although things have moved on in the thirty years since the book first appeared, it has lost none of its relevance and continues to be called upon by musicologists, music theorists and philosophers of music in order to develop or make use of the analogy between linguistic and musical understanding. Lerdahl and Jackendoff recognize at many points, however, that this analogy is stretched, and that Chomskian linguistics cannot be carried over wholesale into the study of tonal music. Syntax, they recognize, does not in music point towards semantics, as it does in language. Moreover, the hierarchical organization that Lerdahl and Jackendoff propose is an organization of individual

---

[13] 'The Rhythmic Interpretation of Monophonic Music', in Longuet-Higgins, *Mental Processes: Studies in Cognitive Science* (Cambridge, MA, 1987).
[14] For example D. Deutsch and J. Feroe, 'The Internal Representation of Pitch Sequences in Tonal Music', *Psychological Review*, vol. 88 (1981), 503–22.

musical objects, such as notes and chords, and not, as in Chomsky, of grammatical categories (verb, noun-phrase, adverb etc.). There are no grammatical categories in music. Moreover, while we can distinguish 'structural' from 'subordinate' events in music, there is much room for argument as to which is which, and there is no one hierarchy that determines the position of any particular event. An event that is structural from the 'time-span' point of view might be metrically subordinate and also a prolongation of some other event in the hierarchy of tension and release. Still, the various hierarchies identified by Lerdahl and Jackendoff capture some of our firmer intuitions about musical importance. The task is to show that there are transformation rules that derive the structure that we hear from a more deeply embedded structure, and do so in such a way as to explain our overall sense of the connectedness of the musical surface.

On the other hand, if music were like language in the relevant respects, then grasp of musical grammar ought to involve an ability to produce new utterances, and not just an ability to understand them when produced by someone else. But there is a striking asymmetry here. All musical people quickly 'latch on' to the art of musical appreciation. Very few are able to compose meaningful or even syntactically acceptable music. It seems that musical understanding is a one-way process, and musical creation a rare gift that involves quite different capacities from those involved in appreciating the result.

Here we discover another difficulty for theories like that of Lerdahl and Jackendoff, which is that they attempt to cast what seems to be a form of aesthetic preference in terms borrowed from a theory of truth-directed cognition. If understanding music involved recuperating information (either about the music or about the world), then a generative syntax would have a function. It would guide us to the semantically organized essence of a piece of music, so that we could understand what it says. But if music says nothing, why should it be organized in such a way? What matters is not semantic value but the agreeableness of the musical surface. Music addresses our preferences, and it appeals to us by presenting a heard order that leads us to say 'yes' to this sequence and 'no' to that. Not surprisingly, therefore, when Lerdahl and Jackendoff try to provide what they regard as transformation rules for their musical grammar, they come up with 'preference rules', rather than rules of well-formedness.[15] These 'rules' tell us, for example, to 'prefer' to hear a musical sequence in such a way that metrical prominence and time-span prominence coincide. There are over a hundred of these rules, which, on examination, can be seen not to be rules at all, since they do not owe their validity to convention. They are generalizations from the accumulated preferences of musical listeners, which are not guides to hearing but by-products of our musical choices. Many of them encapsulate aesthetic regularities, whose authority is stylistic rather than grammatical, like the norms of poetic usage.

Everything we know about language suggests that rules distinguishing well-formed from ill-formed sequences are fundamental, and that these rules are not generalizations from preferences but conventions that define what speakers are doing. They are what John Searle calls 'constitutive' rules.[16] Such rules have a place in tonal music: for example, the rule that designated pitches come from a set of 12 classes of octave-equivalent semitones. But they do not seem to be linked to a generative grammar of the kind postulated by Lerdahl and Jackendoff. They simply lay down the constraints within which a sequence of sounds will be heard as music, and outside which it will be heard as non-musical sound. Moreover these constitutive rules are few and far between, and far less important, when it comes to saying how music works, than the résumés of practice that have been studied in courses of harmony and counterpoint.

This brings me to the crux. There is no doubt that music is something that we can understand and fail to understand. But the purpose of listening is not to decipher messages or to trace the sounds we hear to some generative structure, still less to recuperate the information that is encoded in them. The purpose is for the listener to follow the musical journey, as rhythm, melody and harmony unfold according

---

[15] Likewise, the theory of musical cognition advanced by David Temperley in his earlier work *The Cognition of Basic Musical Structures* is formulated in terms of 'preference rules'.

[16] J. R. Searle, *Speech Acts: An Essay in the Philosophy of Language* (Cambridge, 1969), p. 34.

to their own inner logic so as to make audible patterns linking part to part. We understand music as an object of aesthetic interest, and this is quite unlike the understanding that we direct towards the day-to-day utterances of a language, even if it sometimes looks as though we 'group' the elements in musical space in a way that resembles our grouping of words in a sentence.

This does not mean that there is no aspect to musical grammar that would deserve the sobriquet 'deep'. On the contrary, we recognize long-term tonal relations, relations of dependence between episodes, ways in which one part spells out and realizes what has been foretold in another. These aspects of music are important: they are the foundation of powerful musical experiences and an endless source of curiosity and delight. But they concern structures and relations that are created in the surface, not hidden in the depths. The musical order is not generated *from* these long-term relations, as Schenker (for example) would have us believe,[17] but points *towards* them, in the way that architectural patterns point towards the form in which they culminate. We come to understand the larger structure as a result of understanding the small-scale movement from which it derives.

One of the strengths of *A Generative Theory of Tonal Music* is that it emphasizes these long-term relations, and the way in which the listener – especially the listener to the masterworks of our listening culture – hears the music as *going somewhere*, fulfilling at a later stage expectations subliminally aroused at an earlier one. The mistake, it seems to me, comes from thinking that these perceived relations define a hidden or more basic structure, from which the rest of the musical surface is derived. The perceived relations should rather be seen as we see the relation between spires on a Gothic castle. The pattern made by the spires emerges *from* the supporting structures, but does not generate them.

There is, as Lerdahl and Jackendoff and many others remind us, an act of synthesis, of mental organization, involved in hearing sounds as music. We do not simply hear the sounds that compose

---

[17] See Heinrich Schenker, *Free Composition*, tr. Ernst Oser (London, 1979).

the musical work. We hear sequences of pitched sounds, and we hear *in* those sounds a musical process that is supervenient on the sounds, although not reducible to them. I have argued this point at length in *The Aesthetics of Music*. Music involves movement in a one-dimensional space, in which there are fields of force, relations of attraction and repulsion, and complex musical objects like melodies and chords that occupy places of their own. It exhibits opacity and transparency, tension and release, lightness and weight and so on. I have argued that there is an entrenched metaphor of space and movement underlying all these features of music. Yet those features are part of what we perceive when we hear music, and someone who merely hears sequences of pitched sounds – *however accurately* – does not hear music. (You could have absolute pitch and still not hear music. Some birds are like this.)

What, then, might cognitive science tell us, about hearing and understanding music? It is clear that music is organized in the ear of the beholder, and that all those features to which I have just referred, whether or not based in entrenched metaphors, are features of the organization that we impose upon (or elicit in) the sequences that we hear. So how should the cognitive science proceed? One thing is clear: it cannot proceed simply by adapting cognitive science models from other areas, such as the cognitive science of language. We have to start from scratch. But there is very little scratch to start from, at least in the work of those cognitive scientists who have attended to this problem. Thus Aniruddh Patel, who has made a consistent effort to summarize the relevant findings of neuroscience, begins his discussion of melody from the following definition: melody is 'a tone sequence in which the individual tones are processed in terms of multiple structural relationships'.[18] But what is a tone? Is it identical to a pitched sound, or something that is heard *in* a pitched sound? What kinds of 'relationships' are we talking about, and why describe them as 'structural'? You can see in this very definition a host of short cuts to the conclusion that music is processed in something like the way

[18] *Music, Language and the Brain*, p. 325.

language is processed, and that 'processed' is just the word we need – the very word that suggests the algorithms of computer science. But maybe it is not like that at all. How would we know? It is here, I think, that some philosophy is needed.

When we hear music, we hear movements and relations in a certain kind of space. This space is what is represented in our standard musical notation, and it is one reason why that notation has caught on: it gives us a clear picture of what we hear, unlike, say, the graph notation used by lutenists or the fret-board notation for the guitar, which give us a picture of the fingers, rather than the tones. If we adhere to the strict sense of 'model', according to which a model is the first step towards a computational algorithm, then it is clear that no model can make use of the phenomenal space that is described by ordinary musical notation. A space in which position, movement, orientation and weight are all metaphors is not a space that can feature in a computer program, or indeed in any kind of theory that seeks to explain our experience, rather than to describe its subjective character. It is a space that is *read into, imposed upon, elicited in* sounds when perceived by certain kinds of perceiver – those who are able to detach their perceptions from their beliefs, and to put normal cognitive processes on hold (or 'off-line', to use Gregory Currie's metaphor).[19]

The space of music, I suggest, is a purely *intentional* space: a realm of intentional objects, which has no independent material reality. It is constituted by our way of hearing sound sequences, in terms of geometrical metaphors. In opposition to that suggestion, however, there is a long tradition of musical analysis which attempts to discover something like a real and objective spatial organization in sounds themselves, and to see our appreciation of music as arising from our conscious or pre-conscious ways of latching on to that

---

[19] Greg Currie's suggestion that in the work of the imagination we run our mental states 'off-line' is interesting but obscure. For what is the ground for thinking that the 'on-line' mental state of believing that *p* and the off-line state of imagining that *p* are two versions of a single thing? You don't provide a cognitive science by using computer science as a source of metaphor. See *Arts and Minds* (Oxford, 2004), Chapters 9 and 10.

organization, in something like the way we latch on to grammar in language. Circles, maps and spirals modelling root progressions and key shifts are associated with such names as Johann Mattheson, David Kellner, Gottfried Weber and Leonhard Euler, and played a large part in the great explosion of music theory in the eighteenth century. More recently Christopher Longuet-Higgins has developed a geometrical model of tonal relations, and Fred Lerdahl, in a formidably difficult work, has recast the findings of *A Generative Theory of Tonal Music* in terms of paths taken through 'tonal pitch space' – although, as he here and there acknowledges, his model is numerical rather than spatial, and talk of 'regions' of 'pitch space' involves a kind of metaphor.[20] Yet more recently Dmitri Tymoczko has taken the idea of a musical geometry forward in a novel way, by proposing a complete account of voice-leading and harmonic progression, and mounting a kind of *a priori* argument for the naturalness of the 'extended common practice', by which he means, essentially, Western music from plainsong to pop.[21]

The strongest aspect of Tymoczko's argument is the case that he gives for voice-leading in the common practice. He makes abundantly clear, both theoretically and through detailed examples, that real musicians in the tonal tradition think of chords not as pitch-class sets but as structures emerging from the movement of voices. This is as true of jazz as it is of Bach's fugues or Mozart's symphonies. It explains why Berg's violin concerto is so popular – namely that the harmonies (notwithstanding their atonal character) are almost entirely derived by voice-leading, whether or not they also conform to the serial calculus that supposedly organizes the piece.

In 1973 Allen Forte published his highly influential book *The Structure of Atonal Music,* in which he developed a set-theoretic analysis of serial music.[22] Forte's approach involved rewriting 'simultaneities' as pitch-class sets and reducing them to their 'normal'

[20] Fred Lerdahl, *Tonal Pitch Space* (Oxford, 2001).
[21] *A Geometry of Music: Harmony and Counterpoint in the Extended Common Practice* (Oxford, 2011).
[22] Allen Forte, *The Structure of Atonal Music* (Oxford, 1973).

ordering, with intervals arranged to be as short as octave equivalence allows. This clever book, the influence of which can be discerned in many subsequent academic studies, did an enormous disservice to musicology. For it described harmony while entirely ignoring voice-leading, which is the vehicle of harmonic progression and therefore an integral component of harmonic meaning even in atonal chords.[23] Maybe it is true in some works of serial music that voice-leading has no role: and maybe that is why we hear the result not as 'harmony' but as 'simultaneity'. But that is exactly what leads us to resist that kind of serial music and why it will never have a place in ordinary musical affections. By describing harmonies in Forte's way you deprive yourself of an instrument of musical criticism. You also ignore a whole dimension of musical understanding, a dimension that Tymoczko works hard to make central to the nature and meaning of tonal music. As he shows, the basic sonorities of Western tonal music arise from efficient voice-leading, harmonic consistency and acoustic consonance, and these three features are woven together in the extended common practice.

Forte's mathematics of atonal music issues from an earlier attempt to explain musical understanding, using modulo 12 arithmetic to model pitch-class sequences and simultaneities. For Tymoczko it is not arithmetic but geometry that contains the secret, and his claim is that 'geometry provides a powerful tool for modelling musical structure'.

Many things that we do not understand geometrically can be provided with geometrical models. You can model a game of football by a path evolving in 46 dimensions (two dimensions for each of the 22 players and two for the ball), but the result will not help you to understand or play a game of football, since it is derived from moves that we recognize in another way and adds nothing to our ability to decide or predict them. The geometry is a shadow cast in 46-dimensional space by the light of intuitive practice. Even if we can model the chords of tonal harmony in an 'ordered pitch space' in such a way as to represent

---

[23] See the discussion of Berg's violin concerto, on pp. 301–2 of *The Aesthetics of Music*.

40

the efficient voice-leadings between them, this too may be no more than a shadow cast by a practice that we understand in another way. Tymoczko's 'tool for modelling musical structure' would be 'powerful' only if it either added to our understanding of music or suggested an explanation of how musical elements are processed in the brain. But, after wrestling with Tymoczko's 'ordered pitch spaces', in which chords are assembled in relation to their standard transformations on an infinite Möbius band, I came to the conclusion that this 'geometry of music' is clever but more or less irrelevant.

I was confirmed in this conclusion by Tymoczko's own critical studies in the second part of his book, where, with very few exceptions, he explains his interesting ideas concerning voice-leading, chromaticism and scalar organization more or less entirely in traditional analytical language, using old-fashioned chord grammar and setting out the passages to be explained not in his n-dimensional pitch space but in ordinary musical notation. When expounding his geometry, he writes that

> learning the art of musical analysis is largely a matter of learning to overlook the redundancies and inefficiencies of ordinary musical notation. Our geometrical space simplifies this process, stripping away musical details and allowing us to gaze directly upon the harmonic and contrapuntal relationships that underlie much of Western contrapuntal practice.[24]

He makes this point in the context of an analysis of a few bars from a Brahms intermezzo, giving both a complex geometrical graph and the relevant bits of the score. The graphs are all but unintelligible; but through the score you 'gaze directly' on the notes, and the score offers all the reader needs in order to grasp Tymoczko's argument.

Tymoczko's geometry of chord progressions and harmonic relations was anticipated by Christopher Longuet-Higgins in two 'letters to a musical friend', which appeared in 1962 in *The Music Review*,

---

[24] *A Geometry of Music*, p. 79.

and subsequently in articles collected in *Mental Processes*. Longuet-Higgins (a theoretical chemist by training and a brilliant musician, who invented the term 'cognitive science' and who did as much as anyone else to set up the discipline to which that term now refers) introduced a three-dimensional tonal space, with octaves assigned to one dimension, fifths to another and thirds to another. All the intervals in tonal music can be defined on this space, in which they appear as vectors. Moreover, and this particularly interested Longuet-Higgins, this tonal space distinguishes between intervals that are indistinguishable from the point of view of modulo 12 arithmetic. Thus it distinguishes between a major third and a diminished fourth, for example, even though they are both (in well-tempered scales) made up of four equal semitones.

The tonal space displays the real, hidden, grammar of tonal music, since it preserves the scalar meaning of the intervals in their harmonic representation. A succession of triads defines a path in this space, and this path may either hop around a centre, in which case the music remains in one key, or move from one centre to another, in which case there has been a modulation to another key. Longuet-Higgins gave a precise definition that distinguishes these two cases, and used it to assign notation to difficult examples of highly chromatic pitches, such as the cor anglais solo in the introduction to the third act of *Tristan*. The geometry used by Longuet-Higgins does not emphasize voice-leading, as Tymoczko does, but in other respects it applies the same intuitive idea, that musical relations can be mapped on to geometrical relations by preserving 'betweenness'. It also looks very much like the first step in an explanatory theory, suggesting a way in which the brain 'maps' the musical input, as the visual system maps orientation, distance etc., so as to represent edges, discontinuities and occlusions. Here is one of Longuet-Higgins's typically laconic summaries:

The three-dimensionality of tonal space follows directly from the fact that just three basic intervals are necessary and sufficient for the construction of all others. Given any note such as middle C we may place it at the origin in tonal space and relate all other notes to it by assigning them coordinates (*x, y, z*) which represent the numbers of perfect fifths, major thirds and octaves by which one must move in order to get from middle C to the note in question. In principle, then, the notes of tonal music lie at the points of a discrete three-dimensional space which extends infinitely in all directions away from any starting point. Viewed in this way, the notes of a melody perform a 'dance' in an abstract conceptual space; the appreciation of tonality depends upon the ability to discern the direction and distance of each step in the dance.[25]

There is an important point to be made in response to both Tymoczko and Longuet-Higgins, which is that we already have an idea of musical space which is quite unlike the geometrical orderings set forth in their studies. We hear music as movement in a one-dimensional space ordered in terms of a between-ness relation defined on the axis of pitch (the axis of 'high' and 'low'). This space is folded over at the octave, so that movement in one direction returns to the same place after 12 semitone steps. In its musical use it is endowed with gravitational fields of force, according to scalar measure and key relations. The leading note is drawn towards the tonic, dominant seventh chords tend towards the relevant tonic chords and so on. But this space is a purely phenomenal space. No musical object can be identified except in terms of its place (middle C, for instance), so that position in musical space is an essential property of whatever possesses it. Hence, although we hear movement, nothing moves. The space that we hear is a kind of metaphorical space, but one that is vividly etched on our auditory experience. Moreover, it is a space that contains interesting symmetries and which can be treated mathematically in ways that cast light on our musical experience.[26]

---

[25] 'The Grammar of Music', in *ibid.*, p. 140.
[26] For an example of this, see Wilfrid Hodges, 'The Geometry of Music', in John Fauvel, Raymond Flood and Robin Wilson, eds, *Music and Mathematics: From Pythagoras to Fractals* (Oxford, 2003), pp. 90–111. As Hodges shows, there is another and more useful geometry of music, which

Tymoczko's 'process-based' approach to chromaticism, which emphasizes voice-leading as opposed to static chords, is persuasive, largely because he takes us on journeys through this phenomenal space, rarely troubling to look behind him, at the spooky shadows cast on those Möbius bands. Standard clef notation represents the phenomenal space of music with all the clarity and detail that a critic needs, and when a critic tells us that the G sharp of the opening chord of *Tristan und Isolde* moves chromatically to B while the D sharp moves to D, he describes exactly what we hear as well as what we see on the page – even though the description is literally nonsense, since G sharp cannot move to B nor D sharp to D. Moreover, the one-dimensional space of standard notation reminds us of a fact that Tymoczko rarely adverts to, namely, that voice-leading is not merely a matter of relations between adjacent notes and adjacent chords. It runs through a whole piece of music, creating expectations in each note that reach well beyond its immediate successor. The Prelude to *Tristan* is a wonderful example of this. It does not merely proceed from one unsaturated harmony to the next; each voice pursues its own lonely anxiety-ridden journey through tonal space, moving by semitone or whole-tone steps in obedience to a kind of obsession that seems to owe nothing to the harmonic network of which it is a part.

The ambitious versions of the 'geometry of music' that I have outlined provide models of musical understanding only in a loose sense of that term. The real question is how any given 'model' might be used: is it the first step in a cognitive science of music, such as Longuet-Higgins wished to provide? If so, what would be the neural correlate of the infinite Möbius strip? Here we come up against a brick wall. We can translate tonal music into a kind of geometry. And we can understand how computations can combine variables in more than one dimension. But how do we get from the geometrical models to the computations in the brain?

describes the phenomenal space in which music exists, rather than the imaginary n-dimensional 'model' that tries to keep track of it.

44

If we adhere to the strict sense of 'model', according to which a model is the first step towards a computational algorithm, then it is clear that no model can make use of the phenomenal space that is described by ordinary musical notation. A space in which position, movement, orientation and weight are all metaphors is not a space that can feature in a computer program, or indeed in any kind of theory that seeks to explain our experience, rather than to describe its subjective character.

The idea of a secret order of music is far from new, nor is it new to suggest that this order is geometrical. That was the master thought of the Pythagorean cosmology and of the theory of the universe summarized by Ptolemy and accepted throughout the Western world until the scientific revolution. In a recent work that relies heavily on Lerdahl and Jackendoff (and on many other inputs from psychology and cognitive science), Charles Nussbaum has offered a similar 'clue to all the secrets', arguing that music supplies 'plans of action': it provides 'musical mental models' that 'represent the features of the layouts and scenarios in which ... virtual movements occur'.[27] In another application of Lerdahl and Jackendoff, Diana Raffman has used the generative hypothesis to explain why the 'secret meaning of music' is in fact an illusion – arguing that the syntax of music tempts us to attribute semantic significance to patterns that have no significance other than their musical form.[28] Tymoczko's is the latest in a series of books that promise more than they deliver, since they rely on theories whose application to music is largely wishful thinking. Longuet-Higgins, by contrast, seems to be getting somewhere, since his geometry clarifies distinctions between intervals that we hear but which are not easily represented in traditional notation. Moreover, his geometry is expressly directed towards providing a computational theory of tonal music – a theory that would show how musical objects and transitions might be represented in the nervous system.

[27] *The Musical Representation* (Cambridge, MA, 2007), p. 82.
[28] *Language, Music and Mind* (Cambridge, MA, 1993).

But here is a point at which the defenders of old-fashioned musicology might wish to step in with a long-suppressed protest. Musicology, they might say, belongs to the humanities, not the sciences. It cannot be replaced by mathematical analysis, nor is it a prelude to a theory of musical cognition, whatever that may be. It is devoted to describing, evaluating and amplifying the *given* character of musical experience, rather than to showing how musical preferences might be tracked by a computer. Hence the one-dimensional pitch space in which *we*, self-conscious and aesthetically motivated listeners, situate melodic and harmonic movement ought to be the real object of musical study – the thing that needs to be understood in order to *understand music*.

From this point of view even the three-dimensional pitch space explored by Longuet-Higgins is of little musical relevance, while Tymoczko's Möbius bands might just as well go and tie themselves in knots, for all that they tell us about music. The important point is that the one-dimensional pitch space in which we hear music unfolding is not a space in which the physical sounds that we hear as music actually occur. An account of 'auditory representations' which offers to explain what goes on when we hear music will therefore not be an account of anything that occurs in that imaginary space. No account of auditory sequences and their 'processing' in the brain will be an account of what occurs in the imagined space of music.

I shall conclude with two observations about this imagined space. First, there is a kind of freedom in musical perception which parallels the freedom in the perception of aspects in the visual arts, but which is absent from ordinary cognitive processes. In the Müller-Lyer illusion the apparent inequality of the lines remains even after the subject knows that the lines are of the same length – proof, for some psychologists, of the modular nature of our sensory and intellectual processes, which deliver independent information about one and the same state of affairs. In the case of aspect perception, by contrast, appearances can change under the influence of thought, and will change if the right thinking is brought to bear on them. The nude in Titian's *Venus of Urbino* changes appearance if you imagine her to be looking at a lover, a husband or merely a curious observer.

How you see her depends upon how you think of her size, which in turn depends on how you think of the size of the bed on which she is lying. And so on. In the case of music the structural relations to which Patel refers (see above) are multiply adaptable to the needs of musical thought. Melodies change according to our conception of where upbeats end, where phrases begin, which notes are 'intruders' and which part of the flow, and so on. And it is one reason why performers are judged so intently, namely that how they *play* can influence how we *hear*.

Secondly, we do not hear music as we hear other sounds in our environment. Music is heard as *addressed* to us. We move with it, regard it as calling on our attention, making demands on us, responding to our response. Enfolded within the music there lies an imagined first-person perspective, and to listen with full attention is to relate to the music as we relate to each other, I to Thou. Musical movement is a kind of action, and the 'why?' with which we interrogate it is the 'why?' of reason and not the 'why?' of cause. Hence the imagined space of music is a 'space of reasons', to use Wilfrid Sellars's well-known idiom, and what we hear in it we hear under the aspect of freedom.[29] This feature is integral to the meaning of music, at least to the music that matters, and is one reason why we wish to speak of understanding and misunderstanding what we hear, regardless of whether we can attach some separately identifiable meaning to it. No doubt cognitive science will one day tell us much about the forms of interpersonal understanding. But it will have to advance well beyond the theory of auditory perception if it is to complete the task.

Those features, it seems to me, demand philosophical exegesis. They ask us to look at the phenomenon itself, to identify just what makes an experience of sound into an experience of *music*. Only when we have clarified that question can we go on to ask questions about the neural pathways involved and the way the sounds are 'processed' by them.

---

[29] Wilfrid Sellars, 'Philosophy and the Scientific Image of Man', in *Science, Perception and Reality* (Austin, TX, 1963).

But there is, I think, a more important topic that opens here. Even if we came up with a theory about the processing of music, it would not, in itself, be an account of musical understanding. Indeed, it would tell us as little about the meaning and value of music as a cognitive model of mathematical understanding would tell us about the nature of mathematical truth. All the real problems, concerning what music means, why we enjoy it and why it is important to us, would remain untouched by such a theory. For they are problems about the experience itself, how that experience is profiled in our own first-person awareness and what it means. Meaning is opaque to digital processing, which passes the mystery from synapse to synapse as a relay team passes the baton, or as the algorithm passes the image in a digital camera. The crucial moment of interpretation certainly occurs. But it involves the whole cognitive and emotional apparatus, and achieves an act of understanding of a kind that has yet to find its place in the computational theory of the mind. But here we are in deep water, and there are as many philosophers who will disagree with that last sentence (Fodor, for instance) as there are who will agree with it (Searle, for instance).[30]

---

[30] Jerry Fodor, *The Modularity of the Mind* (Cambridge, MA, 1983). John Searle, *Intentionality: An Essay in the Philosophy of Mind* (Cambridge, 1983).

3

Music and the Moral Life

'The ways of poetry and music are not changed anywhere without change in the most important laws of the city.' So wrote Plato in the *Republic* (4.424c). And Plato is famous for having given what is perhaps the first theory of character in music, proposing to allow some modes and to forbid others according to the character that can be heard in them. Plato deployed the concept of *mimesis*, or imitation, to explain why bad character in music encourages bad character in its devotees. The context suggests that he had singing, dancing and marching in mind, rather than the silent listening that we know from the concert hall. But, however we fill out the details, there is no doubt that music, for Plato, was something that could be judged in the same moral terms that we judge one another, and that the terms in question denoted virtues and vices, like nobility, dignity, temperance and chastity on the one hand, and sensuality, belligerence and indiscipline on the other.

From the dance of the Israelites around the golden calf, to the orgies of Hip-Hop, the musical distractions of ordinary people have called down the maledictions of their priestly guardians. The priests have throughout history tried not merely to control what is sung and played in the temple but also to confine and, if necessary, forbid the revels that take place outside. We no longer think we can do this by law. But we are still deeply concerned by changes in musical practice, in just the way that Moses was when he descended from the mountain and cast the tablets of the law to the ground on seeing the idolatry of the masses. This was perhaps the first recorded protest against 'mass culture'.

Adorno is a latter-day Moses, and his hero Arnold Schoenberg tried to set the episode from the Old Testament to music, as an illustration of the way in which we must never sacrifice the purity of truth to the ease of communication. In the contrast between Moses and Aaron in Schoenberg's unfinished opera we see dramatized the clash of cultures that preoccupied Adorno. There is a culture of long-term thought and abstract conception, represented by Moses, and a culture of short-term pleasure and easy communication, represented by Aaron. Schoenberg's treatment of this theme reminds us that many of the worries expressed, down the ages, concerning the depravities of popular music reflect the fear of idolatry – of false gods, false worship and false emotions. Thus Adorno wanted to show that the freedoms seemingly enjoyed by the American people are illusory freedoms, and that the underlying cultural reality is one of enslavement – enslavement to the fetishes of the market and the consumer culture, which by placing appetite above long-term values lead to the loss of rational autonomy. Popular music was not, for Adorno, something that Americans had been liberated *to*, but something that they must be liberated *from*, in the way that people are liberated from idolatry.

We are clearly in deep water here; and we are not going to save ourselves simply by taking the kind of non-judgemental approach that is so often promoted by courses in music appreciation. In this area to be non-judgemental is already to make a kind of judgement: it is to suggest that it really doesn't matter what you listen to or dance to, and that there is no moral distinction between the various listening habits that have emerged in the age of mechanical reproduction. That is a morally charged position, and one that flies in the face of common sense. To suggest that people who live with a rhythmic pulse as a constant background to their thoughts and movements are living *in the same way*, with the same kind of attention and the same pattern of challenges and rewards, as others who know music only from sitting down to listen to it, clearing their minds, meanwhile, of all other thoughts – such a suggestion is wildly implausible.

Put laconically, the difference between those two ways of responding to music is the difference between preventing silence and letting silence speak. Music in the listening culture is a voice that arises from silence, and which uses silence as a painter uses the canvas: silence is the *prima materia* on which the work is composed, and the most eloquent parts of the classical sonata movement are often the parts when nothing can be heard and the silence shows through. That is seldom, if ever, true of pop music today. Moreover the difference here is surely the kind of thing that is morally relevant – like the difference between temperance and intemperance in eating habits or in sex.

I begin from the question whether musical idioms can exhibit moral virtues and moral vices. It is obvious that we *describe* musical idioms in this way, and it is worth reminding ourselves of some familiar examples. The idiom of the Gregorian chant is almost universally acknowledged to be spiritual and uplifting. The style of Bach's keyboard works is scholarly and dignified. The classical idiom of Haydn and Mozart is courtly, well mannered and correct. The idiom of Beethoven is passionate and defiant. New Orleans Jazz is lively, invigorating, innocent. By contrast Death Metal is oppressive, dark, morbid. Indie music is complacent and easy-going; the American songbook is sentimental and nostalgic.

We should note at once that those judgements are figurative: they involve applying to musical idioms terms whose sense is fixed by their application to human characters. There is no *a priori* way of fixing what these terms mean when they are attached to music. A parallel example might help us to see this. We use metaphors of character, and even of virtue and vice, in describing trees and species of tree. The oak is noble and dependable, the pine dark and brooding, the willow feminine, the cypress melancholy, the maple good-humoured and so on. Nobody thinks that those descriptions convey very much. And even if they convey something, it has no bearing on the moral status of the trees or their real relation to people. The virtues and vices of trees don't rub off on the people who live in their shadow. You don't get noble people living under oaks and light-hearted people under maples. These descriptions are part of an elaborate game we play, not very different from that suggested by Wittgenstein, in asking us to decide whether Wednesday is fat or lean, or that suggested by Gombrich, in asking us to sort everything in the world according to whether it is 'pong' or 'ping'.[31] It is second nature for human beings to extend language in this way, sometimes guided by an impression of similarity, sometimes guided by their own responses, sometimes just playing around. But whether it has any foundation in the thing described or a further foundation in the life of the person so describing it are questions that cannot be settled just by looking at the language.

This doesn't mean that those descriptions of the character of musical idioms are meaningless, or that they are unimportant. But it does mean that we cannot use them to say anything about the moral significance of music. We can understand this easily enough by reflecting on another context in which we use this language – when describing the appearance of people. I may say that Jim has a severe and censorious appearance. But that says nothing about Jim's character: he may be mild and accommodating, for all I know. Appearances can deceive. In the case of music we have *only* appearances to go by. When it comes to music, there is no reality behind the appearance; otherwise Mark Twain might have been right to describe the music of Wagner as 'better than it sounds'.

The same difficulty attaches to the question whether individual *works* of music have a moral character, over and above that of the idiom in which they are composed. Again, there is no hesitation to use virtue and vice words of individual works of music. Bach's *Art of Fugue* radiates authority, wisdom, profundity. Beethoven's *Leonora* no. 3 is noble and life-affirming; Schubert's G major quartet is anguished, dignified and tender in the face of suffering. The last movement of Tchaikovsky's Sixth Symphony is mournful and unsmiling. So it could go on, through all the well-known virtues and vices of mankind. Of course, there are some virtue words, and some

---

[31] Wittgenstein, *Philosophical Investigations* (Oxford, 1952), Part II, section xi. Sir Ernst Gombrich, *Art and Illusion* (London, 1960), p. 370.

vice words, that are seldom called upon when describing music. 'Just', for example, 'cowardly', 'unwise', 'discreet', 'reliable'. Even with such words, however, a game could easily develop, of sorting works of music by means of them. Among just works should we not count the overture to *The Mastersingers* and Brahms's *Academic Festival Overture* – works that attempt to do justice to forms of human life and all that they contain?

Here I want to register a protest against a familiar move in the philosophy of music, and especially in theories of expression. This move tries to ground metaphor in analogy. It goes something like this: we begin from the question what does it mean to describe a piece of music as sad, noble etc.? (Notice that emotion terms and virtue terms tend to be treated together, since they both involve the spontaneous transfer of language from the mental to the musical context.) We respond with a suggestion: we mean that the music is *like* a sad or noble person. In what way like?

In various places Peter Kivy defends an analogy theory of musical character and musical expression, arguing that sad music shares the dynamic properties of sad people: it is slow-moving, drooping, ponderous and so on.[32] And noble music is up-standing, fully presented, with straightforward gestures and clear, honest cadences. Then I want to protest, wait a moment, you haven't advanced us one bit: you said that sad music shares properties with sad people; and then you proved this by describing those properties in two ways – using literal language of people, and figurative language of the music. Music doesn't *literally* move slowly, droop or ponder, for it doesn't literally move. The analogy turns out not to be an analogy at all, but a way of replacing one metaphor with another. I still have the question, what do these metaphors *mean*, and what do they tell me about the thing to which they are applied? And there is a strong tradition of argument, beginning with Wittgenstein's *Philosophical Investigations*, which says that you explain the meaning of a metaphor not by looking at the metaphorical use but by looking at the literal use. The thing

---

[32] See, for example, *The Corded Shell: Reflections on Musical Expression* (Princeton, 1980).

that needs explaining is not the *meaning* of the word 'sad', 'noble' or whatever, but the purpose of using just that word in just this context, where it does not literally apply. And whatever the purpose, it is not that of describing or picking out analogies.

But suppose these analogies exist. Suppose you can give sense to an emotion term or virtue word when used of music by pointing to similarities between the work of music and the mental state or disposition referred to by the literal usage. Would this show that the term identifies something aesthetically interesting and morally relevant in the thing to which it applies? My answer is no. Everything resembles everything else, and most resemblances are insignificant; what makes resemblance interesting is the context that puts it to a use. You may have a striking resemblance to Elvis Presley, but because you can't sing, can't move in a sexy way, can't do anything to put your resemblance on display, it remains insignificant. We notice many resemblances in music. The opening theme of Beethoven's op. 18 no. 1 is like someone signing a cheque: boldly putting down the hand, and then lapsing into a squiggle. But that resemblance (supposing we allow it) has nothing to do with the music or what it means. Naturally, therefore, we need to distinguish accidental from significant resemblances; and that is precisely what we cannot do, if the only ground for the use of mental predicates to describe music is the kind of analogy pointed to by Kivy.

Virtue and vice terms used of musical idioms can, in a way, be taken for granted, as posing no particular problems from the point of view of aesthetics. Like the description of tree species as noble or dignified, the description of an idiom as joyful or aggressive has no particular moral significance. The case parallels that of architecture in the classical tradition. The Ionic Order was considered masculine but adolescent, the Doric Order manly, the Corinthian feminine. And particular styles of ornamentation have been graced with similar epithets down the centuries. But nobody thinks that very much hangs on this, or that these epithets are a clue to the meaning of any particular building, or even to the beauty in general of a particular style. This kind of figurative language comes naturally to us: it is part of our way of being at home in the world that we bring new objects under old categories and extend our predicates to meet the need. The language of the virtues begins to bite only when we apply it to the individual work.

Here is an example. Youthful grace and serenity adhere to the Ionic Order in Greek architecture, much as joy and innocence adhere to New Orleans jazz. That, for us, is the character of the Ionic Order, which possesses this character in something like the way the oak possesses nobility and the weeping willow grief. The use of the word seems apposite, without, however, committing us to any judgement. There are good and bad Ionic buildings, just as there are good and bad works of New Orleans jazz and first-rate and third-rate oak trees. When Cockerell in his amazing designs for the Ashmolean Museum in Oxford used the Greek Ionic Order, however, he produced one of the great works of the classical revival, and one in which youthful grace and serenity are both exhibited. But now the description begins to mean something. I cannot say, 'Look, there is youthful grace and serenity', and then add, 'but of course, it is a piece of architectural rubbish, mere pastiche', without feeling a tension, if not a contradiction, between those two pronouncements. The first has said something about the meaning of Cockerell's building, something that justifies the attention we might pay to it. Cockerell meant us to notice this youthful grace; it represented, for him, an idea of education and its transforming effect on the young mind. The youthful grace of the building, as vivid today as it was when first it was built 180 years ago, is part of what it *means*. And the serenity, amplified by the ingenious mixture of the honey-coloured Oxford stone and the white Portland limestone, is also telling us something. We stand before this building as we might before a serene young person on whose clear brow the light of learning has dawned. Oxford is proud of this building, because the building is proud of Oxford.

There I have begun to use the figurative language in another way, a way that indicates why this building matters and what it means. I am committed, by my description, to a judgement. It is a way of saying *look at this, because* ... Let us go back to music. When Plato banished the mixolydian mode from his ideal Republic, it was in terms similar to those that might be used of an architectural style or a species of tree. No gloomy pine trees on our campus; none of that aggressive Bauhaus fenestration. These are, if you like, aesthetic judgements; but they leave entirely open the rejoinder that a pine tree just here, a jaunty piloti with a glass-wrapped corner just there would help us along. Plato has failed to persuade precisely because he was talking about modes – idioms, as we might describe them – and not about individual works of music. Of course, he could have been right. Maybe in a campus forested all over with pine trees students go crazy; maybe a Bauhaus campus would suffer the death from graffiti that it invites. And maybe when the youth all go to pop concerts and dance to the *aulos* playing in that excruciating mixolydian mode they all start to go downhill, acquire nasty habits, become sexually promiscuous and contemptuous towards their elders, as Plato feared. It could be. But this is all speculation – bypassing the realm of aesthetic judgement, and not in itself vindicating the view that pine trees, the Bauhaus style or the mixolydian mode really exemplify the vices conjured by the words that we use to describe them.

What I mean can be put more simply. The use of the language of virtue and vice to describe musical idioms is simply a special case of a much wider phenomenon, which has aesthetic and non-aesthetic instances. It does not, in itself, say anything about the moral impact or meaning of music. It is a wheel that turns without turning anything else in the mechanism, to use Wittgenstein's image.

When it comes to using these moral terms of individual works, however, we are in a different realm, not only in music but in architecture too. The nobility of Elgar's Second Symphony is there to be heard: it stands before us from the very first bar, and in following the music you are also participating in the unfolding of this virtue. You are in the *presence* of something – the very thing that your words describe when you describe this music as noble. Although the word 'noble' is here used figuratively, you can very quickly understand that it is being used to describe something *in the music*, something that the music is saying, which must be understood by the one who listens properly to it. This music does not merely remind us of the old virtues of imperial Britain: it *exemplifies* and *expresses* them. And that is part of what we appreciate in listening to it, and part of what we react against, should those old virtues seem tainted in our eyes and not truly virtues. The question then becomes: how can you hear such a thing in music?

The question might make us think of figurative paintings. I look at Constable's picture of Salisbury Cathedral, and I describe the Cathedral. If someone asks, 'How can you see such a thing in a two-foot-square piece of canvas?', then we know how to answer. A cathedral is something we see: and that which we see we can also see *in* a picture. Hence there is nothing special about a cathedral that forbids us from seeing it in a picture. Going back to music, however, we encounter a difficulty. Nobility is not something that we hear: it is not an *audibilium*. A virtue of this kind consists in a disposition to behave, to understand, to relate to others. It is displayed over time, by a person's conscious and self-sacrificing behaviour. You don't put your ear to a person's heart and listen for the nobility. And yet you hear nobility in music. So how is that possible? Similarity is significant only if something is *made* of it – as in figurative painting. Nothing is made of the similarities, such as they are, between noble people and the great first subject of the first movement of Elgar's Second Symphony. But much is made of that first subject. A tremendous process of musical development is launched by it, and it is through this musical process that the nobility flows.

But then, how does the nobility in Elgar's music *rub off on* the listener? Remember Plato's worry about the pop music of his day – that it damages the character of those who dance to it. It isn't difficult to see how such a thing might be true. After all, dancing is something you do. It involves relating to your own body, and to the bodies of others, in a conscious manner. Ways of dancing are bound to have an impact on such things as sexual display, courtship and erotic gestures. Ways of marching likewise – think of the goose step. Dancing affects the *embodiment* of the dancer, and embodiment can have virtuous and vicious forms. Thus there is a whole spectrum of conduct, from modesty to lewdness, in the matter of sexual presentation. Modesty has traditionally been regarded as a virtue, and lewdness as a vice. For our ancestors these were, indeed, paradigms of virtue and vice. And it is very clear that these traits of character are displayed in dancing. Plato's thought was that, if you display lewdness in the dances that you most enjoy, then you are that much nearer to acquiring the habit – the vice, so cheerfully celebrated on some of your favourite Greek urns and amphorae. I don't see any reason to doubt that.

Now dancing is not just moving, nor is it moving in response to a sound, a beat or whatever. Animals can do that, and you can train horses and elephants to move in time to a beat in the circus arena, with an effect that looks like dancing. But they are not dancing. To dance is to *move with* something, conscious that this is what you are doing. You move with the music, and also (in old-fashioned dances) with your partner. This 'moving with' is something that animals cannot do, since it involves the deliberate imitation of life radiating from another source than your own body. That in turn demands a conception of self and other, and of the relation between them – a conception which, I would argue, is unavailable outside the context provided by language use and first-person awareness. To say this is not to deny the very remarkable *co-ordination* that can exist between non-human animals. The ability of flocks of birds and shoals of fish to change direction suddenly, each bird or fish responding instantly to the smallest impulse from its neighbour, and the whole moving like a single organism guided by a single will – this is something that moves us to astonishment and wonder. But there is no I–You intentionality that links the fish to its neighbour in the shoal, and no bird has felt that strange fascination with another's self-sufficient movement that Shakespeare conveys:

When you do dance, I wish you
A wave of the sea, that you might ever do
Nothing but that ... (*The Winter's Tale*, IV, iv)

You dance with music, and that means understanding the music as the source of the movement that is also flowing through you. Since the movement in you is a movement of life, in which your position at one moment propels you to your position at the next, so do you understand the music. You are moving in sympathy with another source of life. Yet the thing you are dancing with is not alive, even if it is produced by someone alive – an increasingly rare event in itself. The life in the music is there *by virtue of* the fact that you can dance with it. The ultimate source of the life is you, the dancer. The life in the music is an *imagined* life, and the dance is your way of imagining it.

The moral quality of a work of music rubs off on those who dance to it, to the extent that they move in sympathy to that feature of the music. I don't say that the dancers *acquire* the virtue or vice in question. But they learn to sympathize with it. The process is really not so different from that which occurs in the theatre or when reading a novel. You come to sympathize with a character, and moral qualities are the usual target of this sympathy – not necessarily, of course. Misfortune might awaken sympathy without any judgement of character, but misfortunes suffered by villains don't (unless grossly disproportionate) elicit our sympathy. Few people have difficulty in understanding how virtue and vice can be portrayed in literature, and how the portrait might educate our sympathies, and in doing so bring about some discernible moral improvement.

Hume pointed out that our sympathies tend to coincide and reinforce each other, while our selfish desires conflict and therefore cancel each other out.[33] Hence whatever rubs off on us through sympathy towards a work of art or the people represented in it is of immense importance, and fully entitles us to make a moral judgement. A work of music that moves through its nobility is one that is encouraging sympathy towards that virtue, and as this sympathy accumulates so does the work improve the moral temper of humanity, as surely Mozart did through his operas and Beethoven through his symphonies. And this is the kind of effect that Plato had in mind when he argued against the corybants.

[33] *A Treatise of Human Nature*, Book 2.

Not all dancing is a response to the *moral* qualities of the music. Many people have danced to the Rolling Stones or Bruce Springsteen without directing their attention either to the aggression of the one or the sentimental eroticism of the other. You dance with the music, but not with its meaning. You can compartmentalize, and if you don't do so these days, you will find it very hard to dance, unless you are lucky enough to have mastered Salsa, Scottish Country Dancing, American Barn Dancing or some similar prelapsarian amusement. Such compartmentalization is harder when listening, however, and it is when listening that the moral qualities of a piece of music come vividly to the fore.

This brings me to the crux. What is the relation of listening to dancing? You don't listen *with* a piece of music; you listen *to* it. But the 'withness' of the dance is reproduced in listening. In some way you move *with* the music as you listen to it, and this movement is, or involves, a movement of sympathy. But the movement in the music is purely imaginary. All animals hear sounds in sequences, and group them in perception. This grouping forms part of what the psychologist S. A. Gelfand has called 'auditory scene analysis', and is the auditory equivalent of *Gestalt* perception in the visual sphere.[34] In listening to music, however, another kind of grouping occurs – one that requires an act of imagination. In hearing music we don't hear sequences of sounds only: we hear movement in and through those sounds. We group sounds in terms of this movement that we hear in them. Melodies begin, move on, conclude; rhythms propel the music forward, harmonies create tensions and resolutions which infect the melodic line. Everything is in motion – but it is a figurative motion, which corresponds to nothing real in the world of sound.

You can move with this imaginary movement. The person who listens to music is listening to the imaginary movement, following it, and being led by it in something like the way dancers are led by the music they are dancing to. And you can be moved by this imaginary

34 S. A. Gelfand, *Hearing: An Introduction to Psychological and Physiological Acoustics*, 3rd edn (New York, 1998).

movement, just as you can be moved by a fictional character. Your sympathies go out to Emma or David Copperfield in just the way they would go out to someone real.

So if there is a way in which the nobility of Elgar's music rubs off on the listener it must be through sympathy with the character that the listener hears in, and moves with, in the music. The nobility attributed to the music is not like that attributed to oak trees: it is heard in the individual piece, as presented in and through it. Listening is in some deep way like being in the presence of, and in communication with, a noble person. The similarities here are not between the shape of the music and the shape of a character. They are similarities between two experiences – it is as though we were confronting a noble person, and the acts, inspiration and honest manner of a noble character. We sense the open, responsible way in which that character ventures forth on a musical journey: and as the music unfolds the character is in some way put to the test by it.

That last feature is the important one, since it helps us to overcome the objection that I levelled at Kivy earlier. It helps us to say when resemblances are not just accidental but part of what the music means, part of its character for us and what it is presenting to us. The nobility is being presented *through* the musical line, and understanding that line is an integral part of understanding the character. It is not that the music is telling a story. Elgar's Second Symphony is as 'absolute' a piece of music as any symphony by Brahms. But we are being invited, all the same, into a kind of musical journey, and we go side by side into that journey with a companion – which is the music itself.

Seeing it in that way, we can see how we can make the most radical and far-reaching judgements of character in music. Many people react to the nobility in Elgar with a measure of distaste. This is imperial music, they say: this bold, honest, open melody also has a belligerent and self-consciously superior character, knocking lesser things down as it marches along. And when, in the second subject, you hear another mood, one of tenderness and longing, this too has something imperial to it, as though it were 'home thoughts from abroad', nostalgia for the place that distinguishes me and makes all these world-confronting adventures worthwhile. And when from time to time the music gets lost in those whispering passages, so strangely bleak and directionless, we feel the presence of *doubts*, the very same doubts that rotted the imperial project from within, and which led to its ultimate collapse.

I don't say that is how you *should* hear the Elgar. But you *can* hear it in that way, and it shows how deeply character and our reaction to character are revealed and developed in music – even the most abstract music. As with human character, the moral significance of a piece of music can be undermined by the revealing narcissistic gesture – the gesture that tells you that all this emotionality is not about the other but about the self. That, surely, is what you so often feel in Skryabin – for instance, in the late piano sonatas, with their perfumed harmonies and airy, look-at-me melodic lines, in which the tenderness is so evidently 'fixed'. Someone might wonder about the Elgar in this connection: the constant recourse to the lilting 2 + 1 rhythm, or the equally mesmeric rhythm (3+1)(2+1+1)(2+2) of the last movement: the music might seem stuck in a groove in the same way that certain characters are – unable to revise its fundamental outlook on the world, and hence more interested in self than other when it comes to the crisis. Yet it also confesses to crisis, in the many whispered passages where the forward movement is arrested, and in the tender, vulnerable-seeming second subject. The character displayed in this first movement is clearly a complex one, with moments of bluster, behind which we sense a vulnerable solitude and a quest for domestic affection.

Of course, that raises the question of how much of this is 'read into' the piece by the listener, and how we distinguish that which is read in from that which is 'really' there. I shall conclude with a couple of suggestions. The first is that attributing character to a piece of music is a form of interpretation, and the test of an interpretation lies in performance and reception. If my description of the moral character of the Elgar gives no hints as to how the piece might be performed, and no hints as to how it might be approached when listened to, then it is vacuous as an account of the piece's meaning. In some way the interpretation must translate into a way of playing, and a way of hearing. And surely we are well used to distinguishing performances in this way – criticizing a conductor for *missing* the character of a piece, or misrepresenting it, or spoiling it.

The second suggestion is that an interpretation must be *anchored* in the score. That is to say, it should not be reducible to a vague characterization of the whole piece – comparable to the description of the oak as a noble tree. It should *track the notes,* help the performer and the audience to understand just how one episode follows on another, why this note here, this harmony there. That is the truly difficult task of criticism. It is not enough simply to invent some fanciful story that happens to coincide with the musical movement. There is a test of correctness for criticism of this kind, and that test is the ear of the beholder. It must be that the alert listener or performer, on grasping what the critic is saying, responds with a *changed experience,* thinking, yes, that is how it should be played and heard. This does not mean that interpretation homes in on some single, final judgement – nothing in interpretation is final. It means that there is a test that every interpretation must pass if it is not to be a flight of fancy on the critic's part, and that test is the transformed experience of the listening or performing ear. And from that transformed experience comes the outgoing movement of sympathy towards the character that is heard in the music.

Seeing the moral character of works of music in this way opens the path to a theory of musical expression. Like the virtues and vices that we hear in music, expressive properties are denoted by terms lifted from their central employment in describing the emotional life of people, and applied to the movement that we 'hear in' works of music when we listen to them attentively, appreciating them for what they are in themselves. Terms used in this way form part of a complex and compelling figurative language. As I suggested above, any attempt to explain what they mean by means of analogy or similarity will be question-begging, replacing one metaphor with another and leaning equally on the as yet unexplained idea of 'hearing in'.

Expressive properties, so described, belong to the *meaning* of a work of music. They are not simply associations, reminiscences or evocations. They are what the music is about. A can be about B even if B does not exist, is indefinite or is other than A represents it to be. When we hear grief in a work of music, it is as though the music were saying something about that grief, but no particular grief, no grief that can be found in the world elsewhere than in this music. The grief here is part of the *content* of what we hear, imagined in the work as we imagine the face in the picture. Having said that, we must also emphasize that a work of music is not about its expressive content in exactly the way that a figurative painting is about its subject-matter. Expression and representation are distinct forms of artistic meaning. The representational work of art identifies a subject and says something about it. It has a content, that could be – partially, at least – rephrased in words. Thus a painting and a story can represent the same thing, and represent it differently. The 'aboutness' of representation is shared between a Nativity by Rogier van der Weyden and the sickliest Christmas card. Representation is a property that has no intrinsic aesthetic worth, though it may be executed in more or less worthy ways. A representation succeeds as a work of art when it is also *expressive*, as a kitsch Christmas card can never be truly expressive. Expression, by contrast, is an aesthetic value. For when we speak of 'expression' in the aesthetic context we are really describing *expressiveness*, the ability of a work of art to touch the heart of its devotees. Expressiveness is a mark of aesthetic success, even if it opens a work to criticism. The highly expressive music of Salome's soliloquy as she kisses the dead lips of the Baptist is surely an aesthetic triumph on Strauss's part. But it opens the work to another kind of judgement: are we being invited to identify with a diseased state of mind? Should we be drinking from this jewelled chalice or puking into it?

This points to a distinction that is of the first importance in criticism, the distinction between a transitive and an intransitive concept of expression. Musical scores are often marked *espressivo*. This is not an incomplete instruction: it is not an invitation to ask 'expressive of what?' It is an instruction to play expressively, *tout court*. Of course we can also use the term transitively, to describe a relation; in this sense a performance or a work of music is expressive only if there is a state of mind that is expressed by it. But that is an unusual use of the term, a kind of extension introduced by the critic, an attempt to interpret the music in words rather than to follow the instructions in the score. More usually the term 'expressive' is used of a piece of music in an intransitive sense that parallels the term *espressivo* written on the score. It is used to indicate the music's character as an object of aesthetic attention rather than to identify the state of mind that the music is trying to put across.

Listening to music, I have suggested, is downstream from dancing to it. It is a way of attending to a rhythmical and melodic movement, and making it your own. Dancing is, in its normal manifestation, a social activity: a 'dancing with'. And it conveys an attitude towards self and other that is immediately translated into gestures. Sometimes you may dance alone; but then you are not really alone, since you are dancing with the music – the music becomes your partner, and you fit your movements to the music as you might fit your movements to those of a partner on the dance-floor. Hence there is a great difference between the dancer who *understands* the music to which he or she is dancing and the dancer who merely dances along with it. Understanding involves translating the music into gestures that are like translations of its inner movement.

Why should we seek to understand music in that way? It is surely reasonable to suggest that we build our emotional lives through the relationships that our emotions precipitate, and that much of what we feel is the result of our various attempts to 'take responsibility' for our feelings, and to shape them in accordance with the sympathetic reactions that they provoke. Emotion is, to a great extent, a plastic material, and it is shaped not merely by the attempt to understand its object but also by the attempt to conduct ourselves as we should in the public arena. This 'making outward' of the inner life is what we might call emotional education, and it involves learning how to bring others into fruitful relation with our feelings, so as to reap the reward of their sympathy – though without necessarily being conscious that this is what we are doing.

Something like this can be seen in those festive, ceremonial and ritualized occasions when people allow themselves to *enjoy* their feelings, be they feelings of joy or of sorrow, and when the 'joining in' experience takes over. Much of the work accomplished at these times is a work of imagination, and it is hardly surprising if the occasions when we let ourselves feel to the limit are occasions when we are moved to sympathy towards purely imagined characters – characters around whose lives we can build our own responses without the danger attached to real human encounters. That is why the Greek tragic theatre took place as part of a religious festival and a communal celebration of the city and its gods. This was the occasion in which people could rehearse their sympathetic emotions, and thereby 'learn what to feel' in the difficult conditions that prevail everywhere in the human world except in the theatre.

Those thoughts suggest that emotions are plastic, that they have a social dimension, that we can build them through our sympathetic responses and take responsibility for their outward manifestation, and that in all this there is room for their education. It is not absurd to suggest that, if the theatre can play a part in this education, so too can music. But how? Here is one suggestion: when we move with the music, we are opening ourselves to the 'joining in' experience, moving *with* the music. In doing so we appropriate the gestures made by the music – we 'are the music while the music lasts', to borrow T. S. Eliot's well-known words. We are imaginatively building our own emotional *Entäusserung* by means of the music, in just the way that we might shape our sympathies in adopting the ritual gestures at a funeral or in joining in a military march on some patriotic occasion.[35]

A piece of expressive music does not 'stay put' with its emotional burden, locked for ever in its posture of nobility or wistful sadness. It moves through states of mind, exploring them, coming to hurdles,

---

[35] I take the word '*Entäusserung*' ('making outer, objective, real'), as I take the background argument, from Hegel's *Phenomenology of Spirit*.

obstacles and crises, and perhaps emerging from some deep gloom
into the light and, by doing so, showing that *it can indeed be done*.
Thus Schubert can show us stark terror in the G major quartet gradually interrogating itself, coming to acceptance, finding beauty and
serenity in the very recognition that everything must end. Such a
statement will be plausible as commentary only if the critic backs it
up with a compelling description of the musical narrative. Anybody
can say, 'Here the music is sad, because of the minor key, drooping
phrases and so on'. But not everybody can show how a composer like
Schubert can make music which *lifts itself out of* its own despair, by
purely musical devices – devices that convince us both musically and
emotionally, and which show how emotional processes can be begun
in music, and also ended there. The music is taking you through
something, eliciting sympathetic responses that might in due course
be incorporated into the *Entäusserung* of your own inner life. You are
being, in a sense, socialized, even by the most private and intimate of
music – perhaps especially by this. (Consider those intimate gestures
in Brahms's chamber music, for instance – such as the slow movement of the F minor quintet – invitations to tenderness of a *long-term*
kind, pictures of domestic love which we know can never be realized,
but which remain in the soul for ever, as ideals and reproaches.)

This brings me to a point that has been raised by Jerrold Levinson,
in connection with the variations from Schubert's 'Death and the
Maiden' quartet.[36] As Levinson points out, when we respond to the
emotional content of a work like this we are also, and *at the same
time*, being led through a musical argument. It is not that we are
noticing analogies or picking up allusions. We are exercising our
musical understanding. The music is as though *exploring* a state of
mind, so that the movement takes the emotion forwards, shows its
possibilities of development, resolution, catastrophe and redemption. In Schubert, as the example makes so clear, this is fundamental
to the greatness of the result. Possibilities of feeling are being opened
before us, and opened by the musical syntax. Listeners who bring

---

[36] Talk delivered in Graz, at the Musik-Philosophie forum, November 2015.

their love, their grief, their sorrow to such a work of music find that it is, as it were, seized from them, made to move before their ears, wrapped into a musical process that is also a form of the deepest sympathy, and then – miraculously – brought to the kind of conclusion that life itself seldom offers. And surely that is part of the point of art, that it offers conclusions in a world that is otherwise deprived of them.[37] This is not escapism but its opposite: taking some feeling, however bleak, to its conclusion, and showing thereby that it is in our nature to bear it.

Often the sceptical argument is made, as it was made by Hanslick, that music cannot be an expression of emotion, for the very reason that the same piece of music can be used in operatic or liturgical contexts to set completely contrasting texts, and yet appreciated *as music* in both its uses. But the objection misunderstands the kind of relation we have in mind, when we describe music as expressive. We are really talking of a 'matching' relation – the kind of relation that exists between a piece of music and the movements of the one who dances to it. Think of the many attempts at a choreography for the *Rite of Spring,* in some of which the sacrificial dance becomes a joyful moment of renewal, in others a sadistic assault on the very idea of the feminine. When we dance to a piece, or weave our gestures around it like the listeners to a raga, we are matching one thing to another, making connections, putting ourselves into what we hear and finding ourselves *realized* in it. The connections that we make are tacit, wordless, motivated simply by their felt appropriateness, as the music leads us onwards along contours that it marks out in its own imagined space.

This matching process is governed by the very same concept that shapes the music – the concept of what fits. In just the way that a gesture fits the music to which it is a response, so does one musical event fit its predecessor and successor in the score. The grammatical constraints on the music are thereby transferred to the gestures that

---

[37] On this point see the generous argument of Raymond Tallis, with Julian Spalding, in *Summers of Discontent: The Purpose of the Arts Today* (London, 2014).

we fit to it, so that they participate in the musical order. It is in this way that we are consoled by music – so it seems to me, at least – namely, that it provides order and completion to states of being that drift through our lives in fragmentary or inconclusive ways. That is only a suggestion, of course. But if we look carefully at what goes on in choreography, I think we will see the truth in it. Frederick Ashton's famous choreography for the César Franck *Variations Symphoniques* is an eloquent example, in which the matching relation penetrates the entire musical structure and is also penetrated by it. And, of course, you could choreograph this beautiful work in quite another way, and the result might fit just as well.

If we can develop a theory of understanding expression along the lines that I have indicated, we will surely be more than halfway to our goal, which is to say why expression in music really matters. It matters because it is a manifestation of the moral life, a way of inviting us to shape our sympathies in response to a character imagined in musical form.

4

Music and the Transcendental

When the question of the meaning of music was debated by the German Romantics, the idea began to emerge that there is an especially pure kind of music that would encapsulate what music really and truly means, without the adulteration of words, dance or theatre. At a certain point critics and philosophers began to refer to '*absolute Tonkunst*', the absolute art of sound, in order to distinguish the purely instrumental music of the concert hall, designed to be listened to in silence, and presented in an atmosphere of reverential attention, from the applications of music in opera and song, in dance and *Gebrauchsmusik*, as when meals, ceremonies and sporting events were accompanied by a band. The phrase '*absolute Tonkunst*' probably first appears in E. T. A. Hoffmann's celebrated review of Beethoven's Fifth Symphony, in 1810. By then the claim had already been made – by Tieck, Wackenroder and others – that music offers access to the 'transcendental', its significance lying largely in its power to accomplish this.[38]

Before considering what this reference to the transcendental might mean, we must acknowledge the enormous cultural chasm that separates us from the world of the German Romantics. Their musical culture was a listening culture; ours is a culture of hearing. Much music is heard; not much now is listened to. And among the music

---

[38] See Linda Siegel, 'Wackenroder's Musical Essays in "Phantasien über die Kunst"', *Journal of Aesthetics and Art Criticism*, vol. 30 (1972), pp. 351–8.

that is heard, far more is overheard than is directly heard in the centre of the ear. A new kind of music has emerged precisely to occupy the background, rather than the foreground, of our attention. You hear this music in bars and restaurants all across the world, and people habituated to it can be encouraged to *hear* music only if the music is pushed rudely through the barrier of background noise – say by a loud beat, or a sexy voice, or both. To suggest that music has a special relation to the transcendental, when the primary experience of music is merely that of an unceasing murmur on the auditory horizon, is to strain credibility. But if music is to be appreciated through an act of reverential attention, which isolates it from the surrounding noise and frames it in a sound world of its own, then the suggestion does not seem so absurd.

Even in the old listening culture, however, listening has been only one way of relating to music, and has always depended on another and more intimate engagement with sound. As Férdia Stone-Davis has emphasized, music is first and foremost something that we *do* – it is brought into being by human actions, and those actions do not occur in a cultural void. Performances come to us marked with the intentions and bodily movements of their participants. Music does not leak on to the airwaves from some transcendental source. It arises from the activities of real and present individuals, for whom, as Stone-Davis puts it, music is a process in transition, a process in which performers negotiate thresholds between one action and its sequel, or between self and other.[39]

Music requires us to divide and measure time, to understand movement in time and to link actions to each other in terms of their temporal relations. In which case the claim that music has some special and intimate connection to the transcendental begins to look decidedly odd. Music ought to be more bound than any other art form to temporal, transient and empirical happenings, since that is what it essentially *is*: an event in time, produced by the strenuous

[39] See Férdia Stone-Davis, 'Music and Liminality: Becoming Sensitized', in Birgit Abels, ed., *Embracing Restlessness: Cultural Musicology* (Hildesheim, 2017).

activity of ordinary mortals. So how is it that we are tempted to think of music in another way, as a window on to the transcendental, a place in the order of time where the eternal shines through? It is not the German Romantics only who have seen music in this way. The ancient theory of the 'music of the spheres' was based on a similar idea, and the many attempts to give a mathematical foundation to the theory of harmony have prompted the thought that music expounds, in time, relations and realities that are in themselves timeless. And when this idea was taken up by the German Romantics, it was in the context of a kind of theological anxiety – the anxiety that European civilization was losing its religious anchor and needed another way of reaching and holding on to the transcendental than that provided by religion. The Romantics had the question of God. And music was part of their answer.

The terms 'transcendent' and 'transcendental' have many applications, three of which particularly concern us. There is the theological idea, according to which God is said to transcend the world of creation, and also to transcend our attempts to define or describe Him. There is the philosophical idea, typified by Kant, according to which certain objects of thought transcend the conditions laid down by the understanding, and can therefore be thought only negatively, as lying *beyond* thought, so to speak. And there is what we might call the aesthetic idea, in which we speak of 'transcendent' versions of empirical phenomena. Thus we might refer to Tristan's passion for Isolde as 'transcending' the bounds of ordinary erotic love, while nevertheless being an example of it, or Iago's hatred of Othello as transcending the bounds of ordinary hatred, while yet being hatred. As to whether this third use of the language of transcendence has any bearing on musical meaning, this is an issue to which I return below.

Theologians are often prepared to allow knowledge of God, even though he transcends our cognitive powers; Kant, however, did not allow positive knowledge of the transcendental. There is, in the literature, a lot of having cake and eating it, and it is rare to find philosophers or theologians who take seriously their own conclusion that this or that is really transcendental, since if it is so, how can they know that it is so? The whole concept only makes sense on the assumption that we *can* in some way reach beyond the ordinary empirical world, to the something we know not what that transcends it. Can we or can't we? This is the dilemma that Kant bequeathed to his immediate successors and they did not resolve the dilemma but tried to have things both ways – espousing a kind of idealism that both denied access to the transcendental and then allowed it in through the dialectic of reason – as in Hegel's *Logic*. But in that case, of course, it is no longer transcendental. Hegel called it 'absolute' instead, and the word entered philosophy in this way, just about the same time as it entered the study of music in the writings of Hoffmann and Hanslick.

I have a lot of time for Hegel. Nevertheless, I do not think that the path of absolute idealism is the one that we should take out of the dilemma that I stated. The assumption in Hegel is that whenever we encounter a limit in thought, feeling or conduct we can, as it were, rise above it, and thereby see to the other side. To say that is both to affirm and to deny that there are limits. It is not to advance beyond the limits but simply to muddle them, so that we don't know where they are.

I take it that those who have turned to music in this dilemma have done so precisely because approaching the transcendental through *music* does not require the belief that we can approach it through language, or through our ordinary conceptual powers. In this way we can maintain the belief that the transcendental is incapable of being defined or described while surreptitiously offering a back door to it, so to speak. We offer a way of effing the ineffable. Just such a move was made by Schopenhauer, in the essay on 'The Metaphysics of Music' included in the second volume of *The World as Will and Representation*. According to Schopenhauer, music is a non-conceptual medium which, for that very reason, is able to 'get behind' the world of representations, so as to present the underlying reality, which is Will. Music presents the Will directly, without the intervening veil of concepts. Is this a coherent response to our dilemma? Does it not invite Frank Ramsey's remark to Wittgenstein, that 'what we can't say we can't say, and we can't whistle it either'?

The first step in confronting that response is to recognize that there is more than one kind of knowledge. Philosophers are used to the distinction between knowing that and knowing how, and to the wider distinction between theoretical and practical knowledge. Someone who knows what to do in some difficult situation certainly has a cognitive possession that the merely bewildered lack, but it is not a possession that could be stated as a collection of truths. He could know what to do even if he had no words to express it. And his knowledge exists not as a prediction of some future state of affairs but as a readiness to act, spread over intentions and perceptions that lie below the horizon of language.

Kant was inclined to say that the only way to understand the transcendental is to flip from theoretical to practical reason, to recognize that we are wrong to think that we can have knowledge *about* the transcendental but right to think that, when we reach the limit of empirical knowledge, there is still somewhere to go. We should step sideways, as it were, and recognize that reason does not merely describe the world but also commands us to change it. And really the invocation of the transcendental is a reminder that reason knows the world in another way – as a sphere of action, in which we can freely change the way things are.

Whatever we think of Kant's way out of the dilemma, it is clearly not what people have had in mind in invoking music as a channel to the transcendental. Music is an action, and in certain circumstances it is also an invitation to action on the part of its listeners – for instance, in dancing. But this invitation can be resisted; and it is precisely when resisting, so as to contemplate the musical movement as something objective, outside us, occurring in a space of its own, that we feel its 'transcendental' gravity. It is in these circumstances that music seems to lift us free from our ordinary preoccupations. It works on us then like the Hindu and Buddhist meditation techniques, detaching our thoughts and emotions from the things of this world, and directing them to a realm in which temporal things find their eternal counterparts.

However, what would be the difference, on this view, between contemplating the transcendental by means of the music and just contemplating the music? Granted that fixing your attention on the music conveys a sense of sublime peacefulness or release from this world, why is that not simply an effect of the *music,* rather than of something transcendental that we perceive *through* the music? The very transcendental nature of the alleged object implies that we could not make the difference in practice between the two accounts, and that therefore the invocation of the transcendental is, so to speak, doing no work of its own. It is just something we say, without grounds and without knowing what we mean by it.

It is not only the transcendental that is ineffable: many of our experiences are like this, containing some core content that we cannot put into words, since all words fall short of it. A nameless fear, an indefinable joy, a *je ne sais quoi*, an inexpressible longing and so on. There is an interesting example of music filling in the gap left by words in Beethoven's setting of *'Namenlose Freude'*, 'nameless joy', in *Fidelio.* Here we really do feel that the music has supplied what words could never express – a joy that is not of this world and which unites Florestan and Leonora in a space of their own, visitors from some angelic realm that you and I could never attain to. Is this an example of music opening a path to the transcendental? Not exactly. After all, the words go *some* way to identifying the feeling that the characters are trying to express. We are dealing here with the aesthetic, rather than the metaphysical, idea of the transcendental. Beethoven is presenting an empirical experience that points beyond its own limit, so to speak. He is not taking us into a transcendental realm. His music works in the way operatic music works in general: by taking a defined situation and filling it with a movement of its own.

We can draw a few lessons from the example nevertheless. First, the music is presenting us with something. It does not *describe* the 'nameless joy' of the protagonists, and is therefore not a vehicle of 'knowledge that'. But it makes us acquainted with their feeling: in other words, it conveys a kind of 'knowledge by acquaintance'. And perhaps this is a useful paradigm in art. Susanne Langer wrote of art as a system of 'presentational symbols' (in *Feeling and Form* and elsewhere). I am not sure what she meant exactly. But there is certainly a cognitively significant process that involves presenting something for attention without describing it. The original of this idea is Croce's theory, in his *Aesthetic*, that art expresses the 'intuition' rather than the concept of its subject-matter. And something of that idea survives, too, in Nelson Goodman's theory of expression as metaphorical exemplification.[40] It is as though art drew our attention to things, without reducing them to examples of some general category. Art shows, presents, the individual, shows it as standing forth from the cloak of our concepts, in a naked completeness. The implication is that it takes art to achieve this 'presentation', and that individual things, experiences, people, situations don't do this on their own. It is as though we could reach, through art, to a perfect version of our imperfect states of mind: a version that 'transcends' the ordinary limitations of the human psyche.

Knowledge by acquaintance is not replaceable by knowledge by description, and contains a component that could reasonably be described as 'ineffable' – the critical 'what it is like' which we might attempt to capture in metaphors but which can be properly known only through acquaintance, as feelings are known. It is a plausible claim that this kind of knowledge is conveyed by works of art. And maybe there is a sense in which the ineffable heart of our more elusive experiences can be 'effed' by a work of music, even though it cannot be put into words. The Schubert songs seem so often to work in this way, taking a simple situation and conveying a 'quite peculiar' emotion towards it, an emotion which comes immediately to mind in the music but which we struggle in vain to describe. (Think of the way in which Schubert captures the sentiment of Rückert's 'Du bist die Ruh', for instance.)

This observation connects with what Collingwood says in *Principles of Art* about the 'particular' emotion conveyed by Brahms's song 'Feldeinsamkeit', and with Wittgenstein's remarks in *The Brown Book*, contrasting the transitive and intransitive senses of

---

[40] Susanne Langer, *Feeling and Form* (New York, 1953). Nelson Goodman, *Languages of Art: An Approach to a Theory of Symbols* (Oxford, 1969).

'particular'.[41] When you say that a piece of music expresses a quite particular or peculiar feeling, you are using the words 'particular' or 'peculiar' intransitively, so as to *refuse* any further description of the feeling than the one you have given. You are referring to just *this* particular feeling, the feeling conveyed by 'Feldeinsamkeit', which is the full and sufficient identification of what you have in mind. And you are implying that the feeling could be fully and sufficiently identified only in this way. In the language of literary theory, you are saying that here form and content are inseparable.

When we speak of the way in which a work of music captures or presents some state of mind we are not speaking neutrally, as though recording some conventional or external connection. We are referring to the achieved *content* of the work. In general, works of art have meaning only to the extent that they are meaningful, and meaningful only to the extent that they are successful acts of *communication* with the audience. A work of music that succeeds in effing some ineffable emotion is, to that extent, a successful work of music, one that has crossed the barrier from artistic nothingness into the realm of aesthetic value. Only a minority of works do this.

Thus if someone were to say that music in general acquaints us with the transcendental, then, even if we can make sense of that, it would not amount to very much. 'So what?' is the response. If *all* music does this, even the trite and the meaningless, then this gives us no reason for thinking that music tells us anything that we wanted to know. The only interesting thesis would be that there are pieces of *meaningful* music in which the meaningfulness resides in presenting, in some way, the transcendental, and thereby effing the ineffable.

You can appreciate what I have in mind by turning again to the case of meditation. People use many different props and catalysts in order to meditate. Some burn joss sticks, some play soft music, some listen to ragas, some sit by still waters and dream. But clearly

---

[41] L. Wittgenstein, *The Blue and Brown Books* (Oxford, 1958), p. 158f. R. G. Collingwood, *The Principles of Art* (Oxford, 1938), Chapter 6.

none of those things bears within it the essential reference to the transcendental that the meditating person hopes to recuperate. If there is a case of music actually putting us in touch with the transcendental, then this must be an achievement of the same order as that of Schubert's 'Doppelgänger', as it presents us with the dreadful experience recounted in Heine's poem and so leads us, cynical postmoderns though we are, to know by acquaintance the corrosive jealousy of unrequited romantic love, in those days when you couldn't get on your bicycle and check out the girls across the valley.

If we are to make headway with our quest for a relation between music and the transcendental, then we should think of some *particular* piece of music which is both meaningful as music and points, through its meaning, towards the transcendental, in such a way as to make the transcendental present to our minds. I suspect that many people want to say some such thing of the late Beethoven quartets, which so often have the air of an inner communing with God, or of sacred polyphony set to simple words, like the *Ave Verum Corpus* of Mozart or that of Byrd. But it is seldom clear that we could distinguish, in such cases, between a piece of music that presents us with the transcendental and a piece that presents us with feelings *towards* the transcendental. There is much religious music, and the great examples – Victoria, Palestrina, Bach, Rachmaninov and Messiaen – acquaint us with profound religious feelings. It would be normal for religious people to describe their feelings on hearing such music as directed towards, or about, the transcendental. But that does not mean that the music *expressing* those feelings is about the transcendental. In all musical communication sentiment is passed by sympathy from the music to the listener, but it is *sentiment* that is passed, not the thing it is about. And when this thing is described as transcendental – in other words, as lying in some way beyond the reach of human knowledge – the natural conclusion to draw is that music cannot reach that far.

We seem to have come up against an impassable barrier, therefore. We can assign a role to music in effing the ineffable, when the ineffable is the non-propositional content of our states of mind – a content that can be presented to the imagination but not described in words. But it cannot eff what lies beyond human acquaintance entirely. Is that, then, the end of the story? Not quite.

Consider our knowledge of each other. When I react to your words and behaviour, to your facial expression, to the many signs that you give of your awareness of me, I am reacting to a human being. My emotions and thoughts are focused on you, as revealed to me in the flesh. But that is not how I see you. I see you as a subject like me, another in whose point of view I too appear as another. My feelings and responses reach across to you, but overshoot their target, so to speak, not latching on to the visible embodiment of you but seeking out the I in you. I address my words and looks to the thing that addresses me from your words and looks, and that thing I see as an individual centre of consciousness, located nowhere visible, but standing as though on the horizon of our shared world. I suspect that this is a primary experience of the 'transcendental' – i.e., of that which is somehow beyond the limit of the empirical world. My emotions and responses towards the other reach out beyond the observable other, as though to make contact with this thing on the horizon, this pure perspective which I cannot reach because to reach it I would have to be you.

In other words, there seems to be, contained within our ordinary interpersonal attitudes, an element of overreach, a direction on the world that looks through the world to that which cannot be contained in it. There is, in our outlook on the world, a kind of hunger for the transcendent – a reaching beyond what is given to the subjectivity that is revealed in it.[42] This hunger is satisfied only when we can sense ourselves to be in the 'real presence', the *shakhinah*, by which what is transcendent makes itself manifest in the here and now. Religion lays great store by this experience, which of its nature cannot be given an *a priori* guarantee but which is recorded by all the great mystics and divines as the core of their faith. It is the *mysterium tremendum*

---

[42] I have developed this point in *The Soul of the World* (Princeton, 2014).

et fascinans referred to by Rudolf Otto in his *The Idea of the Holy*.[43] And it is an experience whose ineffability is part of what is valued: for it is a visitation from a sphere that cannot be reached by any merely human effort, and cannot be known except in this way. It is a kind of gift, for which we cannot ask since we lack words to summon it. Hence, in usual religious parlance, it is identified as one manifestation of the Grace of God.

Could it be that music can capture this experience, and make it imaginatively available to us ordinary mortals? I think this is what people have had in mind when they have defended the view that music can reach to the transcendental. Music can put us in the presence of something that has no place in this world, and which moves in a world of its own. And it can do this in a way that seems both orderly and personal, moving with a complete necessity that is also a kind of freedom. Two features of music contribute to this effect. First, the space of music, in a listening culture, is what I call an 'acousmatic space': it is a space full of movement and fields of force in which nothing actually moves, and of which we ourselves could never be a part. In a mysterious way the order of music transforms sequences of sounds into melodies that begin and end, chords that occupy whole areas and gravitational fields that push and pull in ways of their own.

Secondly, the virtual causality that operates in musical space is or aims to be a causality of reason. In successful works of music there is a reason for each note, though not necessarily a reason that could be put into words. Each note is a response to the one preceding it and an invitation to its successor. Of course, sequences in music may sound facile, mechanical or arbitrary, so that the listener has no sense of a reasoned progression. But when that happens we are apt to dismiss the music as trivial or meaningless. Real music is not a sequence of mechanical movements but a continuous *action*, to which the 'why?' of interpersonal understanding applies. The important works exhibit both the freedom and the necessity to which our self-sufficient

---

[43] Rudolf Otto, *Das Heilige*, 1917, tr. as *The Idea of the Holy* (Oxford, 1923).

actions always aspire – each detail *must* be as it is and where it is, and yet each detail must also be freely chosen. It is as though the space of music were awaiting visitation, and whatever appears in it is called upon to live the life of reason, just as we do.

This returns me to the observations made earlier. Stone-Davis is of course right that music is an action, which takes place in physical space, and which creates relations, differences, proximities and thresholds in the world of human communities. However, it is a physical action of a special kind, one that creates a *virtual* action in a space of its own. Just as the painter applying pigments in one space creates a world of imaginary beings in another, so does the musician making sounds in our space create virtual actions and movements in the acousmatic space of music. I have tried elsewhere to say just why this is important, and why it is a mistake to argue, as Andy Hamilton argues, for example, that the physical activity and its attributes deliver the real essence of music, with the acousmatic experience as just one, historically transient, way of hearing it.[44] On the contrary, the acousmatic experience of the listener is the source of what we most value in music, and if it disappeared what remains would not be the art form that has been so central to our civilization since ancient times. In listening to music we enter another space from the one occupied by the performer, and in that space a kind of free causality opens to our perception – a causality in which gestures achieve completion from their own inner urgency, and unimpeded by the obstacles that clutter the physical world. This, it seems to me, is what the Romantics noticed when they singled out music as leading us out of this world into a transcendental reality that we otherwise would not encounter.

Thanks to the two features I mentioned, we hear music as imbued with an intentionality, an 'aboutness' of its own. It is as though it were reacting in its own way to something that we cannot know or observe, since this thing is buried in that space that we cannot enter, audible, so to speak, on its far horizon, but heard only by the music

---

[44] See my review of Andy Hamilton, *Aesthetics and Music* (London, 2007), in *Mind*, vol. 117 (July 2008).

and not by us. Yet we move with the music's sympathetic movement, and it is this, I think, which gives us the impression that we have been put in touch, in some way, with the transcendental. I suggest that this experience is familiar from the world of chamber music, and from the instrumental works of Bach, as well as from much sacred music. The pure polyphony of Palestrina, the plangent Responsories of Victoria, the solo violin sonatas and partitas of Bach and the latter's *Art of Fugue* and *Goldberg Variations* all seem to move in sympathy to some source beyond the limits of this world, but which finds an echo in the sacred space of music.

Of course, the best we can conclude from this is that the music helps us to imagine some kind of contact with the transcendental. It certainly offers no proof that such contact is possible. Perhaps our hunger for the transcendental is a primitive fact about us, which corresponds to nothing real. But about that there is nothing to be said in any case. Of course, the desire to find comfort in the unknowable is always with us, the knowable being so devastatingly devoid of it. But we are led always into contradiction by the pursuit of this desire. Consider St Paul's and the Prayer Book's reference to the 'peace which passeth understanding': is this not already a contradiction – for if it really passes understanding, how do we know it is *peace*? It would not offer comfort to think of this thing if we did not think of it as bringing the peace and reconciliation that we long for. And the same goes for the transcendental realm that we glimpse in the sacred space of music. We feel that music is putting us in touch with another world, beyond the reach of our human knowledge, the very world that appears in the epiphanies referred to by Rudolf Otto in *Das Heilige*. But we also want that world to be good to us, to contain a solace and a vindication, and to ease us as it were into its arms. What would be the point otherwise? And yet music can do this only as the Prayer Book does it, by helping us to see that unattainable world in human terms – providing us like Beethoven's *Heiliger Dankgesang* with an image of healing, like Messiaen's *Turangalîla Symphony* and *Transfiguration* with a vision of the dancing cosmos or like Bach's '*Erbarme Dich*' with a supreme act of penitence, into which we are drawn and which comforts us with the sense that, if there is forgiveness, then it will be granted in return for *this*. These experiences transcend our ordinary ability to articulate them, and do so thanks to the music. But to say that they reach beyond the empirical to the transcendental is to misrepresent their way of working.

This returns me, in conclusion, to the aesthetic idea of the transcendental. Human beings find significance in many things, and attempt to convey that significance in works of art. But works of art also alter and embellish the things that they convey – make the beautiful more beautiful, the moving more moving and the profound more profound. They do this by pushing the empirical phenomenon to its limit, so to speak, to the point where it seems to break free of itself and to cast a shadow in the beyond. That is what Beethoven does in 'Namenlose Freude', and Bach in 'Erbarme Dich'. It is not that there is a transcendent reality which is made present by these sublime expressions of emotion, but rather that they endow empirical emotions with a completeness and purity that in everyday life they could never attain. Always our feelings are mixed, contaminated by other concerns, by needs and distractions. Never in everyday life can we give ourselves completely to love, joy, forgiveness, grief or worship. But these emotions nevertheless conjure a pure world of sympathy, in which they exist in their completed form, unsullied by self-interest, objects of contemplation which bear their meaning entirely within themselves. Music can take us into that world, presenting us with 'transcendent' versions of emotions that we know only in their bounded and empirical form. But, in saying this, we are not endorsing the view that music gives us access to the transcendental. On the contrary, we are saying that it presents us with the *empirical*, the here and now, by showing it in its purified and completed form. And maybe that is the best that we can ask for.

5

Tonality

Many phenomena have been referred to by the one word 'tonality', and it is easy, in exploring this topic, to get lost in definitions. If we mean by 'tonality' the strict use of the diatonic scale and functional harmony as in the 'common practice' of Western art music, then it is clear that tonality is only one possible form of musical organization, and one from which we may very well have moved on. If, however, we take 'tonality' to cover all musical organization in which a given pitch class has the character of a tonic, in which octaves are regarded as equivalent, and in which other pitches are arranged on a definite scale of intervals along the octave, it is less clear that we are referring to an accidental feature of music. Moreover, even if we are using the term in the narrow sense exemplified by the Western classical tradition and Western popular music, it may well be that we are referring to a practice that is in some way a *paradigm* of musical organization – a practice that illuminates the nature and goal of musical organization in all its many forms.

As a result of Schoenberg's musical innovations, and the polemics of philosophical critics such as Adorno and Bloch, 'tonality' came to denote a crux in musical history, a contest in which it was, at a certain point, necessary to take sides.[45] In his *Philosophy of New Music*, first published in 1947, Adorno makes the following claims:

---

[45] Theodor Adorno, *The Philosophy of Modern Music*, tr. A. G. Mitchell and W. V. Blomster (New York, 1973). Ernst Bloch, *Essays on the Philosophy of Music*, tr. P. Palmer, intro. D. Drew (Cambridge, 1985).

- that the diatonic scale arranges pitches which could be arranged in other ways and still be used to make intelligible and enjoyable music;
- that melodies could be constructed without the use of scales, and without a mode or a key;
- that the 12 notes of the chromatic scale could be used in such a way that no one of them emerges as tonic, or as in any other way privileged, without sacrificing the experience of musical order;
- that non-tonal harmonies, construed as simultaneities, will abolish the distinction between consonance and dissonance, opening the way to new forms of harmonic sequence.

Those claims are both interesting in themselves and invitations to experiment. But they are also an intrusion of abstract thought into a realm of empirical knowledge, thereby challenging wisdom that had been slowly acquired over centuries and which was not in any sense the product of a single brain. The fact that Adorno gives little or no evidence for them counts for nothing, since they are *philosophical*, part of an *a priori* attempt to found an alternative to the existing music. For Adorno they promised the renewal of music, the break with a tradition that had become banal and cliché-ridden, and the hope of a fresh start in the face of cultural decline. Those thoughts were wound in to a philosophy that combined Frankfurt School Marxism, the denunciation of popular culture and a high-brow adulation of all that was recondite, unpredictable and difficult to follow. Adorno had the gift of masking his idiosyncratic views as necessary truths, and clothing unsubstantiated speculations in the garments of priestly authority. He was the advocate of an intimidating orthodoxy. And yet the actual arguments, both in Adorno's book and in Schoenberg's original articles,[46] are little more than

---

[46] Many of them collected as *Style and Idea: Selected Writings of Arnold Schoenberg*, the extended edition of which, edited by Leonard Stein, was published in London in 1975. An earlier and shorter collection had appeared in 1951.

rhetorical flourishes, which assume what they set out to prove. The only *proof* of Adorno's position is the proof that has so far not materialized: namely, the emergence of a canon of acknowledged masterpieces, composed according to his principles and accepted into the repertoire. All that we have received from his followers is a reiteration of the cliché that musical organization in our tradition is fundamentally arbitrary, and can be remade according to other rules – permutational, aleatoric, serial and so on – while engaging the perceptions and interests that have emerged over centuries in the concert hall. That cliché commits the paradigm error of philosophy, which is to argue *a priori* for a thesis that can be confirmed or refuted only by experience.

There is in fact nothing arbitrary about the diatonic scale or the place of the tonic within it. While there can be other scales, some sounding strange to Western ears, they are in almost every case attempts to divide up the octave, to provide significant points of rest and closure and to preserve, in whatever remembered form, the natural harmonies delivered by the overtone series. The diatonic scale is one of a number of modes derived from medieval church music, and its history is not a history of arbitrary invention but one of gradual discovery. Equal temperament, the circle of fifths, the chromatic scale, modulation, voice-leading and triadic harmony – all these are discoveries, representing at each stage an advance into a shared tonal space. The result is not the product of decision or design: it is as natural and embedded in our experience as the post and beam in architecture or frying and baking in cookery. If composers are to 'make it new', then they must recognize this natural quality and not defy it, even when venturing into areas where the old discoveries provide no obvious guidance. Yet defiance of nature has become an orthodoxy, and when asked to explain and justify this defiance composers will very often lean on some variant of Adorno's philosophy. In the immediate aftermath of the Second World War much music for the concert hall tended in the direction indicated by Stockhausen's *Gruppen* – elaborate sound effects, organized by arcane systems of rhythm and pitch, which no normal ear can hold together as music but which comes with intimidating programme notes explaining why this doesn't matter, and why the normal ear is an impediment to creative music in any case.

What, exactly, should be our attitude to the dispute over tonality, now that the initial commotion has died down? Any philosophical discussion must begin from the distinction between sound and tone.[47] From the material point of view music is composed of sounds: it is an *art* of sound. But from the aesthetic point of view it is our way of hearing those sounds that is significant: and they are not heard as sounds. They are not heard, that is, as noises are heard, or as the ambient sounds that surround us everywhere are heard, namely, as auditory sources of information. They are heard as tones, elements in an ordered *Gestalt*, in which movement, tension, release and closure are the governing principles. They hold our attention for their own sake and not as vehicles of information about the surrounding world, and they exist in a space of their own, that has no spatial connection with the space in which we live.

I will illustrate the distinction with a simple example, the folk song 'Lovely Joan' (used as the second subject in Vaughan Williams's *Fantasy on Greensleeves*; Ex. 1). The notation here identifies pitched sounds in a sequence. But that is arguably not what we hear when we hear the melody. We hear something begin with an upbeat. We hear this upbeat depart from one place and land in another, and we are instantly aware that the two places are important relative to each other. The melody unfolds as a movement in musical space; there are points of tension, notably the high D in bar 6, and points of relaxation, notably the low D in bar 5. The melody moves towards closure, which is achieved with the concluding one and a half bars, as the melody rises to the leading note, C, and then falls through a sixth, rises again and falls to the C below before concluding on D, which has been heard throughout as the tonic.

That the melody is not identical with the sequence of sounds in which it is heard is shown by a simple observation. The concluding

---

[47] I have spelled this distinction out at length in *The Aesthetics of Music* (Oxford, 1997), Chapter 2.

Ex. 1

phrase, Y, is acoustically identical with the phrase X, which establishes D as the tonic in bars 2 and 3. But it is musically entirely different. X is not heard as a closure at all, but as the launch of the melody
into musical space. In other words, the sequence of sounds occurs
twice, even though the melody has no repeats. We hear the melody
in the sequence of sounds, and this is an act of perception over and
above the perception of the sounds, just as seeing a face in a picture
is an act of perception over and above seeing the coloured patches.
That is why the sound sequence can repeat itself, even though the
melody does not, just as an array of coloured patches can be repeated
on a canvas, even though the one instance is seen as an ear and the
other as a nose.

When hearing a pitched sound as music, we are hearing dynamic
relations, as one tone conjures its successor, creating a field of force
through which the music moves, drawn this way and that by a form
of gravity. It should be noted that, in the example, we are dealing with
a *modal* melody, in which the leading note, rather than the dominant,
has the task of directing the melody towards its final tonic. Features
that are prominent in the diatonic tonality of our classical tradition
are already present in the modal idioms that preceded it.

The dynamic relations to which I have referred indicate some part
of what is at stake in the dispute over tonality, which arose as a result
of the claim, made variously by Schoenberg, Adorno and Bloch, that
the tonal idiom and standard tonal devices had 'become banal', and as
a result could no longer be sincerely used by a composer who wished
for an authentic and modern voice – a voice truly expressive of the
inner life, rather than merely imitative of a form of life that is no

longer available.[48] This dispute naturally raises the question whether there are other ways of organizing sequences of pitched sound that would reproduce the distinction between sound and tone – which would enable us to hear the kind of movement, tension, gravitation, arrival and departure that stand out so vividly in the simple folk tune described above. If not, then it is not clear that modern composers can really do what Adorno and others insist that they do, which is to reject tonality entirely.

The distinction between sound and tone is a special case of the distinction between the material and the intentional object of perception. Sounds are objects in the physical world, albeit objects of a special kind whose nature and identity are bound up with the way they are perceived. They are, as I put it, 'secondary objects', in something like the way that colours are secondary qualities.[49] Tones are what we hear in sounds when we hear the sounds as music. They have features that no sound can possess – such as movement, gravitational attraction, weight and position in a one-dimensional space. They exemplify a special kind of organization – an organization that we hear and which exists only for someone who can hear it. (Someone might be an expert at hearing pitched sounds, and may even be gifted with absolute pitch, but still be 'tone deaf', since unable to hear the musical organization. Sequences don't sound right to such a person, because they never sound wrong.)

The case is usefully compared with that of language. The sounds from which Angela's speech is composed may be as audible to Mary as they are to Peter; but if Mary understands Angela's language and Peter does not, they hear something different. Mary hears *in* Angela's utterance the meaning that Angela is striving to convey; Peter hears only the sounds. The meaning resides in those sounds because they are organized grammatically, and the organization changes the way

[48] The crucial sources are Arnold Schoenberg, *Harmonielehre*, 3rd edition (Vienna 1922), pp. 288–9. Theodor Adorno, *The Philosophy of Modern Music*, tr. A. G. Mitchell and W. V. Bloomster (New York, 1973), pp. 32–5. Ernst Bloch, *Essays on the Philosophy of Music*, tr. P. Palmer, intro. D. Drew (Cambridge, 1985), pp. 97–100
[49] Roger Scruton, *Understanding Music: Philosophy and Interpretation* (London, 2009; repr. 2016), Chapter 2, 'Sounds'.

Ex. 2

the words sound. As I noted in Chapter 2 above, the parallel with
musical perception is strong enough to have motivated generative
theories of musical syntax on the model of Chomsky's generative
grammar.[50] And the comparison helps us to see that musical organization is not the result of arbitrary choices, and cannot be simply
remade according to other rules and other purposes without threat
to its status as music.

In the case of language, grammatical organization is constrained
by the demands of sense. A grammatical sentence must make sense
to native speakers: syntax is therefore constrained by semantics, and
this means that it is not up to speakers to change the rules. Semantic
constraints do not govern the 'syntax' of music – so, at least, I would
argue – and the rules of tonal harmony and counterpoint are not conventions like the syntactical rules of English but generalizations from
the experience of listening.[51] Nevertheless, the organization that we
hear in tones suggests expectations deeply implanted in the musical
ear. And the question of tonality, as I am discussing it here, is the
question of the extent to which those expectations can be ignored or
defied, while still creating music.

Light is cast on this question by the 'wrong note' phenomenon.
You may never have heard the melody of 'Lovely Joan' before, and
yet would recognize that things have gone wrong if F sharp rather
than F natural sounds in bar 3 while all else remains as written. And
then again, if F sharp sounds and the rest of the bar is rewritten as in
Ex. 2, the wrong note is righted, at least for the time being. (The piece
has changed key from D dorian to A dorian mode.) Such immediate
experiences are vital to the understanding of music; composers may

[50] See, for the most ambitious instance, Fred Lerdahl and Ray Jackendoff, *A Generative Theory of Tonal Music* (Cambridge, MA, 1983).
[51] *The Aesthetics of Music*, Chapter 7.

play with wrong notes in that way, making them retrospectively right with a key change, or using them for effect, as in the triads on the harp used to suggest the sparkle on the rose in Act 2 of *Der Rosenkavalier*.

Wrong notes imply right notes, and what makes a note right is its part in the intentional order – the order that we hear *in* sounds when we hear them as music. This order is in one sense the listener's creation. As I have argued in previous chapters, the intentional object of musical hearing is organized by metaphors that correspond to no material realities; and yet these metaphors, and the order derived from them, are shared by all musical people. It is an order that *we* – the musical public – hear, when we hear these sounds as music. And although there is, at any moment, an indefinite number of ways that a melodic line or a chord sequence can continue without sounding wrong, the ideal in our Western tradition has been of an uninterrupted sense of necessity – each melodic and harmonic step following as though by logic from its predecessor, and yet with complete freedom. (Freedom here being 'the consciousness of necessity', in other words the revealed sense that one musical step provides a complete *reason* for the next one, so that each step is free without being arbitrary.)

The question of tonality, therefore, is a question about a shared intentional order. Music is not a natural kind, and we can call any arrangement of sounds music without crossing firm conceptual boundaries. But music is not an arbitrary category. It arose in the course of shared experiences that have encouraged us to group the objects of those experiences under a single label. And those objects have had salient features that have captured our attention and enabled us un-problematically to share our experience of musical events as beginning, developing, journeying through musical space and yearning towards a conclusion. These salient features include all of the following: keys, scales and the special function heard in certain degrees of the scale, notably tonic, dominant and sub-dominant; the distinctions between scalar tones and accidentals, between diatonic and modal scales and between major and minor; cadences, modulations and chord progressions. Not all those features will be exemplified by every piece of tonal music; but they are standardly present. In the central tradition of Western tonal music, melody and harmony run in parallel and the music moves by unforced steps from key to key, employing devices such as the circle of fifths that seem to reside in the very heart of the tonal order. And all this we hear spontaneously.

Already, however, problems of definition, and rival modes of hearing, imbue the idea of tonality with vagueness. Consider the crucial concept of key. Traditionally a key is identified by the tonic, in relation to which the other notes of the scale are understood as subservient in a systematic way.

The triads built on each scale degree are assigned certain 'functions' – both unconsciously, in the hearing of the experienced listener, and consciously, in the writings of musicologists and critics. And theorists have tried to show how these 'functions' are deployed in a musical argument, as tonal music moves through distinct harmonic 'regions', moving from tension to resolution and back again.[52] Riemann's original theory of functional harmony recognized three 'functions' – those of the tonic, the dominant and the sub-dominant – and argued that passages can have a dominant function even though containing no triads of the dominant, with 'secondary dominants' taking over the function of the dominant – though just what that 'function' *is* has never been clearly defined.

The complexities here are seemingly infinite, as we can see from an example. In the passage quoted (Ex. 3) from Schubert's penultimate sonata in A major, harmonies conventionally belonging to C major lead, seemingly without any forcing, into harmonies associated with the distant key of B and back again. But is there a change of key? Speaking theoretically, you could say indeed that the key has briefly slipped sideways by a semitone. But that is not how the passage is heard. Followers of Heinrich Schenker might say that the piece stays in C throughout, since the true tonal centre has not shifted. And it is not only theory (in this case an elaborate and disputed theory) that

---

[52] The foundational source here is Hugo Riemann, *Harmony Simplified, or the Theory of the Tonal Functions of Chords* (London and New York, 1893).

Ex. 3

suggests such a description. That is how the passage is heard: were the piece to offer a full cadence on to a B major chord, we would hear not closure but a diversion of the musical argument, and this diversion would endure until the music works its way either back to the tonality of C or towards a *real* and fully prepared modulation into B. But that modulation is what Schubert is avoiding, since it is precisely the juxtaposition throughout this passage of the tonic and leading note of C that creates its deep poignancy.

Nor can this ambiguity really be removed by the standard ways of notating chords. Although the chord in bar 5 is the tonic triad in B major, it is also the altered triad of the seventh in C major, with sharp third and sharp fifth. Every note and triad of every scale can be, in that way, notated in any key, and there is no way of deriving from the theories and notations available a definitive statement of which key any passage is in. We are trying to capture an intentional organization in material terminology, and it cannot be done.[53] In

[53] Some moves towards this conclusion are suggested in the seminal work by Molly Gustin, *Tonality* (New York, 1969), and her account of the Schubert example is particularly telling.

Part 2, Chapter 7, below, I examine the *Quartettsatz*, a spectacular example of Schubert's ability to change tonal centre continuously, embarking on the wildest of journeys, while preparing an utterly convincing return to what is only occasionally foregrounded as the home key.

Before Schoenberg's decisive break with tonality composers had experimented with certain departures from the diatonic tradition that have been, on the whole, accepted by the musical public. The use of the whole-tone scale by Debussy and others, the 'polytonality' of Stravinsky in *The Rite of Spring*, in which musical development occurs in two adjacent spaces, the squeezing of added notes into traditional harmonies, even Skryabin's adoption of fourth-built chords in place of the third-built chords of diatonic harmony – all these were accommodated by the musical public as extensions of the listening practices that they already embraced. They are genuine departures from diatonic tonality, but do not overthrow its fundamental organizational principles: so, at least, I would argue.[54]

When Schoenberg broke with tonality, he was not satisfied with those local amendments and extensions to its well-known demands. He wished to develop a rival form of musical *order*, which would duplicate the relatedness of tone to tone that we experience in tonal music, while treating all tones as equals from the structural point of view – no tone was to emerge as the tonic. He wrote:

> It is evident that abandoning tonality can be contemplated only if other satisfactory means for coherence and articulation present themselves. If, in other words, one could write a piece which does not use the advantages offered by tonality and yet unifies all elements so that their succession and relation are logically comprehensible, and which is articulated as our mental capacity requires, namely so that the parts unfold clearly and characteristically in related significance and function.[55]

---

[54] See *The Aesthetics of Music*, Chapter 9.
[55] *Style and Idea*, ed. Leonard Stein, tr. Leo Black (London, 1975), p. 279.

Schoenberg's rival principle of unity was to be the 'motif', which, 'consciously used ... should produce unity, relationship, coherence, logic, comprehensibility, and fluency'.[56] The motif is the seed from which everything grows, and can lend itself to other kinds of organization than that provided by tonality – notably to the serial organization which became, in time, Schoenberg's preferred alternative. (For instances of this see Chapter 1 above: 'When is a Tune?')

Although Schoenberg is surely right to emphasize the unity with which we are familiar in classical music, this is not the *only* effect of tonality, nor indeed the most important effect. The effect of unity comes only as a consequence of the journey through musical space, itself made possible by melodic, harmonic and contrapuntal organization, and usually because something more than a motif serves as the guide. By overlooking everything except unity, abstractly described, Schoenberg makes the task of replacing tonality seem far easier than it is. In particular, it enables him to overlook the crucial fact that melodic and harmonic organization, in the 12-tone syntax, come apart from each other, 'that harmony is no longer in gear with the melody it underlies, that the melody therefore is out of focus', as Robin Holloway nicely puts it.[57]

In order to understand where we have got to, therefore, after a century of avant-garde experiments, we need to explore how far the organization that turns sounds into tones is bound up with tonality. Evidently the *diatonic* tonality of Western art-music is not an exclusive and exhaustive framework for musical organization. It has been for a long time clear that pentatonic scales come naturally to the human ear, and are displayed by folk music all around the globe. Since Debussy, Janáček, Puccini and Stravinsky, whole-tone harmony, and also whole-tone melody, have made their way into the centre of the musical experience, as have polytonality, the use of fourth-based harmonies and the octatonic scale. The latter scale was

[56] *The Fundamentals of Musical Composition*, ed. G. Strang (London, 1967), p. 8.
[57] See 'Strauss – Stravinsky – Schoenberg', in *On Music: Essays and Diversions, 1963–2003* (Brinkworth, 2003), p. 153.

championed by Rimsky-Korsakov, as a way of favouring diminished over diatonic harmonies, and has been ubiquitous in modern music, both in the classical register (Stravinsky's *Symphony of Psalms*) and in jazz (Herbie Hancock's *Freedom Jazz Dance*). However, it is worth beginning from the diatonic system, since it highlights features of music that seem to be essentially connected with the listening experience. Here are some of them:

1. Closure. Music in the diatonic tradition works towards colons, semi-colons and full stops, and does so for two obvious reasons. First, because the scale itself has a point of rest (the tonic), connected harmonically with other points on the scale that can perform a similar function; secondly, because harmonic progressions can lead to chords without tension, in which the voices rest together as a settled unity. Hence tonal music admits of both melodic and harmonic cadences – sequences in which accumulated tension is released, as when a suspension is resolved by neighbour-note movement.

2. The musical boundary. Musical elements in the diatonic language have temporal boundaries: they begin and they end, and between those two points they are in continuous movement. This is true even if there is no sound to be heard. Tonal music moves through silences, and is on its way to closure even when there is nothing to be heard, as in the theme of the *Eroica* symphony, last movement, which consists largely of silences, and which moves nevertheless through several semi-closures before arriving at its destination.

3. The topology of musical space. Thanks to octave equivalence the one-dimensional space of music is folded over at the octave, coming back to its point of departure at every twelfth semitone. This feature is fundamental to our understanding of music, since it creates a kind of lattice on which melodies and harmonies are arranged and transposed. Other systems recognize octave equivalence, but they may also avoid emphasizing it, since it creates a natural harmony

that automatically invokes scalar organization. The space of music in the diatonic tradition is both one-dimensional and finite, arranged within a single octave that is multiplied as many times as required.

4. The distinction between the subject, thesis or theme and what is built on it. This distinction, which has been fundamental to musical architecture in the classical tradition, is hard to define precisely. But it is instantly recognizable in pieces composed in the tonal language. We recognize the return of the theme, its occurrence in other places, and the various augmentations, diminutions, ornamentations and variants that make it a mutating presence in the work, a personality that can change its dress and its manner but remain always in essence the same. Atonal music may abound in motivic cells, which repeat or mimic each other, but themes are rare, tunes more or less non-existent. (See the discussion in Chapter 1 above.)

5. The distinction between harmonies and simultaneities. This is perhaps one of the most important of all the marks of tonality. Tones sounding together strike us only rarely as simultaneous but separate events, and more often as parts of a single complex event. This feature of diatonic tonality is replicated in modal, pentatonic, octatonic and whole-tone systems, but it occurs only accidentally in serial music, which is not intended to be heard in that way at all – unless, that is, the composer is surreptitiously over-writing the serial organization with a tonal argument, as does Berg in the violin concerto and *Lulu*. One of the sources of difficulty in avant-garde music today is that simultaneities prevail over chords, so that there is no instinctive recognition in the audience's ear that the various pitches in fact belong together.

6. The specific phenomenology of diatonic space. In diatonic space, and indeed in most musical space derived from the diatonic, modal, pentatonic and whole-tone scales, tones

seem to move *into* each other, to compel each other's appearance, to belong together by a kind of magnetism that makes one tone an introduction to the other and the other a fitting sequel. I do not mean merely that there is a body of rules here, which distinguish right and wrong in note progressions – for if there is such a body of rules, it is the least important fact of the matter. (By contrast, grammar is the *most* important fact of the matter in dictating the sequences of serial music.) I mean that there is a phenomenological 'belonging together' that leads us spontaneously to distinguish right from wrong in what we hear.

These features of tonal music are not unimportant by-products of the tonal syntax. They are *what* we hear, and also how we *understand* what we hear – how we create the links, the patterns and the flow through which we enter into the musical stream and make it our own. They are what the ear demands from and imposes upon sounds when hearing tonally. The question raised by Schoenberg and Adorno is whether those features, so central to our listening culture, can be reproduced without tonality, or some near-equivalent. One of the problems that preoccupied Adorno was that, as he saw it, the tonal idiom has survived in a degenerate version in jazz and its offshoots. Tonality has therefore become irreparably tainted by 'the regression of listening', by which Adorno means addiction to short-term musical thinking, together with the easy discharge of tension in banal chord progression and melodic clichés.[58] This 'regression of listening' was, for Adorno, the great temptation faced by our musical culture. The ordinary listener, challenged by the avant-garde, was presented with an alternative, namely popular music, which had both adhered to tonality and developed in directions that have no precedent in the concert hall. But the effect of this was, according to

---

[58] Theodor W. Adorno, 'On the Fetish Character in Music and the Regression of Listening', in A. Arato and E. Gebhardt, eds, *The Essential Frankfurt School Reader* (New York, 1987), pp. 70–99. 'On Jazz', in *Night Music: Essays on Music, 1920–1962*, ed. Rolf Tiedeman, tr. Wieland Hoban (London and New York, 2009).

Adorno, to associate tonality with certain 'stock effects' and musical clichés.[59] He dismissed the jazz dissonances as 'mere splotches of colour', and argued that 'in the advanced industrial countries pop music is defined by standardization', in which 'every element is essentially replaceable'.[60] Pop music is part of the 'ideology' of capitalist society, a deep untruth, masking the exploitation on which such commodity products are founded. In this way he hoped to link his criticisms of tonality and popular culture to the broader Marxist theory of 'false consciousness': the purely ideological forms of thinking with which the oppressed proletariat responds to, and denies, the fact of being oppressed.[61]

The more specific accusation (made in similar terms by Schoenberg) was that the harmonic language of tonality has 'become banal'.[62] What had once been fresh and compelling had degenerated into something repetitious and mechanical. Words like 'cliché' and 'kitsch' are used to denote the things that the true artist can no longer do, not because they have always led to failure but because they too evidently bear the marks of their former success, and are therefore reached for without the true cost involved in understanding them. It is, surely, one of the strangest of phenomena that artistic gestures that have been used again and again with true effect, such as rhyming couplets and tonal cadences, should suddenly, almost overnight, become impossible, even though they have not changed. The cliché of the diminished seventh, so relentlessly criticized by Schoenberg, Adorno and Bloch, had to be removed from the composer's repertoire. But when we hear it in Mozart or Beethoven it sounds as fresh as it did to them.

That argument, spelled out in a variety of ways by both composers and critics, connects with the fundamental claim of artistic modernism, which is that aesthetic value belongs to the authentic

[59] See *The Philosophy of Modern Music*, p. 34.
[60] *Introduction to the Sociology of Music*, tr. E. B. Ashton (New York, 1976), pp. 25–7.
[61] *Ibid.*, p. 55.
[62] Arnold Schoenberg, *Harmonielehre*, 3rd edition (Vienna, 1922), pp. 288–9. Adorno, *The Philosophy of Modern Music*, p. 34; also Bloch, *Essays on the Philosophy of Music*, p. 98.

voice, compelled by the sincerely lived experience. Music, like the other arts, must belong to the time of its creation, seeking forms and idioms that capture the changed perceptions of the audience to which it is addressed. If it does not succeed in this, then the result is of no real significance, a derogation from the true aim of art, which is to rescue what we humans are, by giving form and meaning to our present experience. The twentieth-century avant-garde therefore had the most worthy of motives, which was, in the words that Eliot translated from Mallarmé, 'to purify the dialect of the tribe'. The aim was to jettison those idioms and devices that had been too much used, and which therefore could no longer be used sincerely. Moreover, in the view of the avant-garde, you do not rescue a cliché simply by giving it a new context, as when Messiaen ends the *Turangalîla Symphony* with an emphatic F sharp major triad. What is needed is not a new context, with the old effects as it were stuck on. What is needed is a new musical order – a syntax from which new effects can grow organically, so as to take their meaning as words do, from their contribution to the whole.

Hence composers looked for other ways of organizing sounds, so as to lift them free from the grooves that turned them in the forbidden direction. The 12-tone serial technique was Schoenberg's answer to the problem: a *systematic* reworking of the basic musical material so as to make the old clichés impossible. If a C major triad should emerge in the course of a 12-tone composition, it would, Schoenberg assumed, no longer be a C major triad, being heard now as a three-membered set, whose meaning lies in its connection to the other nine semitones of an ordered series.

The idea found many supporters. But if music composed in Schoenberg's way has gained a following, it is, in large part, because it is heard in ways that have little or nothing to do with the way in which it was composed. It is heard, as a rule, against the serial syntax. As Fred Lerdahl has pointed out in an important article, the compositional grammar of serial music is permutational, and permutations are hard to grasp by the ear, which latches on to repetitions and prolongations instead.[63] We bring to the serial piece a 'listening grammar' shaped by tonal expectations, and so we hear the music against the compositional grain. It is not that serial music sounds especially harsh or discordant. It is rather that we organize it, in our perception, as moving through musical space in something like the way tonal music moves. We notice phrases in terms of their shape, and hear when the shape is repeated or transposed, as in the example from the Schoenberg violin concerto in Chapter 1. We hear harmonies as increasing or decreasing in tension, and as occasionally moving towards closure. We listen out for themes that have an identity and a memorability in their own right. We hear simultaneities as chords, and follow the voice-leading that takes one chord into its successor. When our expectations are frustrated, the sounds seem to bear no musical relation to each other and the piece disintegrates.

There is no *a priori* reason why a new art form should not arise, involving the creation and appreciation of sounds organized without reference to the standard way of hearing. And there is nothing in grammar or in nature that would prevent us from extending the word 'music' to such a case – music, as I noted, is not a 'natural kind'. But the real question for all seriously musical people is whether sound so organized is capable of delivering anything comparable to what was given to us by the great tradition of tonal melody and harmony, and if so, how.

Composers have wrestled with that question throughout the last century. One notable instance is George Rochberg, the American composer known for his attempts to write string quartets in the spirit, if not quite the style, of Beethoven, and often using quotations from the masters in order to fix himself, so to speak, in the tonal tradition. Rochberg was educated as a modernist and for 20 or more years composed serial music, teaching in the music department of the University of Pennsylvania and obeying all the usual strictures of the avant-garde, avoiding melody and tonal progressions and

---

[63] Fred Lerdahl, 'Cognitive Constraints on Compositional Systems', in John A. Sloboda, ed., *Generative Processes in Music* (Oxford, 1988).

writing music for the educated listener. And then, in 1964, his teen-age son died of a brain tumour. Urgently needing to express his grief, Rochberg found the serial idiom entirely incapable of meeting that need. It seemed suddenly sterile, abstract, intellectual in the negative sense, as though it had been deliberately cleansed of all reference to human feeling.

That was when Rochberg set out to compose in a tonal idiom, mod-elling himself on the Beethoven quartets, because they were the deep-est example that he knew of music that expresses emotion, orders it as only music can order it and in doing so brings consolation to the suf-ferer. The result of Rochberg's return to tonality has been controver-sial. It has seemed to be so complete a reversal, and often so simplistic in its conception of melodic movement, that others have doubted that it is really capable of sustaining the weight of emotion that Rochberg wanted to entrust to it. The charge is repeatedly made, and not only by serial dogmatists, that Rochberg's assumption of tonality is 'pastiche', the imitation of musical expression rather than a real instance of it. It is hard to know how such a charge, which repeats the fundamental claim made by Adorno on behalf of the avant-garde, can be either established or rebutted; but we are left with the thought that the road back to tonality is being blocked by those most capable of taking it.

Against that, however, it must be insisted that it is in the ear of the listener, rather than the theories of the critic, that music exists. Hence not only are there intrinsic limits to musical innovation, but there are requirements to be satisfied, if some new effect is to be heard as part of the music rather than as a simultaneous but independent event. The noise of street traffic outside the concert hall, of the irritating person coughing in the quiet passages, of a door slamming in the back of the room, are not part of the music, and cannot, however intrusive they might be, turn a platitudinous piece into something original. Sounds heard as noise are heard as intrusions, and it does not matter that the composer has explicitly instructed the players to produce those sounds – it is not the composer's *intention* but the lis-tener's *attention* that turns sound to music. And it is this that defines the predicament of tonality today.

The experimental avant-garde presupposes an existing audience, whose patience it depends upon. Jazz, and all the many varieties that have descended from it – Rhythm and Blues, Rock, Pop, Hip-Hop down to EDM, House, Techno and other idioms in which only computers are involved – are all in the business of creating an audience. And they mix diatonic harmony and pentatonic melody in order to achieve this. Here we have the living proof that, despite being sidelined by the concert-hall avant-garde, tonality is what the ear demands. The result may sometimes be idiotic and banal, as Adorno said it must be. Nevertheless, this great expanse of friendly tonality cannot be ignored.

Pop music occurs constantly in the background of modern life. It is inescapable, and forms a kind of ostinato accompaniment to our daily activities, a background throbbing on which its devotees may depend for their moral sustenance. Many of our public spaces are shaped by what Joseph Lanza called 'elevator music',[64] and large numbers of young people go through their days with iPhone speakers in their ears, listening to, or at any rate overhearing, their favourite songs.[65] A new kind of audience has emerged, whose ears have been shaped by repetition, four-square rhythm, familiar harmonic shifts and the repertoire of jazz chords and short-term sequences. This audience is used to music as a form of improvisation on a repeated frame, in which development, of the kind familiar from the classical tradition, is not the important thing. And all the music that this vast audience encounters, whether or not by choice, is robustly tonal. The great question for a composer of 'classical' music – music designed to be listened to in the concert hall – is how to capture the attention of such an audience and to provide a rewarding musical experience without falling foul of the modernist censors who stand at the back whispering 'cliché', 'pastiche' and 'kitsch'.

---

[64] Joseph Lanza, *Elevator Music* (New York, 1995).
[65] Some of the social and psychological effects of this have been explored by Anahid Kassabian in *Ubiquitous Listening: Affect, Attention and Distributed Subjectivity* (Berkeley, 2015).

It is in part the emergence of this new audience that has led composers to be suspicious of the rejection of tonality. Introducing noises, serially organized pitches, cluster chords, stretched tessitura and advanced sound effects into a score that seems, to a musical young person, to have nothing you can really latch on to – nothing you can 'join', either rhythmically or melodically – is merely to lose your audience. In such circumstances it is understandable that there should be an attempt to reclaim tonality, and to use it in some new way that will capture the attention of the young. The question is, how is it to be done?

One approach has been that associated with the minimalists – and in particular with Philip Glass and Steve Reich. The young ear today has been brought up on triads and rhythmical repetitions. Melody has been rudimentary – catchy phrases, with very little build-up and no genuine closure. Influenced by this, Glass has composed music that consists almost entirely of repeated common chords, endless rhythmical figures using the three consonant notes of the triad – in short, the accompaniment to a song that never comes. Many think that the result is just as banal as Adorno predicted. But it has a following, since it corresponds to a certain mood, a kind of distracted disengagement in which the world and its troubles occur only in the distance and in a dream-like version that rules out the possibility of intervention.

In John Adams you find something rather more elaborate – the use of all instruments, strings included, in their percussive mode, in ostinato rhythms that take hold of the orchestra and swing it relentlessly forward, with snatches of melody intriguingly strung on the conveyor belt. (A striking example is his three-movement orchestral work entitled, with tongue in cheek, *Harmonielehre*, expressly responding to Adorno's and Schoenberg's charge that 'you cannot compose like that!') Adams is a highly sophisticated composer, and his music has certainly captured an audience, especially in America. It would have been inconceivable without Rock and jazz harmony. And it is undeniably serious, using the orchestra in novel ways to develop simple material into prolonged statements. But does it mark out a way forward that others might follow, or is it, rather, a kind of trademark music that can be made to order, provided it is made by Adams? We are still waiting for an answer.

If it is true that tonality has declined to the status of a cliché, then it follows that tonality is not – despite the attempts by Lerdahl and Jackendoff to prove the opposite – the equivalent in music of a transformational grammar. The syntactical order of English and its derivation from semantic structures could not decline to cliché, since it provides the overarching medium in which novelties and their degenerate forms both arise. Cliché is an *aesthetic,* not a syntactical defect – a fault of style rather than grammar. And if Adorno is right, we must say something similar about tonality. Even if there are rules of harmony and counterpoint, and the manuals for following them, these are not grammatical conventions, like the rules of language, but generalizations, distillations of our sense over centuries of 'what works', what 'sounds right' to the ear educated in the tonal tradition.

Moreover, if tonality is not a grammar, then the faults that have arisen in the use of tonality will not be cured by inventing a new musical syntax. This new syntax will not in fact *be* a syntax in the linguistic sense, but will be a stylistic innovation, one that may be crystallized in rules and regularities but which will no more be a proof against cliché than a new fashion in dress is proof against the vulgarity of the old one. Everything will depend upon the creativity and taste with which the new idiom is used – and the same goes for the old idiom too.

Hence there is no guarantee that the faults of which the tonal idiom is accused will be avoided – or avoided for long – by adopting a rival set of rules. Just as the revolt against figurative painting soon produced abstract, cubist and fauvist cliché – indeed abstract *kitsch* of a kind that decorates a thousand bars on the Mediterranean seafront – so has the revolt against tonality produced a wealth of atonal clichés – cluster chords, explosions of cross-rhythms on the brass, exaggerated tessitura and a constant searching for acoustic effects.

As a result we are witnessing a return, if not to tonality, at least to idioms that recuperate in altered form some of its principal effects.

In the string quartets of David Matthews, for example, diatonic melodies are backed up by harmonic progressions in which voice-leading and rhythmic movement adapt shapes and goals from the classical and romantic repertoire.[66] James MacMillan, Sally Beamish, Judith Weir, Thomas Adès, Jonathan Bell in Britain, John Corigliano, Michael Torke, David Del Tredici in America: these are just some of the personalities in a growing movement towards a kind of tonal avant-garde. Even if their music mostly avoids keys and traditional harmonic progressions, it emphasizes melodic order and voice-led harmony over pitch-class sets and simultaneities. Meanwhile the language of traditional tonality survives in the scores that first set Adorno's teeth on edge, as he struggled to identify the evils of the Hollywood culture: the scores that puff up the action of movies.

Film music is, in fact, a perfect illustration of the questions that I have been discussing in this chapter, and I return to it below (Part 2, Chapter 13). Its ambivalent reception by the musically cultivated is proof that the debate goes on, inconclusive and repetitious, but with persuasive judgements emerging on both sides. The only conclusion that seems philosophically safe is that the standard effects of tonality touch something deep in the musical ear. Like sugar and alcohol, they easily set up addictive pathways, delivering their rewards too easily and enslaving those who are hooked on them. From time to time a course of avant-garde vinegar may be required to cure the addiction. But the musical ear, it seems, has a natural ability to return to its original pleasures.

---

[66] I give a detailed account of David Matthews's music and his specific way of treating tonality in Part 2, Chapter 10, below.

6

German Idealism and the Philosophy of Music

German idealism began with Leibniz and lasted until Schopenhauer, with a few Central European aftershocks in the work of Husserl and his followers. That great epoch in German philosophy coincided with a great epoch in German music. It is scarcely surprising, therefore, that idealist philosophers should have paid special attention to this art form. Looking back on it, is there anything of this prolonged encounter between music and philosophy that we can consider to be a real advance, and one that we should draw on? Many have thought so, not least because idealism, as it emerged in the post-Kantian period, was prodigal of claims to reveal the secret meaning of things, and to relate our transient impressions to the infinite, the absolute, the transcendental, the ineffable or some other such object of a quasi-religious devotion. Such we find in the writings of Schelling, Fichte, Hegel and Schopenhauer, the last of whom made music not only a primary object of philosophy but an example of it. Music, Schopenhauer wrote, is unconscious philosophy, since in music the inner essence of the world, which is will, is made directly present to the intellect.

My own view is that the value of German idealism for the philosophy of music lies not in those vast claims, made on behalf of music or philosophy or both, but in an argument which begins with Kant's transcendental deduction, and whose influence is felt right down to the times in which we live. This argument is not about music, nor does it necessarily point in a direction that could be called 'idealist' – in the sense of that term as it was understood by Fichte, Schelling and

Hegel. It begins from a specific premise, which Kant called 'the transcendental unity of apperception', taking the term 'apperception' from Leibniz via Wolff. All philosophical enquiry, Kant argued, begins and ends in the point of view of the subject. If I ask myself what I can know, or what I must do, or what I may hope for, then the question is about what *I* can know etc., given the limitations of my perspective. It is not a question about what God can know, what is knowable from some point of view that I could never attain to, or what is knowable from no point of view at all. To answer the question, therefore, I must first understand my own perspective – which means understanding what must be true of me, if I am to ask the philosophical question at all.

I know that I am a single and unified subject of experience. This present thought, this pain, this hope and this memory are features of *one* thing, and that thing is me. I know this on no basis, without having to carry out any kind of check, and indeed, without the use of criteria of any kind – this, I believe, is what Kant meant, in this context, by the term 'transcendental'. The unity of the self-conscious subject is not the conclusion of any enquiry but the presupposition of all enquiries. The unity of consciousness 'transcends' all argument since it is the premise without which argument makes no sense.

This transcendental unity contains also a claim to identity through time. I attribute to myself states of mind – memories, hopes, intentions and so on – which reach into the past and the future, and which represent me as enduring through time. How is this possible, and with what warrant do I affirm my self-identity as an objective truth about the world? Those questions underlie the argument of Kant's 'transcendental deduction', and this is not the place to discuss them. More important is Kant's expanded version of the transcendental subject, as he develops this in his ethical theory and also (although this is not often noticed) in his aesthetics.

The fundamental question of practical reason is addressed to *me*, and it asks 'what shall *I* do?' I can answer this question only on the assumption that I am free. This assumption has a transcendental ground, since it is the premise of all practical reasoning and never the conclusion of it. Transcendental freedom, like the transcendental unity of apperception, belongs to my perspective on the world. It is not a perspective that could be adopted by an animal, since it depends upon the use of the word 'I' – the ability to identify myself in the first person, and to give and accept reasons for believing what I believe, doing what I do and feeling what I feel.

Fichte and Hegel developed those thoughts to provide a new form of insight into the human condition. The immediate awareness that characterizes the position of the subject is, Hegel argued, abstract and indeterminate. It involves no concrete determination of *what* is known or intended by the subject. If we were pure subjects, existing in a metaphysical void, as Descartes imagined, we should never advance to the point of knowledge, not even knowledge of ourselves, nor should we be able to aim at a determinate goal. Our awareness would remain abstract and empty, an awareness of nothing. But as transcendental subject, I do not merely stand at the edge of my world. I encounter others within that world. I am I to myself only because, and to the extent that, I am you to another. I must therefore be capable of the free dialogue in which I take charge of my presence before the presence of you. That is what it means to understand the first-person case. And it is because I understand the first-person case that I have immediate awareness of my condition. The position which, for Kant, defines the premise of philosophy and which is presupposed in every argument, itself rests on a presupposition – the presupposition of the other, the one against whom I try myself in contest and in dialogue. 'I' requires 'you', and the two meet in the world of objects.

The suggestion is illustrated by Hegel with a series of parables, concerning the 'realization' of the subject – its *Entäusserung*, or objectification – in the world of objects. Some of these parables (I am reluctant to call them arguments) are discussed in the literature of political science, notably that of the master and slave. Many of them convey profound truths about the human condition, and about the social nature of the self. But what interests me is the idea from which they begin: the idea of the subject. This idea, it seems to me, is the abiding legacy of German idealism in all its forms. And it is the clue to a philosophy of music. My considered view is that we should abandon the idealist doctrine that the ultimate substance of the world is mental, spiritual or in some other way emancipated from the constraints of space and time. But we should adhere to the idea concealed within that doctrine, which is the idea of the subject, as the defining feature of the human condition, and the feature to which the mystery of the world is owed.

Kant argues persuasively in the *Paralogisms of Pure Reason* that we cannot know the subject under the categories of the understanding – that is, we cannot look inwards so as to identify the I as a substance, a bearer of properties, and a participant in causal relations. To identify the subject in that way is to identify it as an *object*. The subject is a point of view *upon* the world of objects and not an item *within* it. (Again, that is what the word 'transcendental', in this employment, means.) It was Descartes's mistake to look on the subject as a special kind of object, and thereby to attribute to it a substantial and immortal nature of its own.

Nevertheless, even if the subject is not a something, it is not a nothing either. To exist as a subject is to exist in another way from ordinary objects. It is to exist on the edge of the world, addressing reality from a point that lies just beyond the horizon, and which no one else can occupy. This idea has been beautifully elaborated by J. J. Valberg in his book *Dream, Death, and the Self*, and I have tried to say a little more about it, both in *The Face of God* and in *The Soul of the World*.[67] The main points that I wish to emphasize are two: first, that we each address the world from a standpoint in which our thoughts and feelings have a special and privileged place. All that matters to us is *present* to us, in thought, memory, perception, sensation and desire, or can be summoned into the present without any effort of investigation. Secondly, we respond to others as similarly present to themselves, able to answer directly to our questions, able to tell us without further enquiry what they think, feel or intend. Hence we

---

[67] J. J. Valberg, *Dream, Death, and the Self* (Princeton, 2007). Roger Scruton, *The Face of God* (London, 2012). *The Soul of the World* (Princeton, 2014).

can address each other in the second person, I to you. On those two facts, I maintain, all that is most important in the human condition has been built: responsibility, morality, law, institutions, religion, love and art.

There is a consequence that is of vital relevance to the philosophy of music. I call it the 'overreaching intentionality of interpersonal attitudes'. Not an elegant expression, for sure, but no worse, I guess, than the 'transcendental unity of apperception'. What I have in mind is this: in all our responses to each other, whether love or hate, affection or disaffection, approval or disapproval, anger or desire, we look *into* the other, in search of that unattainable horizon from which he or she addresses us. We are animals swimming in the currents of causality, who relate to each other in space and time. But, in the I–You encounter we do not see each other in that way. Each human object is also a subject, addressing us in looks, gestures and words, from the transcendental horizon of the 'I'. Our responses to the other person aim towards that horizon, passing on beyond the body to the being that it incarnates.

It is this feature of our interpersonal responses that gives such compelling force to the myth of the soul, of the true but hidden self that is veiled by the flesh. And because of this our interpersonal responses develop in a certain way: we see each other as wrapped within them, so to speak, and we hold each other to account for them as though they originated *ex nihilo* from the unified centre of the self. You may say that, when we see each other in this way, we are giving credence to a metaphysical doctrine, maybe even a metaphysical myth. But it is not Descartes's doctrine of the soul-substance, nor is it obviously a myth. Moreover, a doctrine that is enshrined in our basic human responses, which cannot be eliminated without undermining the I–You relationship on which our first-person understanding depends, cannot be dismissed as a simple error. It has something of the status that Kant attributes to the original unity of consciousness – the status of a presupposition of our thinking, including the thinking that might lead us to cast doubt on it. Indeed, on one understanding of the matter, the adherence to this presupposition, and the practice that flows from it, is what Kant's transcendental freedom really amounts to.

So, why is this relevant to the philosophy of music? Kant notoriously had little to say about music, which he described as the agreeable play of sensations. In Schelling, Hegel and Schopenhauer, however, we encounter a growing recognition that the subject–object relation has something to do with the power of music, the power that was coming newly into the cultural foreground with the Beethoven cult, with the rise in Germany of academic musicology and with the theory, which was later to dominate musical thinking, that 'absolute' music – music without a text or an explicit subject-matter – is the true paradigm of the art. For E. T. A. Hoffmann (himself strongly influenced by Schelling) Beethoven's music unfolds a 'spirit realm', in which the subject is gripped by an infinite yearning. For Hegel music claims as its own 'the depth of a person's inner life as such: it is the art of the soul and is directly addressed to the soul'. The chief task of music, he writes, 'consists in making resound, not the objective world itself, but, on the contrary, the manner in which the inmost self is moved to the depths of its personality and conscious soul'.[68] Schopenhauer identified this 'inmost self' with the will, and saw music as a direct presentation of the will, which for him was the 'thing in itself' behind appearance. To see what such philosophers were getting at, however, we have to put aside the ambitious systems that commandeer their arguments and look directly at the phenomena.

The first wave of post-Kantian idealism treated the subject–object relation as marking a kind of metaphysical divide: objects on one side, subjects on the other. In Fichte and Schelling there is a kind of creation myth, according to which the world of objects is brought into being by a primeval sundering of the pure and integral subject. The subject remakes itself as object and so stands in opposition to itself in a condition of alienation. (I knows itself as not-I, to use Fichte's idiom.) This movement towards division is contained within the very essence of the real. And it brings about a separation of spirit

---

[68] Hegel, *Aesthetics: Lectures on Fine Art*, tr. Knox (Oxford, 1975), vol. 2, p. 890.

from itself, comparable to that ascribed by St Augustine to original sin. In Schelling art in general, and music in particular, is engaged in repairing that primordial self-alienation. The Absolute makes itself perceivable through the objectification (*Entäusserung*) of the subject. In art, however, and especially in music, the Absolute is led back into its primal unity as self-identity and self-perception.

Poetic and suggestive though that narrative is, I find it impossible to translate into anything remotely approaching a literal truth. Nevertheless, I believe that there *is* an important truth to be glimpsed, refracted and distorted, in the glass of idealist philosophy. Properly understood, the subject–object relation implies that we approach the world of our experience in two quite different ways. To objects we apply the canons of scientific explanation, seeing them as held within the spatio-temporal nexus, and moving according to laws of cause and effect. Towards subjects we exhibit the 'over-reaching intentionality' that goes always beyond the object, in search of the place of freedom that lies on its edge. There is a philosophical question as to how the two approaches can be reconciled, and how one and the same thing – the human being – can be the target of both. But that question is not specific to aesthetics, and demands a general answer that does not depend upon anything we might say about music. The case of music is interesting largely because music attracts the overreaching intentionality that we direct towards the world of persons, even though it does not represent that world but lives and moves in a space of its own. That, so far as I understand him, is the feature of music that occupies Hegel in his far from lucid remarks in the lectures on aesthetics. The same feature underlies Schopenhauer's far more systematic, if ultimately untenable, theory of music as the non-conceptual presentation of the will. But it is a feature that is hard to explain in terms acceptable today.

Here is how I see the matter. I endorse the view, made central by later German Romantics, that music is an abstract (or, as they put it, an 'absolute') art.[69] But it is a view that must be cautiously stated.

---

[69] For the emergence of the concept of 'absolute music' in the period of German Romanticism, see the meticulous study by Carl Dahlhaus, *The Idea of Absolute Music*, tr. Roger Lustig (Chicago, 1989).

For one thing, music, as it is considered by the idealist philosophers, is only one part of a larger cultural phenomenon, one that is to a certain extent the outcome of a transient social order, and indelibly marked by that order. The idealists were writing about the listening culture that emerged in modern times, in which the concert hall began to be the central venue, with chamber music understood as an 'intimate' and peculiarly intense version of a larger public event. The listening culture demands concentrated attention to pure sound, in a place set apart from everyday life, and ringed round by silence. The central event, the concert, has a character that is best understood through the comparison with religious ritual: a collective focusing on an event that is not explained but repeated. (I consider some of the implications of this comparison in the last chapter of *The Aesthetics of Music*.)

While we can only guess at the origins of music in human society, it is plausible to suggest that it began with collective dancing and spontaneous singing, in which the whole tribe joined, and that the musician, the rhapsode and the solo singer came later. Some people make a lot of this thought, arguing that the concert hall is a fleeting and soon to be replaced phenomenon, and that listening, as opposed to dancing, singing along or overhearing on an iPod, is a transient and unimportant episode in the history of music, one that is peculiarly associated with 'bourgeois' society and therefore due to be overthrown in any truly revolutionary order.[70] Those suggestions are exaggerated, as we can see from reading ancient treatises on music, all of which make listening central to the phenomenon. But we must always bear in mind that the emphasis on the intrinsic meaning of music, as an object of attention for its own sake, is itself a historical phenomenon, not to be fully understood in isolation from the culture that produced it.

---

[70] The yawn-inducing attack on the 'bourgeois culture of listening' can be found in Hanns Eisler, 'Musik und Politik', in *Schriften 1924–1948* (Leipzig, 1973), discussed in Chapter 1 of Dahlhaus, *The Idea of Absolute Music*. You find similar stuff in Ernst Bloch, who was perhaps the last idealist in the philosophy of music, profoundly influenced by the Hegelian idea of the subject.

Secondly, we must be wary of drawing too sudden and precipitous a conclusion from the fact that instrumental music is an abstract or non-representational medium. Architecture too is such a medium; but the idealists were not inclined to see architecture as having that special relation to the subject of consciousness that they attributed to music. Music, as we know it, is a non-representational art form. But it is not *this* that enables music to put us in contact with subjectivity, or 'the absolute', or the 'infinite', to use the language of Schelling and Hoffmann. An art form may be abstract and yet purely decorative, like the art of the carpet-weaver or the lace-maker. Common to Schelling, Hegel and Schopenhauer, however, is the thought that music reaches *beyond* abstraction in some way: it contains messages which have a special significance since they are not expressed in concepts, and are maybe inexpressible in concepts since they touch in some way on those areas of consciousness which we cannot put into words, but which nevertheless have immense significance in our interpersonal lives.

I take from the idealist discussions two further ideas about music, concerning musical movement, and first-person awareness. Schelling and Hegel both emphasize the special relation of music to time. Musical works unfold in time, but they also contain movement, organized by rhythm and melody into definite episodes. More – and this is an observation that Hegel comes near to making but never does quite make – musical movement takes place in a dimension of its own, in which there are places and relations that have no physical reality. I argue that nothing *literally* moves in musical space, but that in some way the idea of space cannot be eliminated from our experience of music. We are dealing with an entrenched metaphor – but not a metaphor of words, exactly, for we are not talking about how people describe music: we are talking about how they *experience* it. It is as though there were a metaphor of space and movement *embedded within* our experience and cognition of music. This metaphor cannot be 'translated away', and what it says cannot be said in the language of physics – for example, by talking instead of the pitch and timbre of sounds in physical space. Yet what it describes, the musical movement, is a real presence – and not just for me: for anyone with a musical ear.

It should not surprise us that the terms that we apply to music place it firmly in the arena of personal life. It moves as *we* move, with reasons for what it does and a sense of purpose (which might at any moment evaporate, like the purposes of people). It has the outward appearance of the inner life, so to speak, and although it is heard and not seen, it is heard as the voice is heard, and understood like the face – as 'visitation and transcendence', to use the words of Levinas.[71] Unlike us, however, music creates the space in which it moves. And that space is ordered by fields of force that seem to radiate from the notes that occur in them.

Consider the chord: perhaps the most mysterious of all musical entities. Not every collection of notes makes a chord – not even if they are notes from the same consonant triad. (Consider the 'Hostias' of Berlioz's *Grande Messe des morts*, in which a B flat minor triad on flutes is separated by four octaves from the B flat on trombones, which seems not to belong with the flutes at all, even though it is the root of the triad.) A chord, whether consonant or dissonant, fills the musical space between its edges. And it faces other musical objects from those edges. You can stuff more notes into it, but in doing so you are making it more dense, not occupying space that is not already occupied. And here is another peculiarity of musical space: that two objects can be in the same space at the same time, as when contrapuntal voices briefly coincide on a single pitch or when two chords are superimposed and each retains its separate *Gestalt* character, as in polytonal music. Chords have distinctive relations to the fields of force in which they are suspended. They can be soft and sloppy, like thirteenth chords in jazz – and that regardless of their dissonance. They can be hard and tight, like the final chords of a Beethoven symphony – and that regardless of their consonance. They can yield to their neighbours, lead into them or away from them, or they might stand out as sharp and unrelated.

---

[71] Emmanuel Levinas, *Humanism of the Other*, tr. Nidra Poller (Chicago, 2003), p. 44.

It is a great weakness in the idealists that they make so little effort to identify particular works of music and particular musical phenomena, in order to say *what is going on* in them. They do not confront directly the question that troubles me, which is how we understand musical space, and what *kind* of movement occurs in it. Hoffmann gives concrete descriptions of the Beethoven masterpieces, and his remarks are both inspiring and informative. But he does not tackle the philosophical question, how we can hear in sequences of sounds those bursts of emotion that he describes so well. Schelling seems to be aware of the philosophical question, but he gives us no concrete example through which to comprehend it. Thus he emphasizes that tone (*Klang*) is neither noise nor mere sound but 'the body's intuition of the soul' (*die Anschauung der Seele des Körpers selbst*),[72] and that this feature derives from the fact that music is organized by the principle of temporal succession. Hence music is 'the art that most discards corporeality by representing *pure* motion as such, abstracted from the object, and is borne by invisible, almost spiritual, wings'.[73] So far, however, this is all metaphor. When it comes to building the observation into a philosophical argument, Schelling takes from Kant the theory of time as the 'form of inner sense', and stirs this into his observation concerning the subjective nature of tone to produce the following soup:

> the necessary form of music is *succession*, since time is the general form of the implantation (*Einbildung*) of the infinite into the finite, in so far as it is intuited as form, abstracted from the real. The principle of time in the subject is self-awareness, which is the implantation of the unity of consciousness into the diversity in the ideal.[74]

The least that can be said is that it is hard to disagree with Schelling, for it is equally hard to know what it would be to agree with him. And, without putting too fine a point on it, I would say that it is a

---

[72] *Schriften zur Philosophie der Kunst und zur Freiheitslehre* (1802/3), §76.
[73] *Ibid.*, §83.
[74] *Ibid.*, §77.

general weakness of idealist philosophers that they do not present arguments that can be engaged with from outside their own systems.

However the subject/object distinction might be put to effective use in a more modern, and I hope more lucid, form. The overreaching intentionality that we direct to the world of persons is not confined to that world. In a religious frame of mind we look on the whole of reality as though it were the revelation of a first-person viewpoint: the viewpoint of God. We see things, then, not in terms of the laws of cause and effect, but rather in the terms that we use of people, when we call them to account for their actions. We look for reasons and goals, rather than causes and laws of nature. This is something more than animism, and something less than theology. But it is a human universal, and lies at the heart of our experience of the sacred and the numinous. Whether it is ever a *veridical* experience is, of course, the great question that theologians have to answer, and not a question for my argument here. But the idealist enterprise was precisely to show that this intimation of reason at the heart of the natural world is indeed veridical. Fichte, Schelling and Hegel wanted to provide a substitute for theology in the form of a philosophy that gives access to the viewpoint of God – the 'absolute' perspective which is also the subjectivity of the world.

That ambitious enterprise showed itself to be futile, and it is not my concern to demolish it. But it points to a more circumscribed and more fruitful application of the subject–object relation in the understanding of music. The listening culture that formed the background to the speculations of Schelling and Hegel was based on the transformation emphasized by Schelling of sound (*Laut*) into tone (*Klang*). This is a transformation in the ear of the beholder, and comes about, I argue, when we adopt an 'acousmatic' posture towards the sound world, hearing sounds not as events in physical space but as events occurring in a space of their own, related to each other by the forces that govern musical movement. The acousmatic way of hearing brings with it the overreaching intentionality of our interpersonal attitudes. We are listening for the subject beyond the object, the point of view that harbours the reason, and not just the cause, for what we hear. In representational works of art, such as pictures and poems, the subject is presented to the imagination as something separate from the work – the woman in the picture, the poet who speaks the words. In an abstract art form like music the subject has no identity separate from the work. The subject that we hear, and whose voice this is, lies *in* the notes, a discarnate and incorporeal being who confronts us from a horizon that lies at the edge of these very sounds. And that is what moves us in the great works of the listening culture: works like the quartets of Beethoven and Schubert, which address us from a realm that is entirely emancipated from physical reality.

This suggestion gives rise to another: namely, that through music we can in some unique way *enter into* a subjectivity that is not our own, and indeed not anyone's. This is the suggestion that we find in Schopenhauer, and in conclusion it is worth visiting his account of the metaphysics of music. Schopenhauer was the only post-Kantian who regarded the problem of music and its meaning as a test-case for his philosophy, and his theories had a profound impact on Wagner, whose reading of Schopenhauer fostered his conception of a drama that would unfold entirely through the inner feelings of the characters. These feelings, hinted at in words, would acquire their full reality and elaboration in music. Developing under its own intrinsic momentum, the music would guide the listener through subjective regions that were otherwise inaccessible, creating a drama of inner emotion framed by only the sparsest gestures on the stage – gestures which, for this very reason, would become so saturated with meaning as to reach the limits of their expressive potential.

Schopenhauer saw music as a unique form of knowledge, with a status among the arts that was both exalted and metaphysically puzzling. Unlike poetry or figurative painting, music employs no concepts, and presents no narrative of an imaginary world. Its meaning is contained within itself, inseparable from the ebb and flow of its abstract lines and harmonies. Yet listening to a great work of music we feel that we are gaining insight into the deepest mysteries of being – although it is an insight that lives in the music, and defies translation into words. Schopenhauer's theory offers both to explain and to vindicate this feeling, and at the same time to exalt music to a metaphysical position matched by no other art form. Music, Schopenhauer tells us, 'is the most powerful of all the arts, and therefore attains its ends entirely from its own resources'.[75]

Simply put, Schopenhauer's theory tells us that music acquaints us with the will, which for Schopenhauer is the Kantian 'thing-in-itself', the indescribable reality behind the veil of human perception, whose operations we know through our own self-awareness. The will cannot be known through concepts, since they provide us merely with representations, and never with the thing-in-itself. Our inner knowledge of the will is therefore non-conceptual, a direct and unsayable access to the metaphysical essence. This non-conceptual knowledge is offered also by music. Unlike painting and literature, music is not a form of representation, nor does it deal in Platonic Ideas, which are the common resource of all the other arts. Music exhibits the will directly. And this explains its power: for it also *acts* on the will directly, raising and altering the passions without the intermediary of conceptual thought. Through consonance and dissonance music shows, in objective form, the will as satisfied and obstructed; melodies offer the 'copy of the origination of new desires, and then of their satisfaction';[76] suspension is 'an analogue of the satisfaction of the will which is enhanced through delay'[77] and so on. At the same time, because music is a non-conceptual art, it does not provide the objects of our passions but instead shows the inner working of the will itself, released from the prison of appearances. In opera and song the words and action provide the subject-matter of emotion, but the emotion itself is generated in the music. And 'in opera, music shows its heterogeneous nature and its superior intrinsic virtue by its complete indifference to everything material in the incidents'.[78]

[75] *Die Welt als Wille und Vorstellung*, tr. E. F. J. Payne as *The World as Will and Representation* (Indian Hills, 1958), vol. 2, p. 448.
[76] *Ibid.*, p. 455.
[77] *Ibid.*, p. 456.
[78] *Ibid.*, p. 449.

As it stands, Schopenhauer's theory succeeds in vindicating the expressive power of music only by linking music to his conception of the will as 'thing-in-itself'. Moreover, the theory is in danger of self-contradiction. Schopenhauer denies that music represents the will; but he also says that music 'presents', 'exhibits' ('*darstellt*'), even offers a 'copy' ('*Abbild*') of the will, and what these terms mean is never explained. Moreover, if it is really true that the will is the thing-in-itself behind appearances, then nothing can be said about it. All meaningful statements concern representations and Ideas (the Platonic essences exemplified by individual things). Music belongs in the world of appearance and is, indeed, nothing more than an appearance, which exists only for those with ears to hear it. Hence it is strictly meaningless to speak of an analogy between the movement that we hear in music and the striving of the will itself.

Nevertheless, those philosophical difficulties do not affect the core of truth in the theory. Schopenhauer tells us that the non-conceptual awareness that we have of our own mental states is really an awareness of the will; he also tells us that the will is objectively presented to us without concepts in the work of music. In these two statements we can 'divide through' by the will, to use Wittgenstein's metaphor:[79] reference to the will is an unwarranted addition to another and more intelligible theory, which tells us that in self-knowledge we are acquainted with *the very same thing* that we hear in music. To put it in another way: music presents subjective awareness in objective form. In responding to expressive music, we are acquiring a 'first-person' perspective on a state of mind that is not our own – indeed which exists un-owned and objectified, in the imaginary realm of musical movement.[80]

So understood, Schopenhauer's argument can be detached from his metaphysics of the will, which, like all the metaphysical theories of the idealists, is open to the fatal objection that it assumes a point of view on the world that is strictly unobtainable, and which

---

[79] See *Philosophical Investigations*, Part 1, section 293.
[80] I have defended this view at length in *The Aesthetics of Music*, and assume, for present purposes, an intuitive understanding of what it means.

indeed Kant had shown to be unobtainable in *The Critique of Pure Reason.* Combining the two lines of enquiry that I have followed, we can present a single, plausible and comprehensive theory of musical understanding towards which all the idealists were working, hampered by their gross metaphysical ambitions on the one hand and their musical incompetence on the other, but defensible in other terms than those they appealed to. According to this theory, sounds become music when they are organized in such a way as to invite acousmatic listening. Music is then heard to *address* the listener, I to you, and the listener responds with the overreaching attitudes that are the norm in interpersonal relations. These attitudes reach for the subjective horizon, the edge behind the musical object. The music invites the listener to adopt its own subjective point of view, through a kind of empathy that shows the world from a perspective that is no one's and therefore everyone's. All this is true of music in part because it is an abstract, non-representational art, in part because it avails itself of temporal organization in a non-physical space.

Part II

Critical Explorations

7

Franz Schubert and the *Quartettsatz*

Schubert, who died aged 31 in 1828, left nearly a thousand compositions, the vast majority of which are marked by his distinctive genius. Opera apart, he excelled in every musical genre, writing string quartets that can be set beside the greatest of Haydn and Mozart, symphonies that stand comparison with Beethoven and works for piano that paved the way for Schumann and Chopin. His string quintet in C major is perhaps the most beautiful piece of chamber music ever composed, while his 600 songs represent a flow of unaffected melody without comparison in the history of music. No composer is more relevant to us. We live in a world that is on the run. We run towards huge rewards, and we run from huge disasters. Nothing around us stands still; we seek rest but rarely find it. We have lost touch with what really matters, which is the sense of *being*. And that is what Schubert has in abundance. He is the poet of home and the loss of home. He shows every nuance of love and settlement, and of the grief through which we pay for them. Nothing in his songs is contrived or artificial: everything flows spontaneously from the situation invoked by the poet, and just as life in all its variety gains shape in his incomparable melodies, so too does death lurk in his shifting harmonies, quasi-modulations and asymmetrical forms.

For Schubert's greatest works were written in the shadow of death, which is present in them as in the works of no other composer, save possibly Mahler. In the first movement of the Unfinished Symphony, for example, or in the opening of the great string quartet in G major, he makes us stare into the void, and does so in a way that is neither morbid nor despairing but strangely enriching, urging us to value the moment not despite its transience but because of it. Faced with death, Schubert can recall the sweetest of joys, as in the poignant last movement of the last sonata or in the first movement of the string quintet in C. His vision is clear, undeceived and frightening; and yet he snatches love and joy from the void that stands ready to engulf them, and the result is as life-affirming as any music that we have.

The experience of loss endows Schubert's two great song-cycles (*Winterreise* and *Die schöne Müllerin*) with their sacred character. You cannot listen to these works in just any mood. The space that they define is a religious space, a space lying always beyond the experiences evoked in the individual songs. And they exemplify Schubert's extraordinary ability with words. No songwriter has commanded such a flow of melody as Schubert; but it is melody that seems to arise from the words, as though the poem breathes itself out as music. Whatever the matter in hand – lovelorn, exultant, reverent, nostalgic, furious, heroic, tender, despairing, religious, erotic, through the entire range of human feeling – the Schubertian melody captures the thing as it truly is, free from sentimentality and exaggeration, and with a simplicity and directness that lift us into another and purer way of perceiving.

When I was first introduced to real music, as a teenager, it was common to identify Bach, Mozart and Beethoven as the undisputed masters. Schubert was sometimes mentioned, along with Haydn, Mendelssohn, Schumann and Brahms, as belonging in the second rank. But it would have been regarded as heresy to set Schubert beside the three greats. I have since come to see that Schubert is the equal of Mozart in melody, of Beethoven in musical form and of Bach in sheer musicianship. His ability to combine melodic and harmonic order in a single movement and to endow that movement with impeccable shape is apparent from his earliest works. His setting of Gretchen's lament from Goethe's *Faust* already exhibits the formal perfection that was to be the hallmark of his later song-writing. This consummate masterpiece, which Schubert wrote when he was a mere 17 years old, with its unforgettable spinning-wheel accompaniment and continuous melody working to a dissonant climax as Gretchen remembers the kiss of her seducer, does not merely illustrate Schubert's mastery of dramatic gesture. The harmonic movement carries rhythm, drama and narrative to a single conclusion, as though all three had been contained in a sequence of chords, waiting to be stretched out in this gossamer web of melody.

Schubert's ability to retain an unbroken melodic line while changing tonal centre from bar to bar is no musician's trick but a sign of his complete control of the musical material. Of course, he takes liberties. He does not obey the rules of sonata form; he strays into strange regions. He can be obsessively repetitive. He switches rapidly between major and minor, as at the start of the G major quartet. He can even write an entire movement in the wrong key, like the *Quartettsatz* in C minor (a movement from one of his many unfinished works), which marches into A flat major and stays there or thereabouts, spurning the colder place from whence it came. But none of this is trickery: always there is a purpose to Schubert's innovations, and always they enhance the dramatic power and emotional intensity of the whole.

If I were to identify the distinctive emotion that pervades Schubert's music, I would say that it is a tragic but reconciled love: love not only for people in all their many predicaments but also love for music, and love especially for the music that was brought to him by his muse. Nobody has composed variations like Schubert's – variations on his own melodies, in which he gives way to wonder at their discovery, and holds them to the light so as to discern layer upon layer of significance within them. Most musical people are familiar with the variations on *The Trout* which are contained in the quintet that is named after them and also with the incomparable variations on *Death and the Maiden*, in the eponymous string quartet. Fewer know the variations on '*Sei mir gegrüßt*' contained within a late Fantasia for Violin and Piano – a prolonged and poignant meditation on one of Schubert's most affecting melodies. But it is perhaps in this work that Schubert most directly reveals the source of his inspiration: which is his ability to imagine in music the absent lover who never appeared in reality. When I think of Schubert's death and lament, as I never cease to lament, that he did not live to the age of Mozart, I think of the love that he longed for and never obtained, and wonder yet more at a musical legacy which contains more consolation for our loneliness than any other human creation.

It is this love-longing that informs the remarkable *Quartettsatz*, or string quartet movement, the opening movement of a string quartet that he never completed and which was never performed in his lifetime. He wrote it in 1820, during a transitional period and before he had hit on the concentrated and tragic style of his later chamber works. Yet it is in its way one of the most poignant and emotional of his works for the medium, and one that in no way strikes the listener as provisional or incomplete. It is also pervaded by a strange ambiguity that infects the form, the key and the mood of the piece. It is a sonata movement without a proper first subject, starting and ending in C minor but for the most part in or around A flat major, gripped by icy pincers at both ends but radiant and sunny whenever the only real melody sounds. The ambiguity is enhanced by the opening motif, which slides around the chromatic scale whenever it appears, and seems to be peculiarly foundationless, like a bridging passage with nothing to bridge.

Schubert began writing string quartets at an early age, and is responsible for two or three of the greatest masterpieces in the idiom, as well as for the exquisite C major string quintet. Like all his mature works, the *Quartettsatz* is supremely lyrical but never cloying, with its main melody locked in a grim and rueful setting like a bright jewel in a ring of iron. This is the soul that Schubert constantly shows: the outpouring of love and life in the midst of apprehension. And it is surely why we treasure his greatest works as much as we do: they are all of them, and all in different ways, triumphs of life over death. In all of them there shines a clear and unaffected affirmation out of the heart of darkness. And the *Quartettsatz* is no exception.

As in so much of Schubert, we are being invited to make choices. Music is a realm of freedom. We can choose to hear as a theme what is really an introduction, to hear as an accompanying figure what is really a leading motif and so on. And right from the beginning

Schubert is presenting us with material which we can hear in radically contrasting ways – either as a theme or as an introduction; either as a clear statement of what the movement is all about or as a prelude, from which the subject-matter will emerge when properly prepared. And as the movement unfolds that ambiguity becomes ever more deeply embedded in its structure.

The piece opens with a tremolando figure in C minor, which moves chromatically, first downwards to G, and then soaring upwards, to include every note of the chromatic scale except the one most antipathetic to C, namely D flat. So far this is what you might expect – a chromatic scale used to affirm the key of C minor, tightened by the tremolandos to produce the typically Schubertian sense of apprehension, and avoiding the D flat which would render everything ambiguous. However, the passage ends on that very D flat – and not just the note: the chord of D flat major, held tight in the grip of C minor only because arranged over an F in the bass. To cap it all Schubert gives us two bars in which the first violin does nothing save descend the arpeggiated chord of D flat major – impressing it on us as though it were D flat, not C, that were the principal key (Ex. 1).

I have described the effect in somewhat technical terms, but you don't need the technicalities in order to hear what is going on. It is as though a spirit had arisen out of turbulent clouds and suddenly burst forth into the light – the clouds formed from the key of C minor, the spirit itself, released at last, being in the negation of C minor, namely D flat major. (Major negates minor, and D flat, being removed by a semitone, negates C.)

Ex. 1

Ex. 2

The violin lands from that bright chord back in the darkness, on B natural and in the key of C minor. For 12 bars the movement stays in that key, using the theme, such as it is, of the tremolo passage, and moving always chromatically, until once again the first violin lands on D flat and leads the other instruments in a gentle modulation to A flat major, the dominant of D flat. There then begins the first real theme of the work, a beautiful, serene melody that has been entirely released from the darkness in which the work began (Ex. 2).

Schubert was a master at sudden changes of tonal centre, and the entrance of this melody illustrates the natural way in which he moves from place to place on the scale. However, the melody also reinforces the experience of ambiguity. Is this the first subject or the second subject of the movement? It enters like a first subject, clearing the air after all that chromatic preluding. But since when did a movement in C minor have a first subject in A flat major? But if it is a second subject, then it ought to be in the dominant of the key – which means it ought to be in G. But it is a semitone away from G, in A flat, which is the dominant of D flat major. So if we read back to the opening passage, assuming this is the second subject, that opening passage ought to have been in D flat major. It wasn't, of course – but this A flat melody is reminding us that, concealed within the C minor cloud of the opening passage, was a trapped spirit in D flat major, which burst out briefly in a life-affirming arpeggio and was then recaptured as it fell to earth. So yes, the opening passage really was an introduction, and this A flat melody is the theme for which it was preparing the way.[81]

---

[81] On the question whether the A flat major passage is really *in* that key, see the discussion above, Part 1, Chapter 5.

Ex. 3

The melody is repeated an octave higher, and occupies the longest continuous section of the exposition, concluding finally, after some characteristically Schubertian elaborations, on the chord of A flat minor and a return of the tremolando. The cloud returns, with terrified-sounding scales on the first violin, pressing on the key of A flat minor, until shifting adroitly to a passage which is (more or less) in G, though with once again heavy emphasis on the note (A flat) removed by a semitone. This chromatic bridging passage finally settles on G major, and a new melody enters, and one that raises all the questions raised by the previous theme. Is this (Ex. 3) the second subject? The key of G major would suggest that it is; but then what of that theme in A flat: was that just a passing idea, of no significance, even though it is the theme that listeners remember, and sing to themselves as they leave the concert hall?

One thing to notice about this G major melody is the way in which the semitone conflict – between G and A flat, and between C and D flat – has by now penetrated the whole structure of the piece. It has become part of the musical argument, so to speak. Throughout the melody the viola and cello go on muttering on adjacent semitones, creating a slippery chromatic path on which the melody can scarcely gain a foothold. Hence, despite its clear outline and open-hearted charm, the theme doesn't stand firmly before us and soon gives way to a chromatic passage reminiscent of the opening, moving through C minor to A flat before settling on G major to bring the exposition to a conclusion. The violins and viola ascend bird-like above muttering semitones on the cello, the melody here recalling Schubert's setting of Goethe's poem 'Ganymede', in which the poet compares himself to the boy captured by Zeus, soaring upwards in the eagle's grip.

The exposition has presented us, then, with four ideas: a tremolando motif in C minor; a smiling melody in A flat major and another, somewhat more precarious, in G; and running through all this a chromatic contest between keys associated with C and keys associated with D flat, played out in all kinds of ways in the various melodic lines. The basic feeling is of something serene and life-affirming trapped in clouds of apprehension, from which it briefly frees itself only to be trapped again, but released and ascending skywards at the end, before plunging back to the beginning, as the exposition is repeated.

As it plunges for the second time, into the development section, the music lands in A flat, and picks up a phrase that had first appeared as an elaboration of the original A flat melody – the melody that might have been first subject or second subject, depending how you heard what had preceded it. This phrase is developed for a while over the by now familiar chromatic mutterings on the cello, until D flat major appears once again out of the mists, with a soaring motif on open fifths that is promptly answered by a clenched dominant seventh chord (Ex. 4). This chord is used in such a way that the cello can slip around between C and D flat for four bars, so that we get the point. Schubert is telling us that this movement is in D flat major and the icy grip of C minor is something from which we have by now been freed.

The material so far presented is developed in a variety of ways, Schubert using all his skills at modulation to bring the exposition to an end in an appropriate key. Except that the key is entirely inappropriate. Assuming the C minor tremolando from which we began

Ex. 4

was the first subject, we should be coming back to that motif, and in the home key. But we don't come back to that motif, nor do we come back to the home key. Schubert ends the development in D. Then, after four bars of weird hesitation for solo violin, Schubert introduces the recapitulation in B flat major – not with the tremolando first subject (if it ever *was* the first subject!) but with the sunny melody that first appeared in A flat and which sounded like the first subject then.

Everything proceeds as before, with the cheerful theme moving on to E flat and plunging at the end to E flat minor. From this point on the recapitulation moves towards C in just the way the exposition moved towards G, so that, soaring upwards at the end, it presents us with a quiet C major chord, high in the heavens. But the cellos go on muttering for two bars. For this kind of escape into bliss is only temporary, something from which we will always in the end be wrenched away. The first motif returns, giving us again the notes of the chromatic scale assembled tremolando around C minor rising in a crescendo and reaching what should be, by the rules of classical harmony, the chord on the second-scale degree – D. But no! There is a wrong note: what should be D is D flat, and the chord is that of D flat major, appearing for the last time, defiant, despairing almost, to be promptly hit on the head by a perfect cadence in C minor (Ex. 5).

I don't think you can be in much doubt about the meaning of this piece. It is not telling a story; it is showing a posture towards the world, and showing it by using a form – that of the sonata form first movement – in some way against itself. Everything about this movement is sonata-ish, and yet nothing quite obeys the rules. It breaks the rules in just the way that feelings break through the habits in

Ex. 5

which we have imprisoned them. The melodic material is emblematic of a joy and tenderness that refuse to be captured by the grief and apprehension that enclose them, even though the grief and apprehension are their own. The music is showing, through the sincerity and completeness of its chromatic logic, how fears and griefs can be overcome. We can learn to experience them as the frame, and not as the picture. It is as though the D flat planted in the heart of this music expands to fill the centre, leaving C minor as it were clinging to the edges, containing everything but having no part in the drama. And that is how we should live, boldly laying claim to joy and affection, while aware of the tragic frame in which all such emotions are set.

8

Rameau the Musician

Rameau was renowned in his day as a keyboard virtuoso, and his compositions for harpsichord are among the most colourful in the repertoire, even if attaining only rarely to the emotional refinement and poetry that we find in the *Ordres* of François Couperin. Twenty-five years the junior of Couperin, Rameau belonged to a generation that was beginning to emancipate itself from the musical *lingua franca* of the baroque. Harmonies that had appeared in the works of Bach and Couperin as by-products of scholarly counterpoint were beginning to be seen in another way, as chords – musical objects which have an intrinsic significance and potential, and which can capture voices, so to speak, from the air around them. Although Rameau is known and admired today as a composer of opera, his operatic career began late in his life, when he had already begun to think in a wholly new way about the nature of tonal harmony. His *Treatise on Harmony*, published in 1722, 11 years before his operatic debut, aged 50, with *Hippolyte et Aricie*, was read with enthusiasm and a measure of astonishment by his contemporaries, precisely because it wrote of chords and their uses, and derived from the theory of counterpoint only the notion that the bass must move through melodic intervals, so as to support the structure built on top of it. It is noteworthy in this connection that Rameau's keyboard music often includes extended sequences of broken chords, exploring every aspect of a single harmony before moving on.

The *Treatise on Harmony* is not an easy read. Rameau had to invent a new vocabulary, and to adapt the old language of figured bass, in order to express thoughts that musicologists today would express in another way, knowing the chords by name, so to speak, rather than by their role in a musical language that is no longer spoken. Exactly how we should express Rameau's theories is a matter of controversy. But here are some of the main points that he brings to our attention, at least as I read him:

1. All perfect consonances are composed of two intervals: a minor third and a major third, enclosed within a fifth. If the minor third is below, the result is what we would call a minor triad; if above, the result is a major triad. The major triad is composed of the fourth, fifth and sixth partials of a note sounded two octaves below. That note is the fundamental of the triad, and also the tonic of the key and the 'root' of the chord.

2. All other chords with a clear grammatical role are likewise built from thirds, but all are, in some measure, dissonant.

3. Understanding harmony is largely a matter of understanding the role of these dissonant chords, which have a permanent character and recognizable function. Rameau singles out for special attention the seventh, ninth and eleventh chords, and the diminished seventh. One particular seventh chord – the six-five chord on the sub-dominant – has a special significance for Rameau, and he often uses it to prepare cadences in his operas. In the minor key with major sixth this chord is isomorphic with the famous 'Tristan' chord of Wagner. It is a quintessentially dramatic chord, and that is how Rameau uses it.

4. Many dissonant chords have an actual or implied root – the note which, sounded in the bass, anchors them and determines the ways in which they might resolve into consonant harmonies. As far as I can see, Rameau does not define the nature or role of the 'root' of a chord. But he writes as though dissonant chords are nevertheless rooted in the bass

in something like the way that the triads are rooted. This is clearly true of the dominant seventh, and of other seventh chords built in the same way, by adding more thirds to a triad. In most of these cases there is a note which, when sounded in the bass, produces maximum stability and also moves melodically to the root of another chord that resolves the dissonance. Some dissonances, however, are rootless, like the diminished seventh and the augmented triad, or ambiguous, like the six-five chord which can rest on either of two roots.

5. All harmonic movement involves tracing the relations among roots while making a path towards a cadence. Cadences are of various kinds, perfect and imperfect, complete and interrupted etc.

Tonal music moved on in the aftermath of Beethoven. Diatonic chords with 'altered' notes occur frequently in Wagner, while Skryabin built highly coloured dissonances from accumulated fourths, rather than thirds. Nevertheless, it can plausibly be said that Rameau described the topology of tonal space as it was to be explored during the century that followed. Although it would be wrong to suggest that he anticipated what Schoenberg called the 'emancipation of the dissonance', there is no doubt that his treatment of dissonance was revolutionary at the time. He regarded dissonance as a property of individual chords, rather than as a by-product of counterpoint (as in suspension). Chords, for Rameau, add their spice to whole bars, in which they might be held constant through changes in the melodic line. And in his operas it is clear that the rules of counterpoint have far less significance than the grammatical relations among the harmonies. Rameau is happy to allow the occasional parallel fifths and octaves in the voices, and his chord-based harmony has a drive and conviction that enable him to bypass contrapuntal subtleties and get straight to the point. Look at the 'Air en Rondeau', no. 28 in the score of *Hippolyte et Aricie* (Ex. 1). The second chord here is a pure augmented fourth on C and F sharp, with the F sharp doubled in the bass, leading to a

Ex. 1

Ex. 2

third-built dissonance on G which could be described either as an augmented triad on G with added major seventh or equally as a B major triad over a dissonant G in the bass. You might say that the chord is a kind of appoggiatura resolving on to the E minor chord that follows, except that the E minor chord does not follow – there is a unison B that separates the dissonance from its resolution, emphasizing the free-standing character of the stacked-up thirds. Incidentally, lower down the same page, at bar 381 (Ex. 2), you find one of Rameau's unselfconscious parallel fifths.

Equally important is the free recitative, with its melismatic vocal line over a figured bass, which was a major step towards the music drama as we know it. *Hippolyte et Aricie* shocked many in the audience at its first performance, and one, subsequently famous, number, the second trio for the fates, was cut because the players found it too hard to perform. This trio shows the impact of Rameau's chordal thinking at its most radical, with a rhythmical accompanying figure jumping about over two octaves, and remaining for whole bars on one chord – often a diminished seventh or a six-five chord, and at one point descending chromatically through the minor keys from F sharp minor to D minor, coming then to a dramatic pause on a diminished seventh. This extraordinary passage, anticipating the Mozart of *Don Giovanni*, illustrates the way in which Rameau's harmonic language permits maximum freedom of effect.

In addition to such daring gestures, the opera is without spoken dialogue and is musically continuous, recitative, aria, ensemble, chorus and dance episodes all being woven together to form a continuous musical fabric. This endows *Hippolyte et Aricie* with a unity that is as much musical as dramatic. The plot – downstream from Racine's *Phèdre* – involves the chorus directly in the action, and the dances, when they occur, are not diversions but essential to the narrative. This became a rule in Rameau's operas: the people dance on the stage not as a distraction from the drama but as a fundamental part of it. The dance is not a comment on the story but contained in it. *Anacréon* is a prime illustration of this, and is indeed a leading example of an art form that Rameau made his own – the opera-ballet, or (as he described this particular instance) the *ballet héroique*. His librettist, Louis de Cahusac, had written a book on the dance, comparing ancient and modern practice, and clearly intended his text to be as much danced as sung.

Rameau's place in the history of opera is now assured. The criticism of his contemporaries, many of whom preferred the conventions of Lully, in which spoken dialogue, set dances, commenting choruses and other irrelevances interrupted the dramatic flow, no longer has weight for us. On the contrary, Rameau attempted a synthesis of music and drama that was a model for future composers, and which we now regard as laying out the true path for the opera, the path followed not only by Mozart but also in their different ways by Verdi and Wagner. Rameau was helped to move in this direction by his harmonic discoveries, which enabled him to free himself from the demands of counterpoint and to allow colour and effect to bear the weight of the drama. His music was capable of generating the action by its own impetus, gathering the chorus, the ballet and the principal characters into a single musical movement.

The controversy with the Lullians was not the only one in which Rameau was involved. Far more important historically was the so-called *querelle des bouffons*, a public controversy over the nature of opera, which was connected to other and wider debates surrounding the *Encyclopédie* of Diderot and d'Alembert. It is worth revisiting this episode, since it illustrates some of the strengths and also the weaknesses of Rameau as a musician. The *querelle* was between two factions who were competing for space in the theatres of Paris. On the one hand were those who favoured the French tradition, exemplified by Lully and Rameau, of the *tragédie en musique*. On the other hand were those who championed the Italian *opera buffa*, which was beginning to gain followers in France.

The dispute over *opera buffa* continued another and long-lasting conflict between the Italian *opera seria*, brought to its apogee by Handel, and the operatic styles of the French court. The *opera seria* arose out of baroque counterpoint, and hinged upon the aria as the principal means of musical expression. The action would be taken forward by recitatives and, when the situation of characters was clear enough to permit it, they would step forward with a long aria, usually in ABA form, expounding their sentiments at a length which, while often musically enthralling, was frequently dramatically absurd – not least on account of the *da capo* section, which made every emotion look like a form of paranoia. Rameau, by contrast, made use of arias and ensembles to move the action forward, rather than to comment upon it. (This is particularly true of his use of the chorus.)

The *tragédie en musique* grew out of French classical theatre, which was in its turn profoundly influenced by Greek tragedy, as this was understood by the academicians of seventeenth-century France. From the beginning it was tied to the search for artistic unity and formal integrity, and eschewed the subordination of the plot to moments of autobiographical excess, such as occurred in the extended arias of *opera seria*. The *querelle des bouffons* added a new twist to the conflict between Italy and France. The new comic plots, of which Pergolesi's *La serva padrona* was the most striking, gave prominent parts to the common people, looked with an undeceived eye on class conflict and the puffed-up manners of the aristocracy and appealed to sentiments that might at any time run riot in political form.

The French opera deployed old statuesque dramas involving gods, miracles and heroic passions. It was an art form founded in the conventions and solidities of the French court, and one that spoke of the permanence of kings and of the hierarchies maintained by them. Furthermore, the Italian *opera buffa* was less concerned with dancing and formalized display than with the forward movement of individual feeling, and therefore placed great emphasis on melody. It presented an altogether different image of human life and its goal from that obtainable from the formalized dances of Rameau. The quarrel took on a more radical form with Rousseau, who entered on the side of the Italians, criticizing the French for sacrificing melodic invention to harmonic complexity. In his *Lettre sur la musique française* of 1753 Rousseau went yet further, arguing that there is no such thing as French music, that the very nature of the French language poisoned the sources of melody and encouraged an artificial art, obedient to the rules of harmony alone.

It so happened that Diderot had commissioned Rousseau to write the articles on music for the *Encyclopédie,* and Rameau had complained about these articles, and about the apparent ignorance of their author. This led Rousseau to single out Rameau for special denunciation, even while drawing on Rameau's *Treatise* when later composing his own *Dictionnaire de musique* (1768). All that we now admire in Rameau – the dramatic clarity, the clear enunciation of the text, the power of orchestral effects and the integral musical argument – was denounced by Rousseau as the opposite of music. And to prove his point Rousseau composed a short opera, *Le Devin du village* (1752), in the Italian style. This, notwithstanding its plodding harmonies and four-square vocal line, had an extraordinary success at the opera house. Rousseau also presented a new scheme for musical notation, jettisoning the graphic representation of musical movement and identifying notes and quantities numerically. (The fact that the old notation makes the presentation of harmony and simultaneous voices so clear and immediate was part of what motivated Rousseau to attack it.)

There is something admirable in Rousseau's reckless confrontation with the musical tradition, and also in his ability to crown his philosophical objections with musical works. Yet closer examination reveals that his contribution to the debate is not merely negative

143

but also wedded to negation – determined to find corruption in the surrounding musical culture precisely because it is an established practice and a reservoir of social knowledge. Our notational system developed side by side with harmony and counterpoint. No single person could ever have discovered the knowledge of the human ear and the human heart that these practices contain any more than a single person could discover language. When Rameau came to write his *Treatise on Harmony*, he was not inventing rules or recording the conventions of a game. He was attempting to summarize a body of implicit knowledge, which is in all our heads as listeners and per- formers but which has no first principles, no definitions, no *a priori* system. What Rameau did in his treatise was to render a tradition of implicit knowledge as an *a posteriori* catalogue of explicit principles. His treatise was a moment in the 'coming to consciousness' of music, in which the chord was finally understood as an independent musical object, rich in implications that could be spelled out both musically and dramatically.

Rousseau's system of notation is useless for any musician who has to sight-read multiple parts, and it gives no lucid account of har- monic sequence or voice-leading. It is a match for the old notation only when representing unison melodies. This objection was made by Rameau, and in Book 7 of the *Confessions* Rousseau concedes the point. In the event, however, Rousseau was deterred neither by Rameau's arguments nor by his own recognition of their force. Instead he turned against Rameau and all that the composer stood for. He began to attack harmony and counterpoint as marks of cor- ruption, and to praise unison melody as the pure voice of nature.

Rousseau's attacks were followed up by Diderot's extraordinary satire *Le neveu de Rameau*, in which the *querelle des bouffons* is linked to the wider concerns of the Enlightenment, and in particular to the attempted return to natural sentiment and intellectual clar- ity which, for Diderot, represented the true emancipation of man- kind. Diderot's satire was published only in 1805, in Goethe's German translation, and had no direct influence on events. But it is indicative of the extent to which Rameau had become, during the second half of the eighteenth century, representative of an old art form that was being marginalized by fashion, and even condemned outright by the intellectual firebrands of the day. This is not to say that Rameau suffered any loss of status during his lifetime. By the time of his death he had been appointed composer to the King, and ennobled as a knight of the Ordre de Saint Michel. Following his death, however, he fell quickly out of fashion, with the Italian style, represented by Piccini and Gluck, dominating the Paris opera. Rameau's ballets and operas were thereafter largely unperformed until the movement of revival that began in the 1890s, and which counted Debussy and Ravel among its followers.

What should we think of Rameau's operatic *oeuvre* today? Although he is often praised for his harmonic daring, it should be said, looking back on it, that there are few harmonies in Rameau that could not be found – put, of course, to different use – in Couperin or Bach. What Rameau achieved was the emancipation of harmonic effects from counterpoint, so that they were free to perform a direct dramatic function. Furthermore he made full use of the orchestras at his disposal, and introduced some of the melodramatic gestures that were to be reworked for the concert hall by Stamitz and others of the Mannheim school. His contemporaries rightly admired his ballet music, and the dances in the operas are executed with an exquisite sense of choreography – you can hear the feet of the dancers in the music, which moves in sympathy to the drama in a way that has few subsequent parallels. And – once you accept the conventions of the French classical stage, in which gods that no one believes in create situations that no one could possibly escape, and in which nevertheless everything ends happily with nymphs and shepherds gracefully dancing without any awareness of the cold water that Diderot and Rousseau are about to pour on them – once you accept all that, you can appreciate Rameau as a composer who advanced the cause of music drama by several notches at a time when it was threatened by dead conventions and the lopsided arias of the *opera seria* school.

Rameau had harmony, rhythm and drama. But what about melody? I think it is significant that few musical people retain in their heads a good Rameau tune, apart, perhaps, from the *Tambourin*, contained in the 1724 book of keyboard pieces. His music is melodious, yes; it is a pleasure to sing, and the choruses carry you along in sympathy. But – when compared with Pergolesi, for instance, or with Handel, who preceded him, and Gluck, who came after – we should surely say that Rameau rarely presented us with a heart-rending or even truly memorable tune. His operas work in another way, through a species of melismatic declamation, driven along by strong rhythms and the occasional tense harmony, and with very little lingering by the way, unless in the form of a dance. His own description of them, as *ballets héroiques*, captures their real musical essence, as music for the human body, in all its dramatic predicaments.

9

Britten's Dirge

Continental historians of music are wary of modern English composers, deprecating both the powerful national sentiment that has inspired so many of them and the clear tonal logic of their music, sign of a deep desire to remain in contact with the people. Works like the violin and viola concertos of Walton, the piano concertos of Rawsthorne or the dramatically mawkish but musically radiant *Midsummer Marriage* of Tippett are guaranteed to arouse fits of Anglophobia across the channel, where these tuneful masterpieces have been shunted to the sidings of musical history. According to the Hegelian orthodoxy, musical progress continues in a straight line from Bach to Stockhausen and beyond, and the parochial branchlines in Betjeman-land are dead ends, from which visitors never emerge into the light of real history.

There is one composer, however, who cannot be dismissed in this way, and whose reputation continues to grow both in his home country and around the world, and that is Benjamin Britten. *Peter Grimes* was first performed in 1945, long after the death of tonality had been accepted as a critical commonplace, and its memorable, singable melodies are a triumphant rebuttal of the prevailing orthodoxy. Britten continued to grow thereafter, showing a remarkable capacity to develop both stylistically and critically, in the face of the rapidly changing post-war musical panorama. His was a truly evolving modernism, not a tinkering with intellectual systems but an organic growth from one idiom to its successor, taking in both 12-tone serialism (*The Turn of the Screw*) and oriental heterophony (*Curlew River*), capable equally of strident dissonance (the Cello Symphony), of desolate yearning (*Death in Venice*) and of plangent melody (the *War Requiem*). Not everything Britten wrote was great, and for many people the underlying eroticism has an undigested, not to say adolescent, quality that impedes the real spiritual transcendence at which the composer aimed. Nevertheless, Britten serves as a model of true musical development, as opposed to the fake development imposed on the world by Schoenberg's intellectualizing, and rubbed in with Hegelian glee by Adorno.

Three works of Britten's show clearly that tonality is neither in need of Schoenberg's radical therapy nor really capable of benefiting from it. These works are the Serenade for Tenor, Horn and Strings, op. 31, *The Turn of the Screw* and *Curlew River*, the first of the Church Parables. The Serenade, begun in 1943, was, like *Peter Grimes*, a response to the Second World War. Britten was a pacifist, and had left with Peter Pears for America at the outbreak of war. Like Auden, who had done the same, he felt both guilt towards his country and a profound and searching love for its culture. The Serenade, setting texts by some of the greatest English poets – Keats, Tennyson, Blake – is also part of a lifelong and ambivalent relation to the English church, in both its modern and its medieval manifestations. England, for Britten, was an enchanted land, consecrated by monastic Christianity and the festivals and rites of a national religion. On his return journey by boat in 1942 he composed the *Ceremony of Carols*, setting medieval Christmas poems for children's voices, and he continued to compose music for church settings and liturgical use almost to the end of his life. He was, as might be said, a 'Christian agnostic', one who believed in the Christian stories, ceremonies and rituals, as expressions of deep features of the human condition, but not in the truth of the doctrines that might be given in support of them. It could reasonably be said that the majority of his compositions, following his return to his country in 1942, were contributions to the reconsecration of England: intransitive prayers offered by a pious half-believer.

The Serenade sings of night in all its aspects, and in the prologue and epilogue for solo horn it uses only the natural harmonics of the instrument, evoking Tennyson's 'horns of Elfland faintly blowing', from the poem that Britten sets in the body of the work to such powerful effect. It is hard to imagine more poignant musical commentaries than those the composer gives to Blake's 'Sick Rose' and to Keats's sublime sonnet to sleep. In this brief note, however, I focus on the setting of the anonymous 'Lyke-Wake Dirge', in which Britten hits on a remarkable tune that takes us back to the world of *Piers Plowman* and the Everyman plays. Here is the dirge:

This ae nighte, this ae nighte,
Every nighte and alle,
Fire and fleet and candle-lighte,
And Christe receive thy saule.

When thou from hence away art past,
Every nighte and alle,
To Whinny-muir thou com'st at last;
And Christe receive thy saule.

If ever thou gavest hosen and shoon,
Every nighte and alle,
Sit thee down and put them on;
And Christe receive thy saule.

If hos'n and shoon thou ne'er gav'st nane,
Every nighte and alle,
The whinnes sall prick thee to the bare bane;
And Christe receive thy saule.

From Whinny-muir when thou mayst pass,
Every nighte and alle,
To Brig o' Dread thou com'st at last;
And Christe receive thy saule.

From Brig o' Dread when thou may'st pass,
Every nighte and alle,
To Purgatory thou com'st at last,
And Christe receive thy saule.

If ever thou gav'st meat or drink,
Every nighte and alle,
The fire sall never make thee shrink,
And Christe receive thy saule.

If meat or drink thou ne'er gav'st nane,
Every nighte and alle,
The fire will burn thee to the bare bane,
And Christe receive thy saule.

This ae nighte, this ae nighte,
Every nighte and alle,
Fire and fleet and candle-lighte,
And Christe receive thy saule.

'Whinny' is a Yorkshire dialect word for prickly gorse, and the poem is a fifteenth-century Yorkshire chant collected by John Aubrey in 1686. ('Lyke' = German *Leiche,* a corpse.) Parts of this poem have been set by other composers, notably Stravinsky (*Cantata on Old English Texts,* 1952) and the folk band Pentangle. Here is the tune (Ex. 1): The melody uses an interesting scale, essentially G minor on which is superimposed the hypophrygian mode used in certain

Ex. 1

medieval plainsong chants. (Flattened supertonic, flattened fifth and – although Britten does not avail himself of this – flattened seventh.) It is a small tune, but a haunting one, and proof of Britten's gift as a musical anthropologist, able to capture the meaning of other places, other times and other worldviews, the gift so powerfully manifested in *Curlew River, Les Illuminations, The Prince of the Pagodas* and the many French and English folk-song settings.

The melody is repeated nine times, never accompanied in G minor, but always in a conflicting key, with a scurrying counter-motif in dorian mode (Ex. 2). The accompaniment is brought in just before the final glissando on to the high G, a glissando that imparts an obsessive, incantatory atmosphere to the voice. The double basses and cellos begin the accompaniment quietly in E flat minor, and with each subsequent verse the strings lift the tonal centre, first to a superimposition of F and G, on to B flat and then D, muttering, shuddering, scurrying in agitation at the warning cry. But the tune refuses to alter, sounding its clarion call unmoved by the ever-increasing trouble beneath it.

Ex. 2

The horn is silent until the sixth round of the melody, when it comes in on 'Brig o' dread' in a violent E minor, settling on a constantly iterated G as though to force the melody out of its alien tonality, before subsiding, defeated, on to a low C sharp and finally expiring, *pianissimo*, a semitone lower. This thrilling assault, having failed to eject the melody from its high judgement throne, merely confirms the decree that no human agitation can change. The music has the character of a medieval fresco, with Christ in majesty above the writhing bodies in the pit below. On the last utterance of 'Christ receive thy saule' the double basses collapse on to the E flat minor from which they began, and the chant continues, *senza ritardando*, as though for ever.

Polytonality has given rise to some of the greatest works of twentieth-century music, including Stravinsky's *Rite of Spring* and Szymanowski's first violin concerto. But Britten's polytonality has an originality and force that are unique. The melody against which the various keys unsuccessfully try their strength, and which continues to soar beyond the horizon of our hearing, is not in any key. Its peculiar eight-note scale is like a challenge thrown down to the seven-note scales that one by one compete with it, and its triumph over their many attempts has a kind of metaphysical quality, as though the modal tonality opens a door into the world beyond, where eternal decrees extinguish our transitory agitations. We witness here the unique way in which Britten's poetic imagination is fully integrated into the compositional process. The dirge is not a work of theory, nor is it merely an exercise in polytonal harmony. It is the musical realization of a distinct frame of mind, one associated with England's medieval past, and also reflected in the self-consciousness of a very modern person who wishes to connect with that past and make it part of a renewed vision of his country.

10

David Matthews

During the twentieth century English composers emerged as a distinctive breed, inspired by profound feelings for their homeland and its landscape, and also by a certain cultivated and philosophical distance from the modern world. Like their continental contemporaries, they experimented with polytonality, heterophony, atonal harmony and forms and rhythms borrowed from other places and other times. But – until recently, at least – modern English composers have held back from the repudiation of melody and harmonic sequence. Serialism has had little appeal for them, and for the most part serious English music in our time has shown an acute awareness of the distinction between the art of music and the skills of the sound engineer. In particular, English composers continue to aspire towards melody – or at any rate melodiousness – and towards music that moves forward on a path that listeners can follow and to which they can respond with sympathy.

The attempt to unite modernist harmony with robust melodic thinking is exemplified in the symphonies of Vaughan Williams, the Concerto for Double String Orchestra and Corelli Fantasia of Tippett, the early operas of Britten, the lyrical concertos of Walton, not to mention those all-but-forgotten works by Arnold Bax, Havergal Brian, George Lloyd, and Edmund Rubbra which were aimed at a kind of audience that has now largely disappeared from our concert halls. But the desire to combine modernism and melody continued into my time as one part of the Englishness of English music. And in Robert Simpson and Malcolm Arnold we have seen a determined attempt to retain the Romantic symphony as a paradigm of musical form.

British composers of the post-war generation have been strongly influenced by the kind of melodic thinking that we find in Britten's later work (*Curlew River*, for example, the third string quartet and the *War Requiem*) and in the remarkable triple concerto and *Rose Lake* of the ageing Tippett. But they have also developed a tonal language of their own. In the concertos for orchestra of Robin Holloway, in the operas of Oliver Knussen, Thomas Adès and Judith Weir, in the concertos and symphonies of the Matthews brothers, and in many other works by composers of their generation we find what might be called an 'emancipation of the consonance', and a tunefulness of inspiration that have been a refreshing experience for the music lover. British music in our time offers a new proof that music has an intrinsic grammar, and that this grammar has nothing to do with permutational algorithms, but everything to do with the conquest of musical space by voice-leading and consecutive harmony.

No one more clearly exemplifies this current of musical crafts-manship than David Matthews, who is not merely one of the most prolific composers of his generation but also perhaps the one who has carried forward with the greatest conviction the traditions of modern British (and especially English) music. Matthews's indebt-edness to Britten and Tippett is evident not only from his music but also from his brilliant critical appraisals of both composers, whom he knew, admired and (in Britten's case) assisted during their later years. But – like those two great men, and like so many modern writers and artists in the English tradition – Matthews is a man of universal culture, whose love of the English specificity goes hand in hand with a profound respect for German and Austrian music, for the litera-ture of Greece and Rome, for the art of the Renaissance and for the artistic and philosophical sensibility of Central Europe – not only the Central Europe of Mahler, Bartók and Janáček but also that of Kafka and Zweig, of Havel and Kundera.

His boundless admiration for Mahler shows itself everywhere in his music, not least in the meditative accumulations of melody, such as that which opens the Second Symphony and lasts for a whole movement, or that of the last movement of the Sixth Symphony – an Adagio of Mahlerian proportions in which voice after voice is summoned out of the orchestra to weave its contribution to the elegiac atmosphere. This movement is in fact a set of variations on Vaughan Williams's hymn 'Down Ampney' ('Come Down O Love Divine') and works through many cries of pain to a serene coda, in which Vaughan Williams's beautiful tune appears like a thread of light under dark clouds at the end of day. This, perhaps the most English of all the many English works that Matthews has produced, is also a remarkable tribute to a composer who was for decades regarded with disdain by the musical establishment, precisely on account of the idea of England that inspired him.

As with other English composers, landscape has been of fundamental importance to Matthews, and he has explained its influence on his musical thinking and experience in *Landscape into Sound,* based on his Peter Fuller Memorial Lecture of 1991. But the landscapes evoked in his works are of many different kinds and inspired by many different associations. That which sparked off the powerful *Chaconne* for orchestra is the battlefield of Towton, scene of the most horrendous conflict in the Wars of the Roses, in which 28,000 men died (not to mention the horses). In the preface to the score Matthews quotes Geoffrey Hill's evocation of a field after battle, which

utters its own sound
Which is like nothing on earth, but is earth.

'A medieval battlefield such as Towton', Matthews writes,

has long since mellowed into the peaceable English landscape, the kind of landscape celebrated by our greatest painters and, in music, by Elgar, Vaughan Williams and Tippett. If that pastoral tradition can no longer be sustained in its innocence, perhaps another might replace it, which reconciles our romanticized sense of a picturesque past with the brutal facts of history.

That last sentence captures a vital current in Matthews's thinking, both as a modern Englishman and as a modern composer: the search for an undeceived reconciliation between the romantic and the real, and for an experience of landscape which will be not a form of self-centred illusion but an objective response to the world as it is. One way to achieve this is to concentrate on what is immediate, without specific human meaning, a matter of atmosphere and far-flung suggestiveness. Thus the cello concerto entitled *In Azzurro* evokes a suffusing blue, a synthesis of sea and sky, inspired by a visit to the island of Lundy, in the Bristol Channel, but also connected through the Arabic word 'azure' to places where colours are stronger and more enamelled than they ever are in England.

Matthews may be right that our pastoral tradition 'can no longer be sustained in its innocence'. But he is capable of writing landscape music that has an innocence of its own, such as the short piece for chamber orchestra *From Sea to Sky*, which has some of the joyful expansiveness of Tippett in his double concerto, and which was inspired by early morning walks on the beach in Deal. It should be said here that the reference to landscape is not used to invoke sentiments of a nationalistic kind. His country of birth is only one of the many places that are visited in Matthews's scores, which are the lyrical responses of a wanderer, who is never fully at home but always resonating to new places under new skies. He is possibly the only composer to have included a tango as the scherzo movement of a symphony – and it sweeps along with Latin panache, until stumbling over rhythmically contrary woodwind chords scattered like broken glass on the dance-floor. He has included Mahlerian cowbells and Steve Reich-ish marimbas in his scores, and ranged widely in the geography and history of Europe for his inspiration. His settings of Sappho (*A Congress of Passions*) draw heavily on Cretan folksong. And he has also been profoundly affected by the landscape of Australia, with its slowly unfolding contours evoked by his friend

Peter Sculthorpe, whose music always has to me the character of someone slowly drawing aside a heavy curtain from a scene that consists of another heavy curtain. Matthews's *Aubade* for orchestra, by contrast, draws the curtain from a living landscape, full of the strange birdsongs of Australia, which question the presence of this wanderer from the northern hemisphere but bubble with life regardless.

Perhaps the most striking feature of post-war intellectual life in our country has been its catholicity. The inter-war generation fell under the spell of Eliot, Pound and Wyndham Lewis, and the post-war generation was brought up by schoolmasters and university lecturers saturated in the Eliotian view of European culture. Dante and Baudelaire were our heroes, while we regarded Tennyson and Browning as Victorian relics whose works we did not have time, in the urgency of our modern commitment, to read. We were introduced to the censorious criticism of F. R. Leavis, under whose light we wriggled without ever quite escaping from the glare; we read Rilke in Leishman's editions, and the extracts from the existentialists collected by Walter Kaufmann. The excited discovery of Stravinsky, Bartók and the Second Viennese School, the worry over tonality and whether it was still permitted, the astonished encounter with Rilke, Kafka, Mahler and the Central European soul, the longing for experiences outside the bounds of our Anglican upbringing, and at the same time the stunning message of *Four Quartets*, which told us that those experiences were not out of bounds at all but could be blended with the spiritual heritage of England – all these were shared by our generation and all had a lasting influence. *Four Quartets* brought together the subterranean current of Anglican Christianity with the questioning search for a purified and modernist art that would seek redemption in the immediate moment, observed, internalized and expressed without lies. As the title declares, Eliot had before his mind the great example of Beethoven, whose late quartets show religious questions answered through aesthetic discipline, and redemption achieved by the hard path of artistic truthfulness.

For people of my generation no musical medium has been more important and more personally challenging than the string quartet.

All the crises of twentieth-century art come to a head in the quartet, whose four voices mimic the four voices of the choir and can be used to set out with exemplary clarity the sequential harmonies of the tonal tradition. The greatest of chamber works in the classical style have been quartets – not those of Haydn, Mozart and Beethoven only but the comparable masterpieces of Schubert and the not quite comparable achievements of Schumann, Dvořák and Brahms. There is something about the clarity of tone, and responsiveness to the life and emotion of the performer, which gives stringed instruments a special authority when it comes to exploring abstract forms. In the string quartet tonality is put to the test, and all its devices placed under an auditory microscope. At the same time the instruments converse with each other on equal terms, exchanging the most intimate thoughts and feelings, like members of a family, who will come together after every quarrel. Not surprisingly, therefore, the early modernists used the string quartet both to explore new tonal regions and to challenge the repertoire of the Romantic concert hall. The quartets of Debussy and Ravel take us into a new sound world, as do those of Zemlinsky and Schoenberg. But for us English schoolboys in the 1950s and early 1960s it was the quartets of Bartók that hit us most violently in the stomach, as though it were our own guts that were being pulled around by horsehair.

David Matthews was no exception. Not only has the string quartet featured in his creative output as a favourite medium; he has also used the medium to explore his own art and the possibilities that are open to a composer today. The frame created by the four voices invites tonal treatment, yet the enormous range of intonations available to string players encourages experiment in the realm of colour, timbre and the upper sonorities, both natural and harmonic, of the strings. Moreover, the tradition that began with Mozart and Haydn has consecrated the string quartet as the crucible in which musical sequences, modulations and key relations are tried. In all his quartets, therefore, Matthews has been engaged in an exercise of self-exploration, trying out new forms of tonal thinking, and aiming at the kind of formal continuity and internal cohesion that characterize the classics in the medium. His largest quartet, number 12, is a conscious attempt at late Beethoven, spread over seven movements, each punctuated by adventures into adjacent territory. The quartet contains introductions, cadenzas, two minuets, a serenade, a tango, the whole set in motion by a magnificent prelude and fugue, and carried out with something like Beethoven's combination of meditative seriousness alternating with bursts of unaffected joy. Every now and then, as though overcome by wonder at its own world, the quartet ascends into Messiaen-like birdsong, the birds themselves named in the score as in the *Catalogue d'oiseaux*, and the four instruments striving to escape from their natural sonorities into the clarified air above music.

As schoolboys we were told by enthusiastic gurus that the symphony is dead, that the string quartet ended with Bartók, that tonality is exhausted, and that tunefulness is middlebrow, philistine and in any case no longer 'available'. We were also told (whether or not in the venomous tone of Adorno) that popular music is a commercial imitation of music, a kind of candyfloss on sale in dubious holiday resorts, the sound of which is repulsive to the educated ear. Matthews stood rock-like amid this tide of prejudice. His musical sensibility had been shaped by the symphony and the string quartet, and he thought and felt within the bounds that they defined. Therefore he would compose symphonies and string quartets, and would work to hear them performed. He enjoyed the pop music that was sounding around us in our youth, and found in the Beatles an example of tunefulness and harmony from which there was everything to learn. In his symphonic works we do not hear much pop; but we are given an unusual wealth of melodic ideas, bound together by cogent harmonic progressions, and set in the grand structures learned from Bruckner and Mahler.

The real problem for the tonal composer in our time is how to respect the principles of tonal organization without writing music that is either banal or short-winded. True, there is a late Romantic, or more accurately post-Romantic, sensibility expressed in Matthews's work, and this makes it very personal in its impact. But the treatment of musical elements – of harmony and melody especially – is rigorous and objective, so that each of his movements tends towards a conclusion that is already implied in the opening material. This feature establishes a connection with Sibelius, the great composer singled out by Adorno as the despised voice of reaction in a time that needed revolutionary change.

In his orchestral writing Matthews draws on a data bank extracted from the entire twentieth-century repertoire. Of course, certain effects have a particular appeal for him. He is especially drawn to the use of quiet chords on *divisi* strings, in which the pitches lock together like the knitted fingers of hands in prayer – an effect used consummately by Elgar in the slow movement of the Second Symphony, and constantly recurring in Matthews's symphonies, concertos and symphonic poems. (Rehearsal mark 45 of *A Vision and a Journey* is an instance, with violins divided into twelve, violas into four, cellos into two and double basses playing a sustained open fifth – foundation to an enchanted tower of thirds and seconds touching Heaven with its Gothic finials. A similar instance occurs in the final pages of the cello concerto *In Azzurro*.)

Matthews's harmonies are for the most part adapted from the tonal repertoire, as are his scales. Indeed, there is usually an identifiable tonal centre and sometimes, as in *A Vision and a Journey* and the Twelfth Quartet, a dominant key (in both cases D major/ minor, though much of *A Vision* is in E major). However, rarely does the music bear a key signature, and even when it comes to rest on a firm tonic triad, there is usually a foreign note squeezed in somewhere, as at the end of *A Vision*, where a C, E and B knock the heart out of the D major triad, or at the end of the *Vespers*, where a triumphant B major chord, repeated again and again, is unable to rid itself of the C sharp that has somehow got trapped inside. This way of treating tonal harmony is reminiscent of jazz, and also of the 'thickening' recommended and practised by Janáček. As in Janáček, thickening, properly introduced, imparts tonal structure, while forbidding the cliché-ridden closures of common practice harmony.

Tonality is not a matter of effects, nor even of grammar only. It is primarily a matter of form – a way of developing ideas over a long span of musical argument. Musical ideas, for Matthews, have consequences, and the labour of composing is that of spelling those consequences out. His symphonic writing shows the influence of Bruckner, with long paragraphs held together by continuous lines in the bass. But, like the baroque masters, he never loses sight of the connection with dance, introducing dance forms whenever they seem appropriate, and always allowing rhythmical elements to stand out from the flow.

Four Quartets has left a kind of 'cognitive pathway' in Matthews's thinking. (It is from *Four Quartets* that he took the title for his harrowing symphonic poem *In the Dark Time*.) In the course of many discussions that I have had with him Matthews has often articulated a vision of modern life that made room for the sacred and for the idea of redemption, but divested of the metaphysical commitments of traditional religious belief. In pursuing this vision he has composed two remarkable religious works: the above-mentioned *Vespers* for choir and orchestra, setting poems by Rilke among others, and articulating in a most moving way the religious feelings of a post-religious person; and *The Music of Dawn*, a symphonic poem inspired by the mystical painting of that title by Cecil Collins.

Collins had been a favourite painter of the late Peter Fuller, a close friend of Matthews who died in a car crash in 1990. In Fuller's view Collins typified the neglected tradition of figurative symbolism in English painting, a tradition that reached through Bomberg, Sutherland, Ivon Hitchens and the London Group to Miles Richmond and Cecil Collins. This tradition stands to the English soul in painting as composers like David Matthews to the English soul in music. Matthews was drawn to Fuller in part because they both rejected the cult of desecration and flippancy that had arisen through the art schools and which led in our time to the moral and aesthetic disaster of 'Young British Art'. Although neither could be described as a believer, they were united in their respect for sacred things, and in their belief that it is the duty of modern art to rescue the sense of the sacred from the ruins of formal religion. The sustained melodious enchantment of *The Music of Dawn* conveys some of the intense religious experience that we find in Collins – not an experience that can be contained within the doctrine of any faith but a kind of wonder at creation, and at the consciousness that makes wonder possible.

In a highly suggestive article Matthews reflects on this kind of intransitive sense of the sacred, in the context of a study of Titian's *Flaying of Marsyas*, now in the National Museum in Kroměříž.[82] He raises the question of how this painting, of a subject-matter so horrifying that in other contexts it hardly bears thinking about, achieves an atmosphere of such serenity. The flaying, he suggests, is portrayed as a kind of loving act, and the composition is imbued with calm, as though all conflict had been overcome and reconciled. The savagery of Marsyas is being disciplined and tamed, in a ritual sacrifice that is also a purification.

The painting should be seen, in Matthews's view, as a Renaissance alternative to the Crucifixion. Christianity suggests that man is helpless until he puts his trust in God; but Titian is insisting that man can rescue himself by learning from his mistakes. Hence this image has more to say to us, now, than the Crucifixion, even though it is communicating on the same level as a Crucifixion scene, showing the truth of life in the moment of sacrifice. Christianity, Matthews argues, cannot survive in the modern world, since the ideas of atonement and redemption through faith no longer have a place. But here we find the humanist equivalent, and that is why modern people are so powerfully drawn to this picture.

Titian, Matthews argues, shows us *becoming* rather than *being* – the process of change and the getting of wisdom, a subject that is ignored by contemporary art, which has forgotten that human beings come into the world in order to perfect themselves. In much modern art, and in modern music especially, there is a tendency to reject becoming and to return to a pre-Renaissance idea of being, as

[82] David Matthews, 'The Flaying of Marsyas', *Salisbury Review*, vol. 12, no. 3 (March 1994), pp. 12–14.

something fixed and unredeemable. But in all great post-Renaissance art it is *becoming* that is emphasized, and *being* is seen as something to be *achieved* through becoming. *Stasis* comes through *dunamis*, as in Beethoven's late quartets (and especially that in E flat). The C sharp minor quartet, Matthews argues, is the only one that begins in *stasis* and moves to *dunamis*. And this same quartet ranks with *The Flaying of Marsyas* as one of the supreme achievements of our civilization. Take the two together and you will understand what is lacking in so much contemporary music, namely the dance, that which inhabited the aged fingers of Titian in the same way that it inhabits the voice-led movement of Beethoven's quartet.

Titian's painting inspired Matthews to write one of his most original compositions, *The Flaying of Marsyas*, for oboe and string quartet, in which the contest between pan pipes and lyre, represented by oboe and violin, is gradually subdued and reconciled, and absorbed into the texture of the string quartet. For all the philosophical reflection that went in to this piece it is by no means an academic or 'learned' composition. On the contrary, it shows reflection reworked as emotion, and has a spontaneity that is entirely musical. It exemplifies what I think is the most important feature of Matthews's artistic persona, that he is immediately and totally engaged in whatever is before him, whether it be a painting, a landscape, an idea or a drama.

Matthews's music has many dissonant and angry passages, but they never triumph, and are always overcome by a kind of distancing forgiveness. Even in the *Chaconne*, which marked a transition in his style, and which contains some of his most superimposed dissonances, the ground bass imposes an order which subdues the music to its rhythm, so that this work, which begins with hallucinatory shrieks in the upper range of the double basses, introducing startled cries from across the orchestra, settles at the end on a serene rumination on the ground bass theme, with soft strings in their natural register, accompanied by harp and celesta. The effect is clearly reminiscent of the long-drawn-out 'Ewig' that ends *Das Lied von der Erde*.

This is an appropriate point on which to conclude. Mahler's 'Ewig' summarizes the religious feelings of an artist for whom the source of meaning is earth and her beauty, and who finds redemption not in hoping beyond this world but in being reconciled to leaving it, and leaving it for ever. In Mahler's vision redemption comes through beauty; but the awareness of beauty is not merely an aesthetic thing, existing in fleeting moments of delight. It is a stance of the whole person and informs the whole of life. It has its moral and political expression; and it is best explained, to those who do not know it, as the ability to bless, and to be blessed by, the things of this world. That is surely the condition to which all contemporary music should aspire.

11

Reflections on *Deaths in Venice*

In a recent book, Philip Kitcher takes Thomas Mann's *Death in Venice* as the starting point for an extended meditation on the nature of art and on the consolation that it brings.[83] He moves from Mann's story to the works that have been inspired by it – Benjamin Britten's opera and Visconti's film – and to the music (the adagietto from Mahler's Fifth Symphony) which Visconti used as background. But the argument ranges far more widely, exploring the meaning of both art and life, and also the philosophical question as to how *we* – you and I – should understand the goal and achievement of these melancholy works that attempt to look back on life from its final one-sided boundary. What do they give to us, what do they help us to understand, and why are they so precious? For that they are precious Kitcher does not doubt, and his often beautiful descriptions – of Mahler's sublime *Das Lied von der Erde* in particular – leave the reader in no doubt that he is writing of things that have a supreme value for him.

Kitcher conceives Mann and Mahler (and, I assume, Britten and Visconti) as responding to the challenge presented by Schopenhauer and Nietzsche, which he expresses in the following words:

Human finitude undercuts the worth of what we are and do: our strivings are endless, our accomplishments incomplete. We should either recognize the futility of our actions (abnegating the will) or

---

[83] Philip Kitcher, *Deaths in Venice: The Cases of Gustav von Aschenbach* (New York, 2013).

find the way to transcend the run of common humanity (in some act of self-affirmation). To this challenge Mann's coda and Mahler's *Abschied-Lied* have been taken to *show* the possibility of value in the connection with something that endures beyond the individual self. The novella and the *Lied* evoke a synthetic complex into which readers and listeners can absorb their experiences and integrate them with the endorsement of finite human worth.[84]

By 'synthetic complex' Kitcher means a connection, forged by art, to the wider scheme of things. A work like *Das Lied von der Erde* shows individuals as neither alone nor trapped in their own life-spans but as connected to nature and its cycles, to others who love them or who will, in some future time, re-enact their experiences, their hopes, their loves and their fears. The synthetic complex is a kind of answer to the one who, fully conscious of life's finitude and fragmentariness, nevertheless looks for its meaning: an answer which is the special gift of art since only in art is the connection between the individual and the wider context *shown*, rather than described. Art acquaints us with an *experience* of synthesis, and this is of special value to us since it infects our way of experiencing the contingency and incompleteness of everything we feel and do.

I have used my own words here, in an attempt to summarize Kitcher's concluding argument. The question he addresses is really two questions: the first concerns the value of life, the second the value of art. Here is how he puts the point, in his persuasive account of *Das Lied von der Erde*:

the answer offered by the *Abschied-Lied* is rooted in familiar and elementary features of our lives. The leave-taker has lived and loved, her joys and successes are transient, her life will have an effect for a while, its actions traceable in the enduring, indefinitely renewed world from which she departs, but, like the ripples caused by a stone thrown into a pool, the impact will eventually, perhaps

---

[84] *Ibid.*, pp. 185–6.

even quite soon, diminish to nothing. The connections, transitory as they are, are real, not to be argued away or to be embedded in conjectures about the ensoulment of everything. *The philosophical question asks whether those connections are enough. Mahler's singer affirms that they are – or, to be more exact, that they can be, that finitude is no obstacle to value – and the power of the answer lies in its moving listeners to a corresponding affirmation.*[85]

There is truth in that description of the final movement of *Das Lied von der Erde*. But does it suggest an answer to either of Kitcher's questions – that about the value of life, and that about the value of art? I doubt it, for the following reasons. First, the question about the value of life is a question that is intimately connected with the first-person perspective. It is a question about the worthwhileness of being *me, here, now*. I am seeking the thought, the experience, which will permit a supreme affirmation, a 'yes' that will also be an acceptance of contingency, of suffering, of finitude. That is surely what Mahler is offering with that nine-times-repeated '*ewig*', dying away with shining triads on which seconds and sixths lie glinting and unresolved. But why should the knowledge that my life sends out those dwindling ripples permit an affirmation of it, if the life cannot be affirmed as it is in itself, and as the life that is mine? Surely the search for the 'yes' that affirms my life is like the search for a blessing – the gift bestowed on me by another, which brings reconciliation and peace. And that reminds one of the element that is missing from Kitcher's account, which is the parallel with religion. What Mahler is evoking is surely aptly described as 'the peace that passeth understanding'.

Secondly, I don't think that we can give an account of the value of art in Kitcher's way. It is true, of course, that works of art bring things together in an act of synthesis, that they make connections through metaphor, allusion, symbolism and juxtaposition that create the sense of a hidden order, in which the superficial contingencies and contradictions of existence are resolved. But that does not explain

---

[85] *Ibid.*, p. 171 (italics in original).

the peculiar contribution of *art* to the search for the worthwhileness of life. Those connections could be made, perhaps more laboriously, by philosophy – indeed Kitcher makes a start at making them in the passage I quoted. Why do we need *art* to make them, and what special character does art add to the things that it brings together?

Kitcher is aware of this problem. Throughout the book he is wrestling with it, aware that we get something from a great work like *Death in Venice* or *Das Lied von der Erde*, which comes to us through the aesthetic experience. He alludes to this in the passage last quoted, writing that Mahler's music moves us to 'a corresponding affirmation'. But why and how does it move us? And why do we need art in order to be moved in this way? In a later passage he shifts the emphasis slightly, arguing that the coda to Mann's story and Mahler's *Abschied-Lied* are taken 'to *show* the possibility of value in connection with something that endures beyond the individual self'[86] – and the emphasis on showing (as opposed to telling) seems to connect with a distinctive feature of the aesthetic experience. But why is it important to *show* the possibility of value, and how exactly is that done?

In no way do I wish to dismiss Kitcher's fine and humane treatment of his examples. But the points that I have raised suggest a certain lacuna in his argument, and one that connects to his wider philosophical stance. Kitcher does not believe that religion will satisfy the one who doubts life's value. How, he asks, can our being part of 'a Great Plan for the Universe' lend significance to what we do?[87] Whatever our response to that rhetorical question it is surely relevant to point out that religion is not, in the normal case, just a matter of believing in the existence of a divine plan. There are other aspects, to the Christian religion in particular, which are just as important to the devotee, and which have little or nothing to do with far-reaching metaphysical doctrines. Religions consist of communal rituals, processes of purification, of confession, atonement and forgiveness. People come to the altar burdened by sin and the consciousness of

---

[86] *Ibid.*, p.186.
[87] *Ibid.*, p. 170.

sin, and receive the sacrament that lightens them. In moments of prayer and worship they stand astonished before the absolute simplicity of being, and are renewed by this. They seek redemption and find it in the moment of sacrifice – perhaps, as in Christianity, in the sacrifice of the god himself.

I don't say that any of that is rational or that it provides a theoretical answer to the two questions that trouble Kitcher. Nevertheless religion, described in that way, is an *experience* of the value of life. It imparts a serene blessedness, a benediction that compensates for all the ways in which the worshipper has diverged from the path of righteousness. Is this not an archetype on which works of art draw, when they present to us the spectacle of suffering and invite us to share it in imagination, to step into the already occupied circle of grief and to move there 'in measure, like a dancer'?

If we think of religion in that way, we can see a little more clearly that there are *experiences* of life's worth or meaning which are not just narratives about some Grand Plan, or attempts to connect our lives to a wider universe by some 'synthetic complex'. It is surely just such an experience that is invoked by Mahler at the end of *Das Lied von der Erde*. Kitcher quotes an interesting remark by Benjamin Britten concerning this ending:

> It has the beauty of loneliness and of pain: of strength and freedom. The beauty of disappointment and never-satisfied love. The cruel beauty of nature, and everlasting beauty of monotony ... And there is nothing morbid about it ... a serenity literally supernatural. I cannot understand it – it passes over me like a tidal wave – and that matters not a jot either, because it goes on for ever, even if it is never performed again – that final chord printed on the atmosphere.[88]

Kitcher endorses Britten's rapturous response entirely, except for the one word that seems to explain it, the word 'supernatural'. Britten

---

[88] *Ibid.*, p. 165.

is describing something that is surely familiar to all of us, whether or not we have any theological beliefs with which to embellish it, namely the vision, granted in *this* world, of a light shining from a place beyond it. The moment in and out of time of which Eliot writes in *Four Quartets,* and which the Japanese try to capture entirely without the aid of religious doctrine in the form of the haiku, is promised by both art and religion. It is what each can add, in its own special way, to the life of contingency and finitude: the sense that the moment alone can 'redeem the time'.

Can we make sense of this? Here are a few thoughts, taking off from Kitcher's discussion. Wagner, whose death in Venice occurred only shortly after his great spiritual journey in *Parsifal,* argued that, once religion loses its doctrinal basis, it remains to art to capture its essence in symbols. The essence of religion, he believed, is not contained in truths about God, because there are none that we can know; it is contained in truths about us. But these truths must be put on display in symbolic form if they are to be understood. Two in particular occupied Wagner in his later works: the truth that we find fulfilment in moments, feelings and experiences that have a sacred aura, and the truth that, when we are granted those moments, we do not merely affirm life – we affirm death too, as an inseparable part of it. To experience life as meaningful is to be true to those moments, when we confront what is before us as sacred and necessary, its own sufficient justification. In such moments, as one might put it, we 'come home to ourselves'.

Those moments form the heart of religion in our tradition. They are the experience of benediction, the sense of a serene gaze in which we stand, and which affirms our being. They are what the Jews call *shakhinah* and Christians the 'real presence', the gift that is presented at the altar to the one who comes *in nomine domini*. Strip away the theological doctrines and what remains is the experience of the sacred, of the moment rescued from contingency and presented as complete in itself, its own fulfilment.

The aesthetic experience, as it has been cherished and embellished by our post-Romantic sensibility, is adjacent to the experience of the sacred. It comes about when we are confronted by some sensory aspect of the world and we affirm that aspect as intrinsically worthwhile. This, before us, we think, is not just an instrument, a means for the pursuit of our interests, but an end in itself. It has the quality that Kant beautifully summarized as 'purposefulness without purpose'. Seeing it in that way we also isolate it as a symbol, as something that brings together and fuses the many thoughts and feelings that somehow belong to it. And this 'fusing' (which is what Kitcher refers to, I believe, as a 'synthetic complex') has meaning for us because it transfers the intrinsic value of the aesthetic object to the emotions that are inspired by it. We are consoled by this, because it is a kind of homecoming. This moment, 'printed on the atmosphere', as Britten puts it, is its own full justification. We need look no further for the proof that life is worthwhile, since this is what the worth of life consists in.

I am struggling here, I know. But the connection that I am trying to make between the religious and the aesthetic moments can be understood in another way through the problem of tragedy. Ever since Aristotle, philosophers have puzzled over the tragic experience, wondering what it is that we take from the spectacle of death and suffering, and why the effect is more serenity than calamity. It seems entirely reasonable to suggest that the experience of tragedy involves an acceptance of death, and an affirmation of life *through* the acceptance of death. And it is also reasonable to suggest that this aesthetic experience has much in common with the religious experience, as the victim who is also the redeemer is sacrificed at the altar and his blood shared among the worshippers. The late René Girard has made this primary religious experience the subject-matter of his many imaginative explorations of the idea of the sacred, and even if, at the end of his explorations, some of the mystery remains, it is surely reasonable to suggest that the experience of tragedy contains a residue of that primordial moment of collective worship, when the victim of our aggression turns to us with a blessing.

In many places Kitcher draws attention to another aspect of the aesthetic vindication of our lives, and one that is not, in my view, sufficiently attended to. The sense of meaning is delivered by a great work of art as part of a process. Something is put before us and gradually worked out, so that the ending is experienced as the conclusion and resolution of something. This is why the coda to Mann's story and the *Abschied-Lied* of the Mahler affect us so profoundly. They are the *answer* to what precedes them, the resolution of the given *problem*. We move in sympathy, so as both to share the affirmation that these works express and to feel that affirmation as a necessity, as contained within the very experience of loss. This, surely, is where the value of art lies. Only in the aesthetic experience can we be led in this way to feel from within that our losses are also gains, and that life in its tragic aspect is its own consolation. We come away from the work of art with the sense that something has been resolved by it, and that resolution has been bestowed on us as an enduring treasure. That is surely how we hear those great wrestlings with death in the late Schubert quartets, or the working through from loneliness to praise in the late quartets of Beethoven.

Kitcher's study is a fascinating and painstaking account of some of the greatest works of art produced in modern times, and a rare example of an accomplished analytical philosopher applying his argumentative powers to the most elusive aspects of the inner life. The questions with which the book deals are of the greatest importance for aesthetics, and even if the answers are not entirely satisfactory, they are a real contribution to clarity, in an area where clarity is rarely found.

12

Pierre Boulez

De mortuis nil nisi bonum: of the dead, nothing unless good. But you can take it too far, reinventing someone who was a power-hungry manipulator, by allowing no one to speak for him save his partisans, many of whom owe their careers to promoting him. As the French say, *on a ras le bol* with Pierre Boulez, whose death in January 2016 called forth such a spate of idolatrous prose that the sceptics among us have begun to wonder whether French culture is not after all as dead as its critics say it is, if this minor composer and intellectual impresario can be lauded as its greatest recent product. Yet no one in the official channels of cultural appraisal has sown a seed of doubt.

Boulez has three achievements to his name. First, his compositions, presented to the world as next in line to the serialism of Webern, and the 'place we have got to' in our musical evolution; secondly, his presence in French culture, diverting government subsidies away from anything that might seem to endorse ordinary musical taste towards the acoustic laboratory of the avant-garde; thirdly, his work as a conductor, for whom clarity and precision took precedence over sentiment. His dominating presence in French musical life is proof that, once the critics have been silenced, the self-appointed leader will be accepted at his own valuation. Condemning all competitors as 'useless', and hinting at a revelation, a 'system', that authorized his doings as the musical *Zeitgeist*, Boulez was able to subdue whatever timid protests might greet his relentless self-promotion. His disciples and acolytes have spoken abundantly of his charm, and it is clear that, once the initial period of belligerence was over, and his opponents had been despatched to the dust-heap of history, Boulez was a smiling and benevolent occupant of his self-made throne. But did he rule from that throne over fertile territory, or was this sovereignty an expensive illusion?

Boulez's manipulation of the French subsidy machine has been explored and exposed by Benoît Duteurtre, in a book published in 1995: *Requiem pour une avant-garde*. Duteurtre tells the story of the steady takeover by Boulez and his entourage of the channels of musical and cultural communication, the new power networks installed in the wake of May 1968, the vilification of opponents, the anathematizing of tonal music and its late offshoots in Messiaen, Duruflé and Dutilleux, and the cultural *coup d'état* which was the founding of IRCAM. This institution, created by and for Pierre Boulez at the request of President Pompidou in 1970, reveals in its name – Institut de Recherche et Coordination Acoustique/Musique – that it does not distinguish between sound and music, and sees both as matters for 'research'. Maintained by government funds in the basement of its architectural equivalent, the Centre Pompidou, IRCAM has been devoted to 'sound effects' created by the avant-garde elect, whose products are largely, to coin a phrase, 'plink selon plonk'. Absorbing a substantial proportion of a budget that might have been used to sustain the provincial orchestras of France, IRCAM has produced a stream of works without survival value. Despite all Boulez's efforts, musical people still believe, and rightly, that the test of a work of music is how it sounds, not how it is theorized.

Boulez did, from time to time, produce music that passed that test. He had a fine ear, and no one can doubt that every note in every score was intensely thought about – but *thought* about, and thought about as *sound*. Boulez's was an acoustical, rather than a musical, art, with meticulous effects and sonorities produced in unusual ways, according to arcane theories that are inscribed on the hidden side of notes held close to the chest. He burst into the concert hall as a young man in order to heckle the last attempts at tonal composition, dismissing all who were not serialists, and presenting his seminal *Le Marteau sans maître* in 1955 as showing the direction in which serialism must go.

The instrumentation of that work – alto voice, flute, guitar, vibraphone, viola and percussion – reflects the composer's obsession with timbre and sonority, used here to prevent simultaneities from coalescing as chords. With time signatures changing almost every bar – a 2/4 here, a 5/16 there and so on – and grace notes dropped into every staff, the score resembles a palimpsest from an alchemist's recipe book, and the composer's refusal to describe the serial organization, insisting that it is obvious and apparent to the ear, has led to a quantity of learned literature. The writers of this literature largely assume that *Le Marteau* is a masterpiece and the turning point of post-war music, because Boulez himself has declared so – not in so many words, for he was far too modest for that, but because he pointed speechlessly to its evident perfection.

In a hard-hitting article the American composer and musicologist Fred Lerdahl has told us what the fuss is all about.[89] The inability of the critics to discern the organization, serial or otherwise, of *Le Marteau*, Lerdahl argues, is the direct result of the fact that the listening ear is organized by another grammar than the one here used (ostensibly, at least) by the composer. Here is what Wikipedia has to say about this episode:

> Despite having been published in 1954 and 1957, analysts were unable to explain Boulez's compositional methods until Lev Koblyakov in 1977. This is partially due to the fact that Boulez believes in strict control tempered with 'local indiscipline', or rather, the freedom to choose small, individual elements while still adhering to an overall structure compatible with serialist principles. Boulez opts to change individual notes based on sound or harmony, choosing to abandon adherence to the structure dictated by strict serialism, making the

---

[89] 'Cognitive Constraints in Compositional Systems', in John A. Sloboda, ed., *Generative Processes in Music* (Oxford, 1988).

detailed serial organization of the piece difficult for the listener to discern.

The Wikipedia article chooses there to close the discussion, with a reference to Lerdahl's article. But it misses the real point.

As Lerdahl argues, serialism construes music as an array of permutations. The musical ear looks for prolongations, sequences and variations, not permutations, which are inherently hard to grasp. Hence music (music of our classical tradition included) consists of events that grow organically from each other, over a repeated measure and according to recognizable harmonic sequences. The 'moving forward' of melodic lines through musical space is the true origin of musical unity and of the dramatic power of serious music. And it is this 'moving forward' that is the first casualty when permutations take over. Add the 'plink selon plonk' of the acoustical laboratory and the result is heard as arbitrary – something to be deciphered, rather than something to be absorbed and enjoyed in the manner of a conversation.

You can test this quite easily by comparing one of the many modernist masterpieces that Boulez condemned with a rival composition by the great man himself. From the beginning, in *Le Marteau*, to the interminable instrumental twiddles of *Pli selon pli*, Boulez gives us music that has little or no propulsion from one moment to the next. The fundamental musical experience – fundamental not just to our classical tradition but to all music that has been sung, played and danced from the beginning of time – is that of virtual causality, whereby one moment seems to produce the next out of its own inner dynamic. This is the primary experience on which all rhythmic, melodic and harmonic invention depends, and it is absent – deliberately absent – from much of the music of Boulez.

To say this is not to display an attachment, whether or not 'bourgeois' or 'reactionary', to the old forms of tonality. It is to make an ontological observation: to say what music essentially *is*. So take a piece every bit as adventurous in its sonorities as Boulez, in which traditional tonality is marginalized but which nevertheless adheres to the principle of virtual causality in musical space – say, the violin concerto of Dutilleux, or the powerful chaconne movement from the same composer's first symphony. At once we are in another world, a world that we know, moving *with* the sounds we hear, and hearing them not merely as sounds but as movements in a space mapped out in our own emotions. I have to use metaphors in order to describe this experience – for reasons that I make clear in *The Aesthetics of Music*. But they are metaphors that we all instinctively understand, since they invoke the *phenomenon of music itself.*

There is a reason for referring to Dutilleux, apart from the fact that the 100th anniversary of his birth coincided with the death of Boulez. For he was, in his own way, every bit as adventurous as Boulez, with the same desire to take music forward into the modern world, to build on past achievements and to take inspiration from the great achievements of French music, painting and poetry at the beginning of the modern period. In the 1960s and '70s he was dismissed by Boulez and his entourage as a 'bourgeois' composer, smeared as a 'Nazi collaborator' (in fact he was active in the resistance) and excluded from the privileges of the true avant-garde. But his music, unlike Boulez's, has a regular place in concert programmes and speaks to the ordinary musical listener in accents that are both new and (with a certain justified effort) comprehensible.

If we look back at Boulez's presence in French culture, during the years around 1968 when he was the *Gauleiter* of the avant-garde, we must surely understand him as the instigator of a false conception of music – not only of the place of music in high culture, and in the civilization that is our greatest spiritual possession, but of the nature of music itself. He deliberately, and in my view uncomprehendingly, undid the distinction between musical tone and acoustical sound; he mathematized and scientized a practice that is meaningful only if it is seen as a creative art, and he justified every kind of intellectual pretension, just so long as it was *intellectual*, and just so long as it could be seen as the latest attempt to *épater le bourgeois.*

Of course he was a true musician too. Faced with real music, he had an instinctive grasp of how it might be performed so as to reveal all the currents of thought contained in it. As a conductor he set an example that many have wished to follow, and with reason. Still, even there his personality showed itself. His meticulous version of Wagner's *Ring* cycle shows a conductor who appreciates in thought what can be understood only in emotion. And this version will always be appreciated as a monument to our times, a kind of revenge on Wagner, which is also, when taken together with Chéreau's *marxisant* production, a revenge on Germany. Seeing Boulez in that way, I think, we reduce him to his real size, and can begin to appreciate his true historical significance, as a by-product of a disastrous war.

13

Film Music

There is a kind of listener who first becomes acquainted with the symphony orchestra through film music. And many such listeners want to hear the music again – willingly attending concerts devoted to scores whose original function was to compensate for absent dialogue, and which were heard in fragmented versions that faded in and out of the drama.

So what is the status of film music among the musical arts, and how should it be judged? You often hear the expression 'film music' used pejoratively. 'It's just film music', said of some new symphonic piece, suggests an overblown pursuit of effect at the cost of structure, of atmosphere at the cost of musical form. But perhaps those who criticize music in that way are clinging to a parochial and outmoded conception of concert-hall listening. Maybe film music is the way forward for the tonal grammar and polyphonic architecture that are now so rarely heard in works by the musical avant-garde. Maybe film music is the only safe refuge for the ordinary musical ear, in a soundscape blasted by jagged orchestral explosions and wearisome postmodernist sound effects.

One thing is certain, which is that the most successful film music today exhibits a quite extraordinary level of competence. Melody, harmony, voice-leading and orchestration are all as professional as can be. John Williams's *Harry Potter* scores and Howard Shore's evocative music for *The Lord of the Rings* exhibit a mastery of harmonic sequences, polyphonic organization and orchestral effect that would be the envy of many a composer for the concert hall. Some of the skills employed by such composers can be learned, and there are schools devoted to teaching them. But there are also, in such composers as Williams and Shore, original effects, haunting passages of melody or quasi-melody and a post-Mahlerian sense of just how much can be added without sacrificing polyphonic clarity – all of which are marks of a true musician.

At the same time, when the favourite passages are extracted from their original context and presented in the concert hall, almost invariably it sounds as though something is missing. The melody that seemed so apt and touching on the screen sounds banal or even fake in the concert hall – witness the melodies given to Hedwig's flight by Williams, so brilliantly orchestrated that you notice their emptiness only when the ears are turned fully upon them. It is when hearing this kind of music in the cold, lifted clear of the drama and presented as something complete in itself, that you begin to sympathize with those censorious advocates of the avant-garde who say, no, you cannot compose like that.

Such critics will tell us that tonal chord grammar, even if touched up here and there with Wagnerian chromaticism and the occasional Mahlerian dissonance, has, in Schoenberg's words, 'become banal'. It wasn't always banal. But when used without the fresh melodic material and ingenuous musical narrative of the great masters, it is no longer true art but 'pastiche'. It is not only in music, of course, that we hear this kind of criticism. The accusation of 'pastiche' is used *ad nauseam* to block any attempt that architects might make to build in the traditional manner. But it has a special authority in music criticism, thanks to the polemics of Schoenberg and Adorno. Moreover, in the case of film music the charge often seems to stick. This stuff, however technically accomplished, seems so often to lack the core of sincere inspiration, the heartfelt and heart-stopping theme, and the inspired development that unfolds that theme's potential.

Adorno, who was the first to launch a full-scale assault on the blockbuster scores of Hollywood, saw film music as the last degraded product of the vice instilled by Wagner: the vice of putting effect before cause. Film music, as he described it, used stock devices and ready-made sequences to add a musical halo to whatever was being presented on the screen. Its whole purpose was to add emotion where emotion is lacking, to puff up the empty drama with easily decipherable messages as to what the audience should at any moment be feeling. As Nietzsche put the point in his no-holds-barred assault on Wagner: *espressivo* at all costs.

But Adorno also saw film music in another way: as part of the capitalist assault on high culture. All the music, all the forms of entertainment, by which he found himself surrounded in his exile in California were the products of the capitalist culture industry, whose purpose, in Adorno's eyes, was to reduce art to a commodity, and to provide in the place of the free expression of critical consciousness the 'fetishes' that conceal reality behind a veil of illusions. The musical fetish requires no hard work of aesthetic judgement, no painful exploration of the value and significance of our states of mind. It merely releases us into a warm bath of sentiment that, being unreal, costs nothing. As we respond to the kitschy climaxes on soaring violins, we congratulate ourselves that we are deeply moved. But, Adorno tells us, we are not moved at all, except by the image of ourselves being moved.

Those deep criticisms, expressed in an inspissated language that was Adorno's most lasting contribution to the Marxist repertoire, do not carry weight with everyone. But they suggest, nevertheless, that the adjectives and phrases often used to dismiss or marginalize music for the films – corny, sentimental, fake, kitsch, laid on with a trowel – are identifying a real and pervasive aesthetic fault. And the fault, you might think, comes from the attempt to herd people towards a crowd emotion, to neutralize our critical faculties, to say 'come on, join in, let the tears flow'.

Or is this all just the snobbery of the avant-garde, a kind of musical elitism that belongs to an age from which we have recovered, now that our innocent distractions, once dismissed as 'mass culture', can be enjoyed for what they are, namely fun? Two observations are pertinent here. The first is that it is only *some* film music that conforms to the 'blockbuster' style. It is only the epic narrative, with heroes, battles, the underlying war between good and evil, and (in the grown-up version) the rescue of desirable women by courageous men that can call forth the full orchestral sound, usually amplified, these days, by wordless choirs. And here it is undeniable that there is a repertoire of clichés that film composers do not hesitate to use, and whose nature as cliché is far more apparent in the concert hall than in the course of some heroic battle between good (=handsome) and evil (=ugly) on the screen. The wordless choir is one of them, chanting its ancestral calls to sacrifice over agitated strings and sustained chords on the brass, as the heroic soldiers of the good bravely hold their ground against the forces of evil, mounted on digital monsters that can be killed by nothing short of a power cut.

We should remember, therefore, all those films that have used small musical resources, not to compensate for the schematic nature of the plot, but in order to enhance an atmosphere that originates in the drama. Bernard Herrmann's creepy modernist score for Hitchcock's *Psycho* is a case in point. Hitchcock's drama in no way depends on the music: but if there is to be music for such a gruesome tale, this is it – sparse, icy, setting the nerves on edge like a diamond-edged cutter going through steel. Or, to take a less extreme example, the gentle sadness of Erik Nordgren's score for Bergman's *Wild Strawberries* – a solo violin above a small chamber ensemble, never intrusive, but always picking up the threads of regret and loneliness as the old Professor's life unravels, so as to unravel them a little bit more.

The second pertinent observation is that film scores seem not to survive for long outside the context created by the original screenplay. They inspire a following, of course. But it is a following that associates them with a particular film and a particular story. Of course, this is not always true. There are film scores that have survived because of their intrinsic musical virtues – Prokofiev's *Lieutenant Kijé*, as well as his grand oratorio on the theme of Alexander Nevsky; Walton's music for *Henry V*; and (a particularly telling example) the *Sinfonia Antartica* of Vaughan Williams. But these survive as free-standing musical works, composed according to principles that do not depend on the action that originally accompanied them.

Film music can be fruitfully compared to ballet. Most of the great ballet scores have been, by now, detached from their first choreographies. There are some, of course, that are indelibly associated with the original poetic idea – *Swan Lake, The Firebird, Daphnis and Chloë* – but many more have survived through manifold changes in the choreography and the libretto. The *Rite of Spring* is perhaps the most famous example. Stravinsky's score is a triumph of rhythmic, melodic and harmonic order, which won its place in the hearts of musical people whether or not they had an interest in the ballet as an art form or in the particular attempts, from Nijinsky onwards, to provide a way of dancing to this score.

Why are film scores and ballet scores so different in this respect? Why do ballet scores have such a long and vivid life in the concert hall, achieving a status – especially in the modern era – equal to the greatest of the purely orchestral compositions that changed the course of music? Here is a thought: while dancers dance *to* the music, the film score *follows* the action on the screen. In ballet it is the score that sets the pace, governs the action and in general controls the overall order and movement of the work. In film the score is subservient to the action, can survive only because it adds what the action leaves out and then survives only as a kind of afterimage, the memory of something that has vanished over the horizon of perception.

Those thoughts do not, of course, justify the use of 'film music' as a pejorative term. Perhaps we should be grateful to John Williams and Howard Shore for showing us that this kind of music can still be created – that we can still use the tonal language to create music that resonates in the hearts of ordinary listeners. Perhaps we should be more suspicious than we tend to be of those musical censors who leap to dismiss whatever is spontaneously likeable as cliché, and whatever touches the ordinary heart as kitsch. Nevertheless, we still need guidance: what is the path between avant-garde censoriousness and musical cliché, and how can a serious composer follow that path without some listener in the concert hall turning to his neighbour and whispering 'film music'?

14

The Assault on Opera

The marginalization of the bourgeoisie has led to a crisis in the arts. How can we track down the defeated remnants of the philistine class, in order to disturb them with the proof of their irrelevance? Theatres, galleries, restaurants and public resorts all offer impeccable post-modern fare, addressed to non-judgemental people. TV has been dumbed down below the horizon of bourgeois awareness, and even the churches are rejecting family values and the marital virtues. Yet without the bourgeoisie the world of art is deprived of a target, condemned to repeat worn-out gestures of rebellion to an audience that long ago discarded the capacity for outrage.

All is not lost, however. There is one last redoubt where the bourgeoisie can be corralled into a corner and spat upon, and that is the opera. Believers in family values and old-fashioned marriage are romantics at heart, who love to sit through those wonderful tales of intrigue, betrayal and reconciliation, in which man–woman love is exalted to a height that it can never reach in real life, and the whole presented through heart-stopping music and magical scenes that take us, for an enchanted three hours, into the world of dreams. Siegfried's love for Brünnhilde, shot through with unconscious treachery, Butterfly's innocent passion standing on self-deception like an angel on a tomb, Grimes's death-wish, rationalized as a longing for Ellen's maternal love – these are dramatic ideas that could never be realized through words, but which are burned into our hearts by music.

Is it surprising that our surviving bourgeoisie, surrounded as they are by a culture of flippancy and desecration, should be so drawn to opera? After a performance of *Katya, Pelléas, La Traviata* or *Figaro*, they stagger home amazed at those passions displayed on the stage, by creatures no more god-like than themselves! They will come from miles away to sit through their favourite fairy-tales, and drive home singing in the early hours. They will pay hundreds of pounds for a mediocre seat, in order to hear their chosen prima donna, and will learn by heart the arias which they are never satisfied to hear unless in the flesh. Take any performance of an operatic classic anywhere in the world, and you will find, sitting in close confinement, motionless and devout for the space of three hours, the assembled remnant of the bourgeoisie, innocent, expectant, often martyred by evening dress and dinner jackets, and available for shock.

The temptation is irresistible. Hardly a producer now, confronted with a masterpiece that might otherwise delight and console such an audience, can control the desire to desecrate. The more exalted the music, the more demeaning the production. I have come across all of the following: Siegfried in schoolboy shorts cooking a sword on a mobile canteen; Mélisande holed up in welfare accommodation, with Pelléas sadistically tying her to the wall by her hair; Don Giovanni standing happily at ease at the end of the eponymous opera while unexplained demons enter the stage, sing a meaningless chorus and exit again; Rusalka in a wheelchair from which she stares at a football in a swimming-pool, while addressing the moon; Tristan and Isolde on a ship divided by a brick wall, singing vaguely of a love that hardly concerns them since each is invisible to the other; Carmen trying in vain to be a centre of erotic attention while a near-naked chorus copulates on stage; Mozart's *Entführung aus dem Serail* set in a Berlin brothel; Verdi's masked ball with the assembled cast squatting on toilets so as to void their bowels – not to speak of the routine Hitlerization of any opera, from *Fidelio* to *Tosca*, that can be squeezed into Nazi uniform. Wagner is always mercilessly mutilated, lest those misguided bourgeois fall for his seductive political message; and as for *Madama Butterfly*, what an opportunity to get back at the Americans for that bomb dropped on Nagasaki!

The extraordinary thing is not that this mutilation occurs, but that it is paid for by the taxpayer. Opera productions are expensive, and the more facetious they are, the higher the cost in the props that are needed to grab the attention of an audience lost in wonder as to the meaning of it all. The producers too are expensive. People like Peter Sellars, who have made a living out of the effort to astonish, are international stars. There is a frenzied competition among such avant-garde producers as to who can squeeze the greatest emotion – positive or negative, it hardly matters – from the reviewers. And it seems that, when it comes to claiming subsidies from city councils and arts bureaucracies, what matters is not what the critics say but how loudly they say it. An opera house, to claim the standing required for a state subsidy, must be 'controversial', given to 'path-breaking' and 'challenging' productions. The bureaucrats need to be persuaded that, without a subsidy, something very important to the future of the city or the nation will be jeopardized. And its importance is proved by the protests that are inspired by it.

What should be our response to this ongoing assault on one of the world's greatest art forms? One argument that I frequently hear goes like this. Operas are expensive to put on; to charge the full price to the audience would be to price the art form out of the market. Subsidies are therefore necessary. And subsidies are obtainable only if those who provide them can be persuaded that they are not funding old-fashioned bourgeois audiences, since such audiences have had their share of life and are soon for the chop in any case. Controversial productions are therefore necessary, since the alternative is no productions at all.

There is a measure of truth in that argument. The bourgeois audience is necessary to inspire the modern producer, since otherwise he has no one to offend. But the offence is necessary, otherwise the bureaucrats will think that they are subsidizing the bourgeoisie, which God forbid. The problem is that the argument is based on a false premise. Opera productions do not, in fact, need subsidizing.

For it is not productions that are expensive but producers. They are expensive because, like Richard Jones, Peter Sellars and Pierre Audi, they have a deep psychological need to draw attention to themselves, at whatever cost to the music. This means outlandish props, lighting effects, strange gestures imposed on the singers in opposition to the natural movements inspired by the music.

I am the more persuaded of my view in this matter by small-scale honest performances of the kind that come our way in rural England, or which used to be put on by the great Lorin Maazel at Castleton in Virginia. Every summer we in rural Wiltshire are visited by a small group called Opera A La Carte, under the leadership of Nicholas Heath, who brings classics from the repertoire, from *Don Giovanni* to *Madama Butterfly*, performing them on improvised stages in tents or drawing rooms, accompanying the singers with a chamber ensemble and allowing the magic of the story to spill out over the audience, with only costumes and a few unpretentious props to create the scene. At Castleton, Maazel enjoyed a small theatre, and later a larger one built to his specification, together with an orchestra put together from the young musicians whom he mentored so generously. But again nothing was spoiled by over-production, the music was allowed to speak for itself, and costumes and a few stage effects were enough to create the atmosphere. It is worth adding that the most moving performance of Wagner's *Ring* cycle that I have attended was the concert performance given last year (2016) by Opera North, in which the only theatrical elements were the spontaneous gestures of the singers as they turned to face each other, with the gestures inseparable from their roles. Those gestures, driven by the music, were enough to create the drama, and even the formal dress of the singers did nothing to dampen the effect.

What modern producers seem to forget is that audiences are gifted with the faculty of imagination. This faculty is not extinguished by being bourgeois. Indeed, it is one of the faculties that ordinary decent bourgeois people have to exercise continuously, if only in order to respond forgivingly to the contempt of which they are the target. The obvious truth, that opera stimulates the imagination by presenting a drama as *sung* rather than spoken, seems to escape the attention of the new school of producers, perhaps because so many of them spend their apprenticeship in the spoken theatre. Perhaps they do not fully understand that serious music, by existing and moving in a space of its own, automatically transports us to an imaginary world. Put singers in costumes that distance them from the audience and, even without stage sets and props, they will move in a world of their own. The music itself will tell them where to turn, and with what expression on their faces. Add a prop or two and all the meaning that the composer intended is there in the room, and only the quality of the performance will affect whether the audience can grasp it.

And here is where I think the greatest disservice has been done to opera by the new style of production. In the past a production was designed to *present* an opera; now it is designed to *interpret* it, to attach a meaning to it, whether or not it is a meaning that the work can easily bear. The work is seen as a vehicle for the ideas of the producer, rather than a drama whose meaning lies in itself. Instead of allowing the music to speak, the producer stands in front of it, so to say, moralizing at the assembled bourgeoisie, saying that this or that feature of the text or the music must be pinned to some allegorical or symbolic meaning, and that in any event the whole thing has to be made into a relevant commentary on the psychic traumas of the day – otherwise how can we take it seriously? In short, the magic of opera, its capacity to create an enchanted world of its own, must be neutralized by an interpretation that brings it down to earth, that pins it into some sordid corner, as Peter Sellars did with *Pelléas et Mélisande*, so that the imaginary world intended by the composer is blotted out by a screen of the producer's usually half-baked and in any case self-aggrandizing ideas.

15

Nietzsche on Wagner

Wagner was the most philosophical of musicians and Nietzsche the most musical of philosophers, so a philosophy of music ought to be implied somewhere in their conflict. However, Nietzsche's early adoration of Wagner distorted his later rejection, so that the serious thinking has to be discerned within a cloud of self-loathing. Maybe Nietzsche's reaction would have been more moderate had he not at first offered the unquestioning discipleship that Wagner demanded, presenting Wagner, both in *The Birth of Tragedy* (1882) and in *Richard Wagner in Bayreuth* (1886), as the greatest modern artist and the saviour of German culture. At any rate, the dispute between Wagner and Nietzsche was a divorce, rather than a disagreement.[90] In reacting against Wagner, Nietzsche was also reacting against himself, vomiting forth a poison that he thought he had swallowed, but to which his metabolism had made its own peculiar contribution.

Matters are made worse by the subsequent demonization of Wagner and canonization of Nietzsche. It is hard to go back to this controversy now without regretting the tone taken by Nietzsche and the tone taken subsequently by just about everyone else. Nietzsche's attack on Wagner is an attack on the art, the institution and the man, and it was echoed by Theodor Adorno, so as to foreground those aspects of Wagner which are most objectionable to the modern

[90] For the intricacies of the story see Joachim Köhler, *Nietzsche and Wagner: A Lesson in Subjugation*, tr. Ronald Taylor (New Haven, CT, 1998).

reader – anti-Semitism, the focus on national myths and racial heroes, the use of orchestral magic to fill every moment with an emotion that might seem to be, in Nietzsche's word, 'counterfeit'.[91] And it is partly thanks to Nietzsche that Wagner criticism has become stuck in this groove.

Meanwhile Nietzsche himself has become a kind of idol. Despite his antagonism towards democracy and mass culture, despite his unashamedly racist attack on the Germans and all things German, despite his advocacy of 'health' and strength against the 'sickness' of compassion, despite his contempt for socialists, vegetarians, feminists and women generally – despite committing every sin condemned by the morality of 'political correctness', Nietzsche is now a cult figure. His perspectival approach to truth and knowledge, his debunking of morality in general and Christian morality in particular, his genea-logical approach to art and culture and his emphasis on power and domination as the real 'truth' of the human condition – all these give him a head start in the postmodern search for anti-authoritarian authorities. His texts are therefore read for what they permit – which is just about everything – rather than for what they condemn – which is also just about everything. The result is that, in the Nietzsche–Wagner stand off, Nietzsche is dealt all the winning cards. And this is a pity since it obscures the very real strength of Nietzsche's position, and the seriousness of the grounds on which he questions Wagner's art. Although Wagner the artist can be defended against the charges levelled by Nietzsche, those charges force us nevertheless to explore the music dramas at the deepest level. And they contain interesting hints of a philosophy of music.

Nietzsche expressed his adoration towards Wagner in his first pub-lished work, *The Birth of Tragedy*, which appeared in 1872. Fourteen years later Nietzsche reissued *The Birth of Tragedy* with 'an attempt at self-criticism', in which he dismisses the book as 'badly written, ponderous, embarrassing, image-mad and image-confused, senti-mental, in places saccharine to the point of effeminacy, uneven in

---

[91] Theodor Adorno, *In Search of Wagner*, tr. Rodney Livingstone (London, 2004).

tempo, without the will to logical cleanliness', and much more to similar effect. And certainly *The Birth of Tragedy* has none of the lapidary quality that we associate with the later works. For all that, it is an important work, and one that is vital to understanding Nietzsche's conception of the artistic enterprise.[92] It registers a decisive break with a reading of Greek art and literature that had been orthodox in German-speaking countries since Winckelmann and Goethe. According to this reading, Greek civilization epitomized the human spirit in its sunlit, self-knowing form. The art of the Greeks was an art of reason, and their literature an exploration of the virtues through which the rational being confronts and overcomes adversity. The Greek ideal was one of clarity and harmony, and this ideal was conveyed by their poetry, their architecture and their art.

Nietzsche was not the first to cast doubt on that wishful picture. In *The Art Work of the Future* (1859) Wagner had pointed to the religious nature of Greek tragedy, to the connection between tragedy and religious ritual and to the paradigmatic nature of tragedy as an art. *The Ring of the Nibelung* was conceived with the *Oresteia* in mind, and Wagner understood the Greek gods in Aeschylus in the same spirit as he depicted the German gods in *The Ring*, namely as personifications of the unconscious forces by which the human will is governed. Nietzsche went further, identifying Dionysus, the god of tragedy, as one of two dominant psychic principles, the other being Apollo, the god of philosophy. While Apollo represents the reason and enlightenment that had been singled out by Winckelmann and Goethe as integral to the Greek ideal, Dionysus was the god of dark passions, unconscious yearnings and ritual destruction. Tragedy invites this god into the public arena, where his demands can be acknowledged and purged. And the true vehicle of tragedy is not words, in which the rational and critical intellect is sovereign, but music and dance, in which bodily rhythms and animal passions find their expression.

[92] This view is endorsed by Julian Young, *Nietzsche's Philosophy of Art* (Cambridge, 1992), though for reasons slightly different from those I give. In my view *The Birth of Tragedy* is the only one of Nietzsche's works that contains an argument detachable from the author of it.

Nietzsche argued that Greek civilization had been misjudged by Winckelmann, Goethe and Schiller, and that a new understanding had since supervened, one that acknowledged the function of Greek religion in presenting and appeasing the irrational aspects of the human psyche. This thesis is one to which Nietzsche returns in later works, writing, for example, in *Twilight of the Idols,* that 'it is only in the Dionysian mysteries ... that the *basic fact* of the Hellenic instinct finds expression'.[93] And he connects that 'basic fact' with life, health and sexuality. The thesis was later defended by E. R. Dodds in *The Greeks and the Irrational* (1951), and has been effectively normalized by modern scholarship. But it was associated in *The Birth of Tragedy* with the new German spirit, manifest in the art of Wagner. Like the Greeks, the Germans had their myths and legends, in which the unconscious forces of life claim recognition and acknowledgement. If the Germans were really to do what Winckelmann and Goethe wished for them, and to replicate the achievements of Greek civilization, it would be not through philosophy but through music, not through reason and enlightenment but through myth and legend.

Here Nietzsche introduced a theme that was to dominate his later thinking: the theme of health. Myth, he argued, is the healthy part of a culture: 'myth alone saves all the powers of the imagination and of the Apollonian dream from their aimless wanderings.'[94] Without myth the Apollonian principle of reason has no life on which to reflect. Hence the 'Socratism which is bent on the destruction of myth' is the sign of an unhealthy and degenerate culture. And Nietzsche discerned this unhealthy 'Socratism' in the Germany of his day, arguing that 'now the mythless man stands eternally hungry, surrounded by all past ages, and digs and grubs for roots, even if he has to dig for them among the remotest antiquities'.[95] In the face of this disinherited condition, Nietzsche implies, the Wagnerian rebirth of tragedy through music and myth brings with it the possibility of a return to

---

[93] *Twilight of the Idols,* 10.4.
[94] *Birth of Tragedy,* p. 135. Page numbers refer to the Kaufman edition, *The Birth of Tragedy* and *The Case of Wagner* tr. Walter Kaufmann (New York, 1967).
[95] *Birth of Tragedy,* p. 136.

health. Nothing less is at stake in the destiny of German music than the defence of German culture from decadence. The terms are those that Nietzsche would later use to condemn the art of Wagner, but they are here used to praise it. So, right from the start, Nietzsche's discussion of Wagner presents us with two major questions in aesthetics: on what grounds can we distinguish healthy from decadent art, and what is the aesthetic significance of the distinction?

In the last work published in his lifetime, *Twilight of the Idols*, Nietzsche ventures an explicit account of his aesthetic (sections 19 and 20): 'The "beautiful in itself" is scarcely a term,' he writes,

> not even a concept. In the beautiful man sets himself up as a measure of perfection; in certain cases he prays to himself therein. Nothing is beautiful; the human alone is beautiful: in this naivety all aesthetics is contained – it is the first truth of aesthetics. Let us add a second truth at once: nothing is ugly save *decadent* humanity [*der entartende Mensch*].

Nietzsche is here giving the *central* place in aesthetic judgement to the distinction between healthy and decadent forms of human life. He adhered to this position throughout his literary career. As he puts the point in the posthumous *Ecce Homo*, 'what has most profoundly occupied me is in effect the problem of decadence', and in taking up arms against decadence, he was 'joining forces against everything sick in me, including Wagner, including Schopenhauer, including the whole of modern "humaneness" [*Menschlichkeit*]'. And he returns to the point in *Contra Wagner*, arguing that 'my objections to the music of Wagner are physiological objections: why should I trouble to dress them up in aesthetic formulas? After all, aesthetics is nothing but a kind of applied physiology.'[96] Wagner's music, he suggests, is the cause and effect of a bodily sickness.

Nietzsche was not the first philosopher to place the idea of health at the centre of his worldview – Feuerbach had defended a 'healthy

---

[96] *Contra Wagner*, in W. Kaufmann, ed., *The Portable Nietzsche* (New York, 1954), p. 664.

sensuality' in his *Principles of the Philosophy of the Future* (1843), a work that profoundly influenced Wagner. And the concepts of decadence and degeneration were moving to the centre of intellectual life at the time of Nietzsche's mature works. Krafft-Ebing's *Psychopathia Sexualis* appeared in 1886, and in a compendious and influential work published in 1892 Max Nordau summarized the *fin de siècle* as the period of decadence, taking Nietzsche himself, along with Baudelaire, Zola, Wagner, Poe and many more, as symptoms of the disease.[97] Nevertheless Nietzsche was probably the first thinker to take the distinction between health and disease as definitive of what is at stake in the artistic enterprise. And this distinction had an added importance for him on account of his genealogical method.

This method conditions all Nietzsche's fundamental positions in philosophy, so that for him to describe a work of art as decadent and to say that it arises from and is rooted in a decadent form of life are ultimately equivalent claims. Tragedy, according to *The Birth of Tragedy*, is healthy precisely in what is most obscure, and what flows unconsciously beneath the reasoned clarity of the conscious motives. For health means life, life belongs to the body, the body belongs to the community, and the community is true to its inner nature only when responding to the unconscious forces by which it endures. In the collective dance the social organism lives and renews itself.

The tragic hero is precipitated out of the dance through the fault of consciousness, and for this fault he must pay. Hence the original dichotomy – Dionysus versus Apollo – shows itself in another: that between the formless flow of unconscious life and the *principium individuationis* that asserts itself in defiance of life. Those Schopenhauerian terms are used to alert the reader to the danger of the enlightened, Apollonian spirit that stands outside the collective life of a culture, in a posture of critical isolation. That, for Nietzsche, is the primary source of decadence. The tragedy reaffirms the original

---

[97] Max Nordau, *Entartung* (1892), tr. as *Degeneration* (London, 1895).

flux, in which human life constantly renews itself through negating the claims of individuality. Nietzsche quotes Isolde's dying words by way of explaining what he means:

In des Wonnemeeres
wogendem Schwall,
in der Duft-Wellen
tönendem Schall,
in des Weltathems
wehenden All –
ertrinken – versinken
unbewusst – höchste Lust.

Isolde's 'highest joy' lies in the renunciation of the individuated self, sinking at last into the unending flux of becoming – the world breath's wafting whole, which is the equivalent in Wagner of Schopenhauer's directionless and ever restless Will.

Nietzsche was later to turn his back on Schopenhauer as he turned his back on Wagner. But some of the most important ideas adumbrated in *The Birth of Tragedy* survive into his mature writings on music. For Nietzsche the primary musical phenomenon is dance, and dance is organized by rhythm. Dance is a social phenomenon: we dance *with* others, and usually in groups. So music is one part of a complex social whole, which is the group or tribe *moving together*, in response to a pulse whose significance lies deeper than reason. The primary form of this collective movement is religious ritual, and it is from religious ritual that tragedy is born. The art of tragedy, Nietzsche claims, delayed the destruction of the Greek myths by perpetuating the Dionysian ritual in which music and dance occupied a central place.[98]

Those ideas are more suggested than dwelt upon in *The Birth of Tragedy*. But they are of considerable importance in understanding the dispute with Wagner. Equally important is the conception of art

[98] *Birth of Tragedy*, p. 138.

that the two men shared, and which they had inherited from Hegelian philosophy. Art, for both Nietzsche and Wagner, was the highest of human activities – higher than science, and higher too than religion. Indeed the destiny of art, according to both Wagner and Nietzsche, is to rescue through symbols the human truth that religion conceals, the truth about *us*. This truth is not what religion tells us, but it is what religion *means*. And both thinkers turned to music as epitomizing the spiritual transformation that is the true goal of every artist. 'Only music,' wrote Nietzsche, 'placed beside the world, can give us an idea of what is meant by the justification of the world as an aesthetic phenomenon.'[99]

Here, then, is a suggestion as to the source of the dispute with Wagner. Both men believed that the human world is in need of justification. They believed that the *religious* justification was either empty (Wagner) or pernicious (Nietzsche). But both believed that the religious need is a non-accidental feature of the human psyche, and one that demands satisfaction. This satisfaction is to be found in art, which supersedes religion and provides an *aesthetic* justification of the world ('the justification of the world as an aesthetic phenomenon'). And for Nietzsche, at least, no other justification is possible: hence the need for tragedy, which involves the overcoming of horror by aesthetic means. The difference between Nietzsche and Wagner begins at this point. For Nietzsche an aesthetic justification of the world is one that affirms life and health against decline and sickness. It is in direct conflict with the Christian justification, which elevates meekness, compassion and other such allegedly life-denying dispositions over the life-affirming virtues on which the future of mankind depends and of which Nietzsche went on to give an alarming description. As he puts it in *The Genealogy of Morality*: 'The *sickly* are the greatest danger to man: *not* the wicked, *not* the "beasts of prey".'[100]

---

[99] *Ibid.*, p. 141.
[100] *The Genealogy of Morality*, 3.14.

For Wagner, by contrast, the aesthetic justification of the world involves foregrounding our capacity for renunciation. Art is not a vindication of life but a redemption from it, and the theme of redemption is the recurring motif of the Wagnerian music drama, from *The Flying Dutchman* to *Parsifal*. The music drama retains, for Wagner, the fundamental significance of the Greek tragedy. That is to say, it is not merely a *picture* of a moral process. It is an *enactment* of that process, into which the spectator is drawn as a quasi-participant, as in a religious ritual, so that the redemption portrayed on the stage takes place also in the psyche of the observer. This 'Eucharistic' conception of art became ever more prominent as Wagner's art developed, so that *Parsifal* is described as a 'festival play for the consecration of the stage': in other words, as a religious ceremony. And Wagner attempted to confine the performance of *Parsifal* to the sacred precinct of Bayreuth (mercifully without success). In some way the work of art *redeems* the one who stands within its emotional ambience. The spectator *undergoes* the music drama, and his emotions are rearranged by it, as they are rearranged by the religious ritual. The hunger of the knights of the Grail for the Eucharistic meal is a symbol of the hunger that calls out in all of us, for a spiritual transformation that art alone can now provide. This transformation frees us from our enslavement to the world, and gives us the strength and the serenity to renounce it. And – if we are to follow the path taken by Tristan, Isolde, Parsifal, Hans Sachs and the Dutchman – we will recognize that the erotic, which seems to invite us *into* life, is in fact the original call to renunciation, the deep burning in the soul that tells us that we are 'not of this world'.

The Wagnerian idea of redemption closely corresponds to the Christian one; and it was part of Wagner's brilliance to recognize that in all its forms redemption requires sacrifice – the very sacrifice that is portrayed in the Greek tragedy and enacted in the Christian Eucharist: the sacrifice of the whole human being. The human must be 'offered up' if we are truly to transcend it: only then do we free ourselves from the resentments and conflicts with which human communities are poisoned. That which is 'offered up' is life itself – either in the promissory form of erotic yearning (Sachs, Parsifal) or in the realized form of a living victim (Siegfried, Tristan, Brünnhilde). This idea has both a religious and a secular meaning, as is clear from *Parsifal* and *The Mastersingers,* and has since been developed in surprising and ingenious ways by René Girard.[101] Wagner's vision of redemption through sacrifice is both a theory of human communities and a moral exhortation. And the moral exhortation is tried and tested, not in life, but in art – in the realm of imagination, that enables the spectator of the drama to 'live through' a sacrifice that he cannot actually live. (If he did so, life itself would cease.) That vision of redemption was once available through religion. In *Parsifal*, however, art replaces religion, taking the instruments of redemption and infusing them with an *aesthetic* life.

For Nietzsche the whole idea of redemption, conceived in that way, is a denial of life and an invocation to decadence. In the third essay of *The Genealogy of Morality*, devoted to the demolition of asceticism, he ridicules *Parsifal*, wondering whether the composer had not intended the work as a kind of satyr play, a grotesque sequel to *The Ring*. And in *The Case of Wagner* he sets out to demonstrate the decadent quality of the Wagnerian hero, who is not a hero at all but an *entartete Mensch*. He also sets out to show the *aesthetic* disaster that ensues when such a character is made central to a large-scale music drama. The goal of the book is to reject Wagner's moral vision, and also to suggest that the attempt to build that vision into a sustained work of art leads to music that is fundamentally sick. The moral faults of the vision translate directly into aesthetic faults in the music, and at the same time an immersion in the music involves a corruption in the soul of the listener, whose psyche is jeopardized by this surrender to a polluted ideal.

Claims of that kind place an enormous critical onus on the one who makes them, and it is fair to say that Nietzsche does not discharge that onus. He does not succeed in showing that the Wagnerian

---

[101] *La Violence et le sacré* (Paris, 1972). *Des Choses cachées depuis la fondation du monde* (Paris, 1978).

philosophy of redemption is either decadent in itself or aesthetically destructive. Nor does he succeed in showing just *how* a moral vision displays itself in musical form, and just *how* music invites the sympathy (and possibly corrupt sympathy) of the listener. The belief that music has a moral and character-forming potential is at least as old as Plato; and the belief that works of art are to be judged in terms of the life contained in them has survived into our times as a critical commonplace, though one that stands in need of a philosophical underpinning. But it seems to me that Nietzsche does not really provide that underpinning.

Nietzsche's attack has three parts. First there is the accusation of decadence, which is directed not only at Wagner but at the world of which Wagner was a part, and specifically at the *German* conception of that world. Then there is the attack on the claims that Wagner makes for his art. For Wagner his *Gesamtkunstwerk* involved an adventure of music into new expressive domains, so as to explore the depths of the human condition through the 'endless melody' that speaks to what is unconscious and hidden. Against those claims Nietzsche argues that Wagner is really a 'miniaturist', that his musical techniques are incapable of generating real development and that the whole thing is a kind of confidence trick, a simulation of musical life, which ignores the real source of music in rhythm and dance. Finally Nietzsche argues that the heroic in Wagner is a sham. His characters need to be unmasked, to be deprived of their mythic costumes and returned to the bourgeois context from which they have been lifted into legend. Wagner's portentous music does not offer them redemption, since it merely disguises the fact that they are the ordinary sick refuse of nineteenth-century society – as far from tragic grandeur as Flaubert's Emma Bovary.[102] The Wagnerian drama is a species of 'counterfeiting', in which the heroic passions and vast deeds reveal

---

[102] Cf. Ruskin's critique of George Eliot, whose characters he dismisses as 'sweepings out of a Pentonville omnibus', 'Fiction, Fair and Foul', in *Works*, ed. E. T. Cook and A. Wedderburn (London, 1909), vol. xxxvii, p. 372. The similarities between the Ruskinian and the Nietzschean postures towards the modern world led me to the character of Merope, in *Perictione in Colophon* (South Bend, 2002).

themselves, when held up to the critical light, as thin wisps of sickly passion, puffed up by musical bombast. The promises of 'redemption' and 'transcendence' both depend on the forgery conducted by the music, and the fact that these promises are taken so seriously by so many is indicative of the equally decadent and counterfeit nature of the surrounding culture.

Those powerful criticisms issue in off-putting passages like this:

Wagner's art is sick. The problems he presents on the stage – all of them problems of hysterics – the convulsive nature of his affects, his overexcited sensibility, his taste that required ever stronger spices, his instability which he dressed up as principles, not least of all the choice of his heroes and heroines – consider them as physiological types (a pathological gallery!) – all of this taken together represents a profile of sickness that permits no further doubt ... Precisely because nothing is more modern than this total sickness, this lateness and overexcitement of the nervous mechanism, Wagner is *the modern artist par excellence*.[103]

Nietzsche is aware that to justify his claims he must say something about the music – about what it *does* and *how* it does it. His attack is directed against all three musical dimensions – melodic, rhythmic, harmonic – as Wagner makes use of them. Nietzsche claims that Wagner's supposedly 'infinite' or 'endless' melody conceals an absence of genuine melodic inspiration.[104] He implies that there is even a kind of *fear* of melody in Wagner – certainly fear of those gripping tunes that Nietzsche identifies in *Carmen*, and which he associates with 'French' finesse, as against 'German' bombast. (This reverses a thesis of *The Birth of Tragedy*, which had contrasted the healthy world of German myth with the unhealthy clarity of French

---

[103] *The Case of Wagner*, p. 166.

[104] That Wagner was the enemy of melody was a critical commonplace in the early reception of his works. An article in *The Times* of 21 July 1853 claims that Wagner's music 'threatens to exclude melody altogether'. Wagner's champion Francis Hueffer responded with *Richard Wagner and the Music of the Future* (1874), defending the Wagnerian conception of melody as inseparable from the musical and dramatic texture. (Thanks to Gulliver Ralston for these references.)

civilization, applying in a local way the contrast between *Kultur* and *Zivilisation* made fashionable by Herder.) The real melody, for Nietzsche, is the melody that gives direct and immediate pleasure to the listener, the melody that engages with the spontaneous will to dance. He is short on examples, other than *Carmen*, but we can all agree that the *Habañera* from that great work is quite another kind of thing from the Prize Song from *The Mastersingers,* which constantly develops, and reaches closure only as a temporary pause in its seemingly unending growth towards the final chorus.

Nietzsche is dismissive towards the Wagnerian 'leitmotif', which he compares (obscurely) to a 'toothpick', used to get rid of the remainders of food.[105] And he associates the Wagnerian musical process with a 'degeneration of the sense of rhythm',[106] while praising Wagner for having inspired the study of rhythmics, then being initiated by H. Riemann.[107] In *Contra Wagner* – the fragments collected in Turin in 1888 – Nietzsche takes this criticism further, interestingly connecting the '*endlose Melodie*' with the rhythmic disintegration, as he perceived it, of Wagner's music – its inability to *dance.* He illustrates through an image that occurs also in *The Case of Wagner*:

One walks into the sea, gradually loses one's secure footing, and finally surrenders oneself to the elements without reservation: one must *swim.* In older music, what one had to do in the dainty, or solemn, or fiery back and forth, quicker and slower, was something quite different, namely, to *dance.* The measure required for this, the maintenance of certain equally balanced units of time and

---

[105] *The Case of Wagner*, p. 174.
[106] *Ibid.,* p. 184.
[107] *Ibid.,* p. 179. H. Riemann's *System der musikalischen Rhythmik und Metrik* did not appear until 1903. It is now unjustly neglected. In unpublished work Kathy Fry has drawn attention to Nietzsche's phrase-structure analysis in the 1870–71 notebooks of *Tristan*, Act III, scene ii (the passage of rhythmical disorder, as Tristan tears the bandage from his wound). Nietzsche here attempts to show that a strophe/antistrophe form emerges at the higher level, so that what looks like disorder is in fact another kind of order. I am grateful to Kathy Fry for drawing my attention to this passage, which again shows Nietzsche praising Wagner on an aspect of his work that would later draw forth severe condemnation. See G. Colli and M. Montinari's critical edition of Nietzsche, *Werke II:3 Vorlesungsaufzeichnungen 1870–71* (Berlin, 1993), p. 192.

force, demanded continual *wariness* of the listener's soul – and on the counterplay of this cooler breeze that came from the wariness and the warm breath of enthusiasm rested the magic of all *good* music. Richard Wagner wanted a different kind of movement; he overthrew the physiological presuppositions of previous music. Swimming, floating – no longer walking and dancing.[108]

The faults Nietzsche discerns concern Wagner's attitude to the listener. The composer's floating rhythms are denying the impulse to move with the music in a healthy and reciprocal way: Wagner is not responding to, not *wary* of, the listener's soul. Finally Nietzsche is dismissive of Wagnerian harmony, which he describes (in connection with *Parsifal*) as 'a rope of enharmonics', on which ugly things perform their gymnastics.'[109] He means, I take it, that the harmonic progressions are not genuine but the result of taking chords whole from one tonal centre to another, as in the enharmonic changes used in classical music for special effect, and normalized by Schubert in his *Lieder*. This use of enharmonics, Nietzsche implies, negates true harmonic movement, so that the music slops around like a sea instead of moving forward like a river. Thus Wagner's music is a failure in all three dimensions of musical order: melody, rhythm and harmony. And the failure stems from the adverse *use* of music, to inflate the sentiments attached to scenes and characters that do not really contain them. To put the point directly: the defects of form stem from defects of content. Because the content is faked, so is the form.

Nietzsche was, of course, aware of the originality and brilliance of Wagner's music. In an illuminating study Georges Liébert has shown the extent to which Nietzsche's love–hate relation with Wagner was really a love–hate relation with himself, and in particular with his own self-image as a musician. Liébert shows how deeply self-deceived the philosopher was, both in his initial admiration for the composer and

---

[108] *Contra Wagner*, p. 666.
[109] *The Case of Wagner*, p. 168.

in his subsequent petulant break with him.[110] At the very moment when he was publicly denouncing *Parsifal* as a work of sickness, decadence and deception, Nietzsche sent to Peter Gast a wonderful description of the Prelude to that work, and confessed, in his notes written at the time of *Beyond Good and Evil*, that he knew 'of nothing that grasps Christianity at such a depth and that so sharply leads to compassion'.[111] *Parsifal* captures the dramatic and emotional logic of the Christian vision, and Nietzsche's own musicality compelled him to recognize this, and to see it as an artistic triumph.

Furthermore, the faults that Nietzsche discerns in Wagner's music are very obviously the faults shown by his own compositions. These have now been published, and many issued on CD. There are some charming songs in the manner of Löwe, some grandiose attempts at choral and orchestral fantasias, and massive splurges for piano with fraught romantic titles such as 'Hymn to Friendship'. Nietzsche was at best what he so unjustly and outrageously accused Wagner of being[112] – a miniaturist, whose short-breathed successes are inspired by solitary and lachrymose emotions that could not be pursued at greater length without morbidity. The works for which he would have wished to be remembered are formless improvisations, with lunatic bass-lines and grotesque progressions, entirely devoid of melodic or harmonic logic.

Nietzsche knew this, of course, and had turned to literature with a sense of opting for second-best. He even described *Also sprach Zarathustra* as a work of music, hoping to gain by metaphor what he could not achieve in fact. And throughout his troubled and lonely literary career he took what consolation he could from the fact that he, unlike his critics, had the soul of a musician and could hear his way into the secret heart of things. His prose was an attempt to convey the wordless truths, the primeval needs and hopes, which find their true voice in music. But the spirit of Dionysus eluded him, who

---

[110] Georges Liébert, *Nietzsche and Music,* tr. David Pellauer and Graham Parkes (Chicago, 2004).
[111] Letter to Peter Gast (Heinrich Köselitz), January 1887.
[112] *The Case of Wagner,* p. 171.

claimed it as his own. And in his attack on Wagner's music he was taking revenge for this.

According to Nietzsche, Wagner's music only *pretends* to the emotions that it claims. Hence the dramas themselves fall apart. The characters are real only by moments, and only in those histrionic gestures that show Wagner's art to be the art of the showman. True drama, Nietzsche holds, is not theatrical, and it is precisely Wagner's mastery of the theatrical idiom that disqualifies his dramas from bearing the meaning that he wishes for. Wagner is an actor, a showman, and everything he does is devoted to *effect*, even though there is no dramatic content in terms of which the effect could be justified. Hence the paradoxical-seeming description of Wagner as a 'miniaturist'. It is only by moments that the magic works. But, in a famous passage, Nietzsche turns that criticism around, acknowledging that some of those moments, at least, are not mere theatre, but sparks of lyrical insight without compare in the history of music:

> There is a musician who, more than any other musician, is a master at finding the tones in the realm of suffering, depressed, tortured souls, at giving language even to mute misery. None can equal him in the colours of late autumn, in the indescribably moving happiness of the last, truly last, truly shortest joy; he knows a sound for those quiet, disquieting midnights of the soul, where cause and effect seem to be out of joint and where at any moment something might originate 'out of nothing'. He draws most happily of all out of the profoundest depths of human happiness, and, as it were, out of its drained goblet, where the bitterest and most repulsive drops have finally and evilly run together with the sweetest. He knows that weariness of the soul which drags itself, unable to leap or fly any more, even to walk; he masters the shy glance of concealed pain, of understanding without comfort, of the farewell without confession – indeed, as the Orpheus of all secret misery he is greater than any; and some things have been added to the realm of art by him alone, things that had hitherto seemed inexpressible and even unworthy of art – the cynical rebellion, for example, of

which only those are capable who suffer most bitterly; also some very minute and microscopic aspects of the soul, as it were the scales of its amphibian nature: indeed he is the master of the very minute. But he does not *want* to be that![113]

Take away those moments, however, and what remains? A great work of counterfeit: fake transcendence,[114] fake characters, fake emotions and – in the end – a fake redemption offered by Parsifal, the 'holy fool'. None of this is believable, since none of it comes from the heart – it is all icy abstraction, rooted in the Hegelian conception of music as a vehicle for the 'Idea'.[115] Thus 'everything that ever grew on the soil of *impoverished* life, all of the counterfeiting of transcendence and beyond, has found its most sublime advocate in Wagner's art'.[116] Nietzsche does not spell out this criticism in detail, but it is clear that he believes not merely that the raw material provided by Wagner's characters is insufficient to meet their allegorical and metaphysical purpose but also that it is impossible that any characters *should* meet that purpose, and moreover that it is decadent to *want* to meet it. For the longing for redemption, as Wagner presents it, is a sickness, a renunciation of life and health for the sake of a bogus spiritual purity. Although Nietzsche does not explicitly say so, I suspect that he regarded the Wagnerian 'redemption' as a kind of cliché, an idea worn thin by too much use, brought in to the later dramas only because the characters, lacking the will and integrity that makes true tragedy possible, have to be content with 'redemption' as second-best. Hence Nietzsche's ironical comment, *re* the placing of a wreath on the composer's grave by the German Wagner Society, on which was inscribed the last words of *Parsifal*: 'Redemption for the Redeemer': 'Many (strangely enough) made the small correction: "Redemption from the Redeemer". One breathed a sigh of relief'.[117]

---

[113] *Contra Wagner*, p. 663.
[114] *The Case of Wagner*, p. 183.
[115] Ibid., pp. 177–8.
[116] Ibid., p. 183.
[117] Ibid., p. 182.

In response to those charges I will say only this: Nietzsche's advocacy of 'life' is at best an excusable compensation for the invalid existence that the philosopher was obliged to lead, at worst a surrender to all that is most destructive in human nature. If compassion for the weak is decadence, if sacrifice is decadence, if the transcendence of sexual desire is decadence, if the renunciation of power for love, and divine arrogance for human pity are decadence – then roll on decadence. And if health comes only with a life 'beyond good and evil', in which pity and renunciation play no part, then away with health.

But there is truth in Nietzsche's claim that the Wagnerian characters do not always live up to the metaphysical and moral burdens that he places on them. Only every now and then – alone in the forest, confronting the Rhine daughters, dying in a long-delayed access of consciousness – does Siegfried represent the tragic truth of human freedom. And whatever we think of his personal qualities and allegorical meaning, Siegfried is certainly very far from the 'marvellously accurate archetypal youth' whose portrait Nietzsche praises in *Richard Wagner in Bayreuth*.[118] Only in the encounter with Kundry as seductress does Parsifal become fully alive as a human being. On the other hand, there are few creations that are as hair-raising and persuasive as Wagner's Kundry. There is nothing since the Greeks to compare with the portrait of Wotan, and little outside Dickens and Victor Hugo to match Alberich or Mime.

Much more interesting philosophically is Nietzsche's sketchy attempt to read the charge of decadence into the *music*, to associate the moral failure (as he saw it) of the dramas with a failure of musical form. The insight that inspired *The Birth of Tragedy* is of lasting importance. Music is not a conceptual idiom. All attempts to assimilate the organization of music to the organization that we know from language are, it seems to me, doomed. We understand music by moving with it, and what we understand is not a thought but a 'field of sympathy' into which we are inducted by the music as we are inducted into a ritual by the gestures of a priest. Dance is the

---

[118] *Untimely Meditations*, Cambridge, 1997, p. 201.

primary form of this collective movement, and dance has a place in religious ritual for that very reason. If there is corruption in the music of Wagner, it must be found, therefore, in the musical movement. In this Nietzsche is right; and he is right to question the melodic, rhythmic and harmonic organization of the Wagnerian idiom in those terms. What kind of human being is it that the listener is invited to 'move with' in this music? In surrendering to this movement am I surrendering something of myself that I should be withholding? Or am I, as Wagner wants me to believe, entering a sacred place, in which the sympathetic response to the music will effect a new order in my feelings? Can I through this music achieve the order of sacrifice and renunciation that will bring the peace and quiescence that the Greeks sought through tragedy, and which we moderns must seek through a new form of art – the 'art work of the future' that will replace religion not by refuting it but by doing its work, and doing it better?

Wagner believed that he had to refashion all the ways in which music moves. His endless melodies are not, however, the redundant contraptions that Nietzsche claimed them to be. Nor does his music display a rhythmic disintegration. The use of the broken triplet of the 'look' motif in the prelude to *Tristan and Isolde* is one of the finest examples in music of a syncopated rhythmic order generated from the smallest possible cell, which spreads its accent through the whole entity of which it is a part. The result is not rhythmic disintegration but integrated rhythm *without closure*. Likewise the harmonic movement of the prelude is not a tightrope of enharmonic changes but a supreme instance of voice-led modulation *without closure*. And the melody is moving according to the same principle and in a way that enters the memory of every musical person. This is musical art of the highest order. This three-dimensional movement without closure is used to convey a state of mind 'from within' and without words – without even the possibility of words.

That having been said, however, Nietzsche's questions need to be answered. What would show this supreme musical competence to be also moral competence, so to speak – the expression of uncorrupted human life, of a kind that invites and deserves our sympathy?

The sting might be drawn from Nietzsche's charge of decadence, without conferring on the Wagnerian drama the supreme significance that it claims for itself. Not counterfeit, but not necessary either – a byway of modern life that teaches us nothing. Such might be the moderated judgement of a Nietzschean today. But we have reached the point at which Nietzsche's onus needs to be discharged. His own advocacy of life is far more obviously a sham, in my view, than Wagner's post-Christian philosophy of redemption. And his defence of closed rhythms and catchy tunes is too short-breathed to carry any intellectual weight. One wonders what Nietzsche would say in response to Lady Gaga, Meshuggah or EDM, or in response to a popular film culture dominated by 'special effects', ludicrous metamorphoses, and relentless violence without any moral or emotional rationale. Would he be thereafter a little less inclined to apply the label 'decadent' to Wagner, or would he recognize that there are forms of 'life' to which a dose of old-fashioned decadence might reasonably be preferred?

16

The Music of the Future

In 1860 Wagner published a now famous pamphlet entitled *The Music of the Future* (*Zukunftmusik*). In it he expressed his view that it was not enough for music to be merely contemporary – *zeitgenössisch*; it had to be *ahead* of itself, summoning from the future the forms that already lay there in embryo. And of course Wagner was entitled to write in this way, given what he had achieved in *Tristan und Isolde*, which was finished the year before his essay appeared, and which introduced the chromatic syntax that was to change the course of musical history.

We should not forget, however, the wider context of Wagner's argument. The obsession with the future comes from Ludwig Feuerbach, and ultimately from Hegel's philosophy of history, which represents human events as motivated by the always advancing logic of the dialectic. For Hegel history has a *direction*, and this direction is revealed in laws, institutions and sciences, as well as in literature, art and music. Each period is characterized by its *Zeitgeist*, shared among all the products of the culture.

In Feuerbach the *Zeitgeist* idea is allied to the belief in progress, understood in terms of the life and energy of human communities. The future, Feuerbach believed, is not merely a development of the past; it is *better* than the past. It marks an increase in knowledge and therefore in power over our own destiny and therefore in freedom. It is not easy now, after the communist and fascist experiments, to endorse the belief in progress that they both so vehemently shared.

But somehow, in the arts, the belief survives. Modern people spontaneously incline to the view that each artistic form and style must be superseded as soon as it appears, and that the true values of art require constant vigilance against the diseases of nostalgia and pastiche. Each composer faces the challenge: why should I listen to *you*? And each claims originality, authenticity, the plain fact of being me, as a vindication. Hence each tries to avoid repeating what has been done already or relying on formulae that, by dint of over-use, have become clichés. In everyday life clichés may be useful, since they evoke stock reactions and settled beliefs. In art, however, clichés are inherently meaningless, since they prevent the work that uses them from *saying* anything of its own.

Wagner's emphasis on the future of music was influenced by the Hegelian theory of history and Feuerbach's use of it. But it was also rooted in a real sense of tradition and what tradition means. His innovations grew organically from the flow of Western music, and his harmonic discoveries were discoveries only because they also affirmed the basic chord grammar of diatonic tonality. They were discoveries within the extended tonal language. Wagner was aware of this, and indeed dramatized the predicament of the modern composer in *Die Meistersinger von Nürnberg*, which is his own striking reflection on 'tradition and the individual talent'. In that opera the plodding C major tonality of the Mastersingers is brought to life not by remaking it entirely but by moving it onwards, through the use of chromatic voice-leading, altered chords and a new kind of melody in which boundaries are fluid and phrases can be repeated and varied at liberty within them. In the course of the opera the chorus brings the new melody and the old harmony into creative relation, and the work ends jubilantly, with the new incorporated and the old renewed. This is nothing like the radical avant-garde departures that have dominated music in more recent times.

Right up until Schoenberg's experiments with serialism, musical innovation in the realm of 'classical' music proceeded in Wagner's way. New harmonies, scales and melodic ensembles were imported into the traditional musical grammar, new rhythms and time signatures were adopted, and with Stravinsky and Bartók organization was inspired more by dance than by the classical forms. Whole-tone and octatonic scales led to music in which, while there was melodic and harmonic progression, there was often no clear tonic, or two competing tonics, as in much of *The Rite of Spring*. Schoenberg wrote of 'floating tonality', others of atonality, meaning the loss of the sense of key, and the use of harmonies which, even if tied to each other by voice-leading, seemed to be unrelated and, by the old standards, ungrammatical.

None of that involved any rejection of the classical tradition: composers like Debussy, Bartók and Stravinsky were renewing that tradition, and what they wrote was not merely recognizable to the ordinary educated listener but also interesting and challenging on account of its new harmonic, melodic and rhythmical devices. Both the continuous development of the Romantic symphony in Sibelius, Vaughan Williams and Shostakovich and the incorporation of modernist harmonies into the tonal language lay within the scope of the existing language: these were developments that issued naturally from the pattern of musical discovery that has characterized Western classical music from the Renaissance.

As things stand now, however, there is absolutely no guarantee that a new work of music will be recognized as such by the educated musical ear, or that it will be possible to hear it as an addition to the great tradition of symphonic sound. A radical break seems to have occurred, with two consequences that the listening public finds difficult to absorb: first, modern works of music tend to be self-consciously part of an avant-garde, never content to belong to the tradition but always overtly and ostentatiously defying it; second, these works seem to be melodically impoverished, and even without melody entirely, relying on acoustical experiments to fill the void where melody should be.

I don't say the emphasis on acoustics is necessarily a fault from the artistic point of view. A composer like Nathan Davies, who uses live filtering to give the effect of resonators, extracts tones from white noise and turns those tones towards music. The effect of this is striking, at times entrancing: the tones emerge from the white noise purified, to be used as though new. But until those tones *are* used, and used in melodic and harmonic structures, the result will remain at a distance from the audience, outside the reach of our musical affections. It is only the loved and repeated repertoire that will ensure the survival of music, and to be loved and repeated music requires a dedicated audience. Music exists in the ear of the listener, not on the page of the score, nor even in the world of sound. And listeners, deterred by the avant-garde, are in ever shorter supply: not in the specialist festivals, of course, but in the wider culture of our cities, where music will survive or die.

I identify four developments that have led to the place where we now are. Thanks to these developments a new kind of music has emerged which is less music than a reflection upon music, or perhaps even a reflection on the lack of music, or on the impossibility of music in the age in which we live.

The first development is, in many ways, the most interesting from the philosophical point of view, and this is the radical attack on tonality by Theodor Adorno and his immediate followers. Although Adorno linked his argument to Schoenberg's 12-tone serialism, and the new approach that it promised, the force of the argument is largely negative. It concerned what he was *against,* rather than what he was *for.* And Adorno carried weight in the post-war period because he was an ardent critic of the culture of capitalism, one who had attempted to adapt the Marxist critique of bourgeois society to the new social and political realities. His critique of tonality was part of a systematic theory of the death of bourgeois culture. Tonality had to die because the bourgeois order had to die. And the desire nevertheless to cling to tonality, in the manner of Sibelius or Copland, even in the manner of the neo-classical Stravinsky, is bound to lead, Adorno thought, to empty clichés or sterile kitsch. Such is the inevitable result of attempting to make use of an idiom that has died.

This argument of Adorno's, which is an application of the Hegelian *Zeitgeist* theory, is not easily answered, even if it is easily doubted. All artistic people are aware that styles, idioms and forms are living things that can also die, and that there is a need, integral to the artistic enterprise as such, to 'make it new'. This does not mean being iconoclastic or radical in the manner of the modernist avant-garde. It means conveying a message and an inspiration of one's own. The true work of art says something new, and is never a patchwork of things already said. This is the case even when the work employs an idiom already perfected by others, as when Mozart, in his string quartets, writes in the language of Haydn.

Thomas Mann wrote a great novel about this, *Doktor Faustus*, meditating on the fate of Germany in the last century. Mann takes the tradition of tonal music as both a significant part of our civilization, and a symbol of its ultimate meaning. Music is the Faustian art, the defiant assertion of the human voice in a cosmos of unknowable silence. Mann therefore connects the death of the old musical language to the death of European civilization. And he re-imagines the invention of 12-tone serialism as a kind of demonic response to the ensuing sense of loss. Music is to be annihilated, remade as the negation of itself. The composer Adrian Leverkühn, in the grip of demonic possession, sets out to 'take back the Ninth Symphony'. Such is the task that Mann proposes to his devil-possessed composer, and one can be forgiven for thinking that there are composers around today who have made this task their own.

This brings me to the second development that has fed into the obsession with the avant-garde, and that is the invention of serialism. I call this an invention, rather than a discovery, in order to record the wholly *a priori* nature of the serial system. The new harmonies and chromatic melodies of *Tristan* were *discoveries:* musical events that came into being by experiment, and were adopted because they sounded right. In retrospect you can give quasi-mathematical accounts of what Wagner was doing in the first bars of *Tristan*. But you can be sure that you will not thereby identify Wagner's own creative process, which was one of trying out new combinations and seeing where they led.

By contrast, serial organization was an invention – a set of *a priori* rules laid down by Schoenberg and adapted and varied by his successors. These rules were to provide a non-tonal grammar for music, determining what comes next independently of whether its coming next sounds right or wrong to the normal musical ear. It is not the tone or the scale but the maths that matters. There is no reason, of course, to think that serial organization should not also lead to sequences that *do* sound right, or come to sound right in time. But their sounding right is quite independent of the serial organization.

One of the advantages of working within a framework of *a priori* rules is that you can say just why this note occurs in just this place: the series requires it. But in another sense you lack such an answer, since the series requires the note regardless of the heard relation to its predecessor. Moreover the grammar of serialism is not based on the scale or any other way of grouping tones dynamically, in terms of what *leads to* what. In listening to music we listen out for progression, prolongation, question and answer – all the many ways in which one tone summons another as its natural successor. Serialism asks us to hear in another way, with the brain rather than the ear in charge.

The result of this is that, while we can enjoy and be moved by serial compositions, this is largely because we hear them as organized as tonal music is organized, so that 'next' sounds 'right'. We may notice the serial structure, but it is the progressive, linear structure that we enjoy. In a great serial composition, such as the Berg violin concerto, we hear harmonies, melodies, sequences and rhythmical regularities, just as in the great works of the tonal tradition, and we do so because we are hearing *against* the serial order. It is as though the composer, having bound himself in chains, is able nevertheless to dance in them, like a captive bear.

The third development, associated particularly with Boulez, Stockhausen and Nono, is the move towards total serialization. Composers decided to serialize time values, unpitched sounds and timbres, hoping thereby to exert total control over everything. Interestingly enough, this development went hand in hand with the emergence of aleatoric scores, in which instrumentalists are handed bundles of notes that they could choose to assemble in any order, or scores that ask for indeterminate sounds. Randomization had the same effect as serialization, which was to deprive musical elements of their intrinsic ways of relating to each other. Whether we impose a dictatorial serial order or present notes in unordered bundles, we undo the demands of melody, harmony and rhythm, which are inherent in the traditional grammar, and replace them with systematic requirements that can be explained intellectually but not, as a rule, heard musically.

In 1970 Stockhausen composed a two-piano piece, *Mantra*, for the Donaueschingen festival. In a subsequent lecture delivered in Britain, which can be seen on YouTube, he sets out the 12-tone series on which the piece is based. He plays the notes one after another, assigning an equal time value to each, and tells us that this melody occurred to him at a certain point, and that he decided to work on it, composing flights of new notes around each of its elements, arranging the series in conjunction with its own retrograde and so on. What was most striking to me about Stockhausen's description of what he was doing was the word 'melody', used of this sequence that is not a melody at all. Of course there *are* 12-tone melodies – for example, the melodies assigned to some of the characters and situations in Berg's opera *Lulu*. But all that makes sequences into melodies is absent from Stockhausen's theme: it has no beginning, no end, no tension or release, no real contour apart from its pure geometrical outline. It is a sonic object, but not a musical subject. And as he explains what is done with it you understand that it is treated as an object too – a piece of dead tissue to be cut up beneath the microscope. We understand the distinction between subject and object because we ourselves exemplify it. The true musical theme is a subject in something like the sense that I am a subject: it has a consciousness of itself, a meaning and a point of view. This is simply not true of the helpless dead sequence that Stockhausen presents in his lecture.

The effect of such innovations was to replace the experience of music by the concept of music. The typical avant-garde work is designed as the concept of itself, and often given some portentous title by way of illustrating the point, like Stockhausen's *Gruppen*: a work for three orchestras in which notes are amalgamated into groups according to their acoustical properties, and tempos are defined logarithmically. Much can be said, and has been said, about this momentous, not to say megalomaniac, composition, and indeed its great success, like that of Boulez's *Le Marteau sans maître*, is not independent of the fact that there is so much to say about it, some of which Stockhausen himself had anticipated in his article '… wie die Zeit vergeht …', published in the third issue of *Die Reihe*. The score is not a notation of musically organized sounds but a mathematical proof, from which the sounds can be deduced as theorems.

The eclipse of art by the concept of art occurred at around the same time in the visual arts, and for a while the game was amusing and intriguing. However, this particular bid for originality has dated much more rapidly than any of the harmonic discoveries of the late Romantics. Do it once, and you have done it for all time. This is certainly what we have seen in the realm of conceptual art in our museums and galleries. And it is what we have heard in the concert hall too. In conceptual music the creative act is always, from the musical point of view, the same, namely the act of putting an idea about music in the place where music should be: the act performed once and for all by John Cage in *4′33″*. The elaborate theorizing engaged in by Arthur Danto in order to connect the conceptual art and music of our time with Hegel's thesis of 'the death of art' is simply the last gasp of the *Zeitgeist* illusion: the illusion that all that happens in the realm of culture happens by a kind of historical necessity, so that, at any point in the process, 'there is no turning back'.[119]

This leads me to the fourth development, which is in many ways the most interesting, namely the replacement of tones by sounds, and musical by acoustical hearing. Edgard Varèse, Pierre Schaeffer and their immediate successors awoke composers and audiences to the many new sounds, some of them produced electronically, that could enter the space of music without destroying its intrinsic order. These experiments are not what I have in mind when referring to

---

[119] Arthur Danto, 'The End of Art: A Philosophical Defense', *History and Theory*, vol. 37, no. 4 (1998), pp. 127–43.

the replacement of tones by sounds and musical by acoustical hearing. I am thinking of a more general transition, from *Tonkunst* to *Klangkunst* – a transition of deep philosophical significance between two ways of hearing and two responses to what is heard.

Sounds are objects in the physical world, albeit objects of a special kind whose nature and identity are bound up with the way they are perceived. Tones are what we hear in sounds when we hear the sounds as music. As I have been arguing in this book, the organization that we hear in music is an organization that *we* – the musical public – hear, when we hear these sounds as music. And although there is, at any moment, an indefinite number of ways in which a melodic line or a chord sequence can continue without sounding wrong, the ideal in our tradition has been of an uninterrupted sense of appropriateness – each melodic and harmonic step following as though in dialogue with its predecessor, and yet with complete freedom. We are moved by music because music moves.

Of course, there are sound effects too: sounds from the real world intrude into music, like the unpitched sounds of the percussion section, or the recorded birdsong that intrudes into Respighi's *Pines of Rome*. But when we hear these sounds as part of the music they change character. They are no longer noises, no longer events in the ambient soundscape, like the coughs from the audience on a cold winter's day. They are caught up in the musical movement, becoming one with it, and dependent on the forward propulsion of which they are now a part. Thus a single piece of music, with no repeats, may nevertheless contain multiply repeated sequences of sounds. As objects in the material world sounds are identified and counted in another way from the way in which melodies, which are intentional and not material objects, are counted. (See above, Part 1, Chapter 5.)

The intrusion of acoustical ways of thinking into the practice and teaching of music is something we owe to Boulez and Stockhausen, and to the educational practices that they established. In Stockhausen sounds from everyday life are accorded exactly the same value as sounds within music – they are, as it were, invited in from the surrounding world, as in the work *Momente*, in which all kinds of

sounds and speech forms are brought together in a potpourri of fragments. As Stockhausen himself says, this work has no real beginning
and no end: like all his works, it starts without beginning and fin-
ishes without ending. For it lacks those elements of musical grammar
that make beginnings and endings perceivable. It starts nowhere and
stays at nowhere until ending nowhere. The same is true of Boulez's
Pli selon pli, in which the exotic instrumentation and serial organization do not conceal the fact that no moment in this work has any
intrinsic (i.e., musical) connection to the moment that comes next.
The experience of 'next', and the inevitability of the next, have been
annulled. In a concert devoted to music of this kind the audience can
know that the piece has ended only because the performers are putting down their instruments.

Music (music of our classical tradition included) has until now
consisted of events that grow organically from each other, over
a repeated measure and according to recognizable harmonic
sequences. The 'moving forward' of melodic lines through musical
space is the true origin of musical unity and of the dramatic power
of traditional music. And it is this 'moving forward' that is the first
casualty when pitches and tempos are organized serially, and when
sounds are invited in from outside the music.

This is not to say that acoustical processing may not have a part,
and an important part, to play in bringing sounds into a musical
structure. Joanna Bailie, to take just one example, has used the
recorded and digitally processed sounds culled in public spaces as
inputs into music for which instrumentalists and singers create the
musical frame. The atmospheric effect of this is unquestionable.
However, in the work of such composers we see the reassertion of the
musical against the acoustical ear, and perhaps even a path back to
the place where music reigns in a space of its own.

All those four developments are of the greatest musicological
interest, and I do not deny that they can be used effectively, to produce works of real power. But it is also clear to my way of thinking
that they are responsible for a growing gap between serious music
and the audience on which it depends, not necessarily financially

(since, after all, there is a massive machinery of subsidy that keeps the avant-garde in business), but at least spiritually. If avant-garde music is ever to step down from the world of concepts into the world of tones, then it will be because the audience exists in whose ears this transition can occur. Take away the audience and you take away the concrete reality of music as an art. You turn music into an arcane exercise in the acoustical laboratory, in which groups of patient instrumentalists pump out sounds according to formulae which mean nothing, since meaning lies in the ears that have fled from the scene.

Adorno may have been right that the old grammar was exhausted, that post-Romantic harmony had taken tonality as far as it could go, and that music must therefore find another way into the future, whether or not led by the avant-garde. The great question that we must still confront is whether rhythm, melody and harmony are still available to us, in whatever modified forms, as we endeavour to write music that will be not only interesting, as so much avant-garde music undeniably is, but also enjoyable and calling out for repetition. We all know Schoenberg's remark, that there is plenty of music still to be written in C major. But where *is* that music? Or rather, where is that way of writing, downstream from C major, that will restore to C major its undeniable authority for all of us, as it was restored by the final chorus of *Die Meistersinger*?

Two aspects of modern culture place obstacles in front of us, as we search for the new idiom that will renew our musical tradition. One is the insistent presence of easy music; the other is the dictatorship exerted on behalf of difficult music. By easy music I mean the ubiquitous products of pop and Rock, which influence the ears and the attention span of young people long before they can be captured by a teacher. The audience for new music must be discovered among young people whose ears have been shaped by the ostinato rhythms and undemanding chord grammar of pop. To offer serious music to such an audience you must also attract its attention. And this cannot be done without rhythms that connect to young people's own bodily perceptions.

Serious composers must work on the rhythms of everyday life. Bach addressed listeners whose ears had been shaped by allemandes, gigues and sarabandes – dance rhythms that open the way to melodic and harmonic invention. The modern composer has no such luck. The 4/4 ostinato is everywhere around us, and its effect on the soul, body and ear of postmodern people is both enormous and unpredictable. Modern composers must in some way acknowledge this, if they are to address young audiences and capture their attention. And the great question is how it can be done without lapsing into banality, as Adorno told us it must.

Americans tend to accept popular music and the culture around it as providing the raw material on which the serious composer gets to work. From Gershwin to John Adams it has been normal to take some aspect of the popular music of the day and to show its connection to other and more long-term ways of musical thinking. Just as Gershwin rewrote jazz sequences in the language of counterpoint, so does Adams lift the ostinato four-in-a-bar of the Rock group into an orchestral empyrean, where the flat-footed dance gives way to a gravitationless rhythm that moves and develops with the harmony. Adams uses the tonal language, not to make the kind of profound statement that we know from Beethoven or Bruckner, but nevertheless to lift the young ear out of its groove and to make it listen. There is a lesson to be taken from this, which is that the ear of the listener is plastic, moulded both by the surrounding culture and by the everyday sounds of life as it is now. In a way Stockhausen acknowledged this, with his works that snatch sounds from the surrounding world, and work them into his quasi-mathematical textures. But the textures are feeble, with no musical propulsion, no intrinsic 'next' to bind one event to its neighbours. Adams wished to provide that propulsion, into which the sounds of the modern world could be dropped and immediately reshaped as music. But maybe there is something mechanical here too – an ostinato that uses rhythmic pulse to carry us through whatever harmonic and melodic weaknesses we might otherwise hear in the score. (I am thinking here of the ironically entitled *Harmonielehre*.)

The contrary obstacle also lies before us: the dictatorship of the difficult. Bureaucrats charged with giving support to the arts are, today, frightened that someone will accuse them of being reactionary. To some extent we are all frightened of being accused of being reactionary. The history of the French salons in the nineteenth century, and of the early reactions to musical and literary modernism, has made people aware of how easy it is to miss the true creative product, and to exalt the dead and the derivative in its stead. The safest procedure for the anxious bureaucrat is to subsidize music that is difficult, unlikely to be popular, even repugnant to the ordinary musical ear. Then one is sure to be praised for one's advanced taste and up-to-date understanding. Besides, if a work of music is easy to assimilate and clearly destined to be popular, it does not need a subsidy.

It is surely in this way that Boulez rose to such an eminence in France. At the same time as vilifying his opponents and anathematizing tonal music and its late offshoots, Boulez achieved a cultural *coup d'état*, which was the founding of IRCAM. This institution reveals in its name – Institut de Recherche et Coordination Acoustique/ Musique – that it does not distinguish between sound and tone, between *Klangkunst* and *Tonkunst*, and sees both as matters for 'research'. It gives institutional blessing to the *Zeitgeist*, telling us that musical history has come to a stop, and that 'the rest is noise'.[120]

We have lived in fear of the *Zeitgeist* for far too long, and we must exorcize this ghost. We must tell ourselves that it is possible to be modern without being avant-garde, without lapsing into sound effects, and instead thinking in the old musical way, in terms of grammatical sequences, with a beginning, a middle and an end, sequences that linger in the ears and the memory of the listeners, so that even if they never hear the piece again, they sing it to themselves inwardly and find in it a personal meaning. It seems to me that, if there is, now, to be a music of the future, it will, in that way, belong with the music of the past.

[120] See the admirable history of modern music by Alex Ross: *The Rest Is Noise: Listening to the Twentieth Century* (New York, 2007).

And we must allow ourselves, now, to explore the *real* history of modern music, the history of the meandering, searching, undogmatic spirit of the twentieth century, which discovered in the bequest of tonality so many hitherto unexplored ways of articulating the anxiety and longing that come about when a civilization mislays its God. There would be a place in this history for Schoenberg's *Moses und Aron*, certainly, for Berg's *Wozzeck* and *Lulu*. But these works are neither more important historically nor greater musically than Britten's *Peter Grimes*, Janáček's *Katya Kabanova* or Shostakovich's *Lady Macbeth of the Mtsensk District*.

Any attempt to write the real history of modern classical music should pay attention to the writings of Robert R. Reilly, the music critic for *Crisis* magazine for 16 years, who is still reviewing concerts and operas for *Ionarts*. His reviews of recordings have been collected in a single volume, reissued in an expanded edition by the author in association with Jens F. Laurson.[121] The result is a wanderer's guide to the forbidden land of real contemporary music, a map of the vast catacomb of serene and consoling masterworks, hidden beneath the field of fashionable noise. The downpour of state and academic subsidies, which keeps the noise industry going, does not seep through to this underworld, which is nurtured solely by the passion of its devotees. But it is the place to which real music has retreated, and Reilly's aim is to show how easily you too can visit it, thanks to the adventurous recording companies who have been there first. Moreover much of this real music has found its way on to YouTube, and readers can summon up the pieces that Reilly describes as they read his penetrating descriptions of them.

It should be said that Reilly is no ordinary music critic. A former US Army armoured cavalry officer, who has served in government under President Reagan and in the United States Information Agency, and who has also been director of Voice of America, he could fairly claim to have been conducting the battle for our civilization simultaneously

---

[121] *Surprised by Beauty: A Listener's Guide to the Recovery of Modern Music*, by Robert R. Reilly, is published by the Ignatius Press in San Francisco.

on all available fronts. He has written with knowledge and insight about the historical origins of Islamism in the Ash'arite theology that came to dominate Muslim thinking in the eleventh century. His book – *The Closing of the Muslim Mind* – is beginning to have the influence that it deserves, as we ask why it is that Islamists have no other recourse, in the encounter with those who disagree with them, than to kill as many as they can. What goes wrong when people seriously believe that they *believe* something while forbidding all debate as to its truth? This – the question on which civilizations turn – has troubled Reilly as it ought to trouble us all.

If I were to single out the features of Western civilization that justify our defence of it, and which seem to be so palpably absent from the barbarism with which the Islamists wish to replace it, the tradition of classical music would be high on the list. Reilly clearly sees things in the same way, and is as distressed as I am by the fact that a deliberate attempt has been made to bring that tradition to an end. The noise industry has conquered the faculties of musicology and composition, has begun to marginalize harmony and counterpoint in the curriculum and set up shop with acoustic laboratories in the heart of every music school. It has equipped itself with theories, critics and schools of composition that maintain a vigilant and censorious presence in the culture. The fact that the resulting music is entirely without appeal has been put out of mind as irrelevant. The point is the charm of the theory, not the sound of the result. A concert hall from which the audience has fled is not a cultural disaster if a group of state-subsidized zombies is making noises at one end of it.

As I pointed out above, music is not an arrangement of 'pitched sounds' in mathematical permutations. It is a dynamic process in virtual space, a form of movement in which static sounds become goal-directed tones and simultaneous pitches are magically blended into chords. The whole enterprise of acoustical research, which for Boulez and Stockhausen spelled the way forward into the music of the future, was based on a false conception of the musical ear. It was precisely by building on theory rather than intuitive understanding that the music of the future ceased to be music and became instead a dance of spectres in a mausoleum of sounds.

Those observations leave us with the great question that is at the forefront of Reilly's writing about modern music: the question of a 'live tradition'. How can the tradition of the classical concert hall survive the assaults of the avant-garde? Conscious repetition of learned effects does not amount to real musical content, and mere competence will always leave a 'so what?' impression in the listener's mind, as it does for me with the works of Lowell Liebermann or Morten Lauridsen. Might there then be some truth in the argument that we can no longer write tonal music, since the result will always be repetitious and banal, a rearrangement of stock effects that have lost their meaning for the authentic musical ear?

Surely the way to answer that question is not to go on producing theories and counter-theories, but to listen. We need to go down for a long spell into the forbidden land of melody, and hear what its denizens are up to. And the result, Reilly shows, is truly surprising. There really are melodies down there, and they really do soar and move and enchant as tunes have always done, even if the word 'tune' seems not quite to capture their character. There is harmony, rhythm and development too. It all goes on as before, vital but unacknowledged, like the rituals of a forbidden religion. Reilly is voluble in his praise of melody: he finds it especially in Samuel Barber, whom he credits as a founding father of modern American music, the one who never betrayed the heart for the head and who showed how to be entirely original while speaking to every musical person.

Reilly's search for melody leads him to concentrate on the modern symphony, whose practitioners have remained true to the classical heritage, taking intelligible thematic material and developing it in comprehensive arches across musical space. It was precisely this heritage that Adorno most fervently attacked, since the symphony represents the bourgeoisie, subdued after a day in the office, slowly and peaceably recuperating in the concert hall as another group of workers toil in tuxedos for their comfort. The great symphonies of

Sibelius, with their romantic evocation of the landscape beyond the villa window, were seen as an offence against modern life, as were the comparable outrages of Nielsen, Vaughan Williams and Roy Harris – all escapist fantasies for the after-dinner hours of the bourgeoisie.

Yet composers continue to be drawn to the symphony, the concerto and the string quartet, and Reilly has uncovered and described for the reader much of this hidden treasure – hidden because those who create it believe that beauty and humanity are essential to the artistic enterprise, and that clever mathematics can never be a substitute for real musical form. Among symphonists who have called forth Reilly's praise several are all but unknown – including the Dane Vagn Holmboe, composer of 13 symphonies in a hectic idiom of their own, the Irishman John Kinsella and the American Stephen Albert. Indeed reading Reilly's gripping chapters, with YouTube on the screen, is both an education in itself and a source of shame to those like me, who have defended tonality all these years without realizing that it is a live tradition, constantly renewing itself in defiance of an academic orthodoxy that denies its right to exist.

One modern symphonist has commanded the affection of concert-going audiences throughout the contemporary world, and that is Dmitri Shostakovich, whose great, cloying and self-dramatizing works, with their no-holds-barred assault on the listener's emotions, both real and fake, have somehow defeated the critical outcry from the avant-garde. The special circumstances under which Shostakovich lived and worked, forced to address the people in officially sanctioned accents while covertly reaching out to his fellow sufferers from the regime of violence and lies, have silenced the scoffers and the kitsch-hunters. This is serious music for a serious audience in a serious world. It is gripping, eloquent and, in its demonic way, enjoyable, replete with melodies – some banal, and none exactly lovely, but melodies nevertheless. Shifting between mirthless animation and moping self-pity, the symphonies have achieved a popularity beyond any other modern instances of the form, notwithstanding their essentially uniform colour, aptly described by Robin Holloway as 'battleship grey'.[122]

Is it only the special and deplorable situation in which Shostakovich composed that explains his mysterious grandeur? Can we learn from him, and can we, in our pampered conditions, risk such a direct appeal to the audience? Reilly does not answer those questions; instead, in a learned and wide-ranging essay, he reflects on the desolation that haunts Shostakovich's works. 'If Shostakovich's symphonies are tombstones,' he writes, 'the 15 quartets are the flowers he lays on the graves.' Of the last quartet, composed of six uninterrupted adagios, Reilly draws a parallel with Haydn's *Seven Last Words of Christ on the Cross*, suggesting that, appearances to the contrary, Shostakovich, a professed unbeliever, was not a nihilist but a seeker after consolation, who believed that the spirit of song and dance will eventually banish despair. But Reilly admits that in the grotesqueries of the Fourth Symphony we confront torment, death, brutality, violence and drunken destruction with little respite and no redemption promised.

That period of history is over. And Americans never had to suffer it in any case. So how does the symphonic tradition fare in America? Reilly quotes Stephen Albert, who decisively rejected 12-tone serialism, with its implied premise that 'the past has no meaning. 'What was going on,' Albert wrote, 'was the massive denial of memory. No one can *remember* a 12-tone row. The very method obliterates memory's function in art.' Albert turned to Shostakovich for inspiration, and also to the earlier masters such as Sibelius and Stravinsky. Shostakovich was the initial inspiration also for another American symphonist, Steven Gerber, who gradually worked towards his own very American idiom with his *Spirituals for String Orchestra* and *Serenade Concertante*. And the good news to which Reilly constantly returns is that the younger generation is taking composers like Albert and Gerber seriously. This we discover in the violin concertos of

---

[122] *On Music*, pp. 297–300.

Jonathan Leshnoff and Jennifer Higdon, both works of beauty and both increasingly popular.

For Reilly the case of Albert's teacher, George Rochberg, is of the first importance. In 2016 I had the honour to deliver the annual lecture established in memory of Dr Lloyd Old at the City University of New York. The theme of the lectures, established by Dr Old's sister, Constance Old, is modern music and where it is going, and I had the benefit of a string quartet, provided by the Barry S. Brook Center for Music Research and Documentation, in order to illustrate my argument. I tried as best I could to rehearse what is at stake in the dispute between the classicists and the avant-garde, and then I handed it over to the audience to judge. The quartet played three pieces: the first movement from Tippett's fresh and energetic second string quartet, Webern's bagatelles for string quartet and the third movement of George Rochberg's sixth string quartet, which consists of variations on Pachelbel's canon in D.

The Webern produced pursed lips and furrowed brows, as the audience strove to match the terse stabs with which the instruments puncture the silence – a wonderful effect, of course, but one on the very edge of musical meaning. The Tippett, moving in a space of its own but never far from tonal harmony, seemed to produce no response from the audience at all. But when it came to the Rochberg, the majority were visibly moved, the members of the quartet playing with great emotion, completely at one with the work, as they were not really at one with either the Webern or the Tippett. I was back in the world of the classical concert, in which audience and musicians are united by an unseen web of sympathy, producing music together out of their shared and rapt attention.

As soon as the lecture ended, however, I found myself surrounded by keen graduate students from the Brook Center, telling me how absolutely awful the Rochberg movement is, how it is impossible to write like that and mean it, and how the piece should never be played. The contrast between the young musicians to whom the future of their art was being entrusted and the audience on which they will depend for their livelihood could not have been more striking. The break with tradition was clear. As for Tippett – yes, honest stuff as far it goes. But going round in circles in an enclosed English garden.

The argument goes on, riveting, vital and inconclusive. No one is more accomplished in defending the tonal tradition, or better informed about its real recent achievements, than Robert Reilly. His book should be on every serious music lover's shelves, and readers should consult it whenever, in a world of relentless and erudite noise, they are surprised by beauty, and wish to hunt down the criminal responsible.

17

The Culture of Pop

In writings that seethe with undigested venom, Adorno dismissed
the popular music of America as a 'fetishized' product of the 'culture
industry' – a collection of songs as musically insipid as they were morally and politically corrupting.[123] The ranting dismissal of everything
within earshot, which made no distinction between the voice-led
harmonies of Gershwin and the sloppy strumming of a Bluegrass
band, ought to have disqualified Adorno as a serious critic. But his
deft combination of fastidious disdain and *marxisant* diatribe struck
a chord with many American musicologists. In the wake of Adorno
it was a widespread view that, according to the highest authority –
namely, that of a real live German-educated Marxist – American
popular music is all rubbish, every single note of it. And then, of
course, came the inevitable reaction. Rather than dismiss everything
in the name of the Marxist utopia, why not accept everything, in
the name of the world as it is? Adorno's blanket dismissal of popular music is therefore indirectly responsible for the equally offensive
habit of regarding pop music as an art form on a par, from the critical
point of view, with the music of Bach, Brahms or Stravinsky. The step
from modernist dismissal to postmodernist endorsement turns out
to be so small that academic musicology has needed no real exertion
to achieve it.

---

[123] See Theodor W. Adorno, *The Culture Industry*, ed. J. M. Bernstein (London, 1991).

One conclusion to draw from this fragment of cultural history is that we should take the word 'popular' seriously – far more seriously than it was taken by Adorno. *Pace* Adorno and Horkheimer, the songs of the Great American Songbook[124] were not imposed upon the American people by an unscrupulous 'culture industry' eager to exploit the most degenerate aspects of popular taste. The musical language of the songbook arose 'by an invisible hand' from spontaneous music-making, with a large input from Afro-American music, both secular and religious. When that music later spread across the world it was not by an imperialist venture of a conquering civilization but by the same process whereby it arose – the spontaneous taste of ordinary people.

The cultural context of pop is not that of an 'industry' and its manufactured appetites: if the industry is there, it is as a response to those appetites and not the source of them. At the same time (and here Adorno has a point) this cultural context is unlike anything that has been documented in the work of anthropologists. Popular culture is not a system of moral or religious norms, does not find expression in customs and ceremonies, is not induced through rites of passage and is often enjoyed in solitude and without any essential reference to a community of initiates. Its very fluidity and openness enable it to flow over all traditional forms of social order and to break down the barriers between them. Through its music popular culture has become a globalizing force, creating adherents wherever people can reach into cyber-space and grab its products with a mouse.

Pop music makes room for technical virtuosity, like the guitar-playing of Jimi Hendrix, for melodic invention (as in the riffs of Metallica), for the occasional harmonic *trouvaille*, as in the opening sequence of AC/DC's 'Highway to Hell', and often imaginative accompanying figures, as in 'Baba O'Reilly', by The Who. Like music in our classical tradition, and like jazz, ragtime, blues and folk, it has

[124] I use this phrase as shorthand for the music centred on the 32-bar strophic song with jazz-based harmony, from the songs composed by Jerome Kern and George Gershwin down to those sung by Barbra Streisand and Mel Tormé. See the poignant articles devoted to 'The Great American Songbook' by Terry Teachout, in *Commentary* magazine, from summer 1999 to 2002.

rhythm, harmony and tone colour – even melody (though not much of it). However – and this, I think, is what principally distinguishes pop from its jazz-based and folk-based predecessors – these seem to be generated from a point *outside the music.*

This is particularly evident in the case of rhythm, generated by percussive sounds that may have little or no relation to anything else that is happening. Often the music itself draws attention to this – opening with some mesmeric sound effect or cheesy crooning, and then bringing in the drum kit with a barrage of amplified noise, as though a gang that had been waiting quietly on the staircase were suddenly to break down the door. The device is frequently used by the group Oasis – in 'My Big Mouth', for example. The ingress of external rhythms which you hear in the opening bars of that piece can be usefully contrasted with an example from an earlier period – 'Lay Down Sally', by Eric Clapton – in which the guitarist (Clapton himself) generates rhythm from an accompanying figure, which precedes the statement of the principal melody. The melodic outline of this figure distributes beat and accent over the bar-line, and does so from the figure's own internal movement. When bass and drum enter, they do not force on to the music any rhythm that is alien to it, but pick up the existing accent. Beat, as deployed in contemporary pop, is often the antithesis of rhythm, corresponding not to any internal phrase structure of the music but to the stomping and head-shaking of the performers – as in the antics of Pete Townshend or Johnny Rotten.

In an unusually insightful study of the cultural context of Rock, the poet Ruth Padel argues that this music is about 'being a man': it is a venture into the 'vast wishing well of masculinity', even when sung by women to words and music of their own. And she calls her book *I Am a Man*, by way of emphasizing the point. Those words come from a song by Muddy Waters – surely the real founder of Rock, the one who first released this wild child from the boarded tenements of downtown America.[125] And in Muddy Waters's day rhythm was

---

[125] Ruth Padel, *I Am a Man: Sex, Gods and Rock 'n' Roll* (London, 2000). The line from Muddy Waters is prophetic of the tradition that he founded: 'I am a man; I am a rolling stone.'

rhythm, not beat. The Rock idioms of Elvis, Chuck Berry and the Beatles are rhythmically articulate, in the manner of the dance music that they displaced. It is only much later, in the wake of the Rolling Stones, that beat took over, and with it a new species of masculine anguish.

Pop melodies are made up, as a rule, from curt modal or diatonic phrases, with little internal variation or prolongation, and avoiding foreign keys. Of course, things were not always so, and are not universally so even now. The melodies of the Beatles, for example, were often highly adventurous, with internal rhyming and modulations into neighbouring keys, as in 'She Loves You'. But the Beatles belong to another era, and their once insolent songs sound quaint and innocent beside Oasis, Nirvana or The Verve. In the place of melody it is quite normal to hear a kind of ritualized shouting on one note, with small fluctuations of pitch at the chorus, as in AC/DC's 'Highway to Hell' and 'Thunderstruck', or 'No Child of Mine' by Guns N' Roses.

Even when this kind of pop aims to be lyrical, melody may be synthesized from standardized phrases, which could be rearranged in any order without losing the effect. It is not that pop is always tuneless: rather that the tune, when delivered, frequently has a 'borrowed' character. Consider the hit by Mary J. Blige, 'Get to Know You Better'. Here the melody is assembled from a small set of notes, arranged around the flat lyrics, and without internal movement. The effect is emphasized by the yukky thirteenth chords and droopy vamping which open the piece, with a sound that suggests someone trying carefully to puke into a wine glass. This kind of logogenic melody[126] is without clear phrase structure, and avoids cadences and harmonic rhymes. It exists simply to pin the words to the underlying beat, thereby generating a lyrical atmosphere without being truly lyrical. It is an *ersatz* melody, which could not survive outside the 'processing' inflicted on the song.

---

[126] For the distinction between logogenic, harmonegenic and orchegenic melodies see 'When is a Tune?', Part 1, Chapter 1, above.

(In fairness it should be said that in other songs – such as 'Be Without You' – Mary J. Blige recaptures some of the melodious sentimentality of the American Songbook, driving the accompaniment into the background, where it belongs. But such songs belong to another and older tendency, and one that is continuous with the domestic feelings and ordinary griefs of people who know they must one day grow up.)

The externalization of harmony comes about by treating the harmonic dimension of music purely vertically, as a sequence of chords with no voice-leading between the parts – a feature noticed and deplored by Adorno, in his comments on the chord notations for strummed guitar.[127] The chords are taken from the shelf and laid out in a sequence. Whether sounded in distorted form on the electric guitar or churned out of a keyboard and synthesizer, these chords are often lifeless relics of harmony, which do not move but merely replace each other, since none of their notes bears any melodic relation to its successor. A good illustration of this is the piece which the October 1997 issue of *Guitarist* describes as a modern classic: 'In Bloom', from Nirvana's second album, in which the chords succeed each other in exactly the arrangement that is implied by the shift of the hand along the frets of the guitar, and in which the illogical sequence is led by none of the voices – not even the bass.

It is in the nature of strumming that it obscures voice-leading, being largely indifferent to the distinction between a chord and its inversion. The same issue of *Guitarist* tells you how to hit a C major seventh: easy – you just stop the A string on C and the D string on E and strum the lot! But the result is a first inversion of the chord with three Es in it and only one C – a monster that topples on to its neighbour as soon as it is sounded. In fact, out of context, it is not a C major seventh at all, but the chord of E minor with added minor sixth: acoustically identical but musically as different as can be. It is a significant fact about the contemporary pop idiom that the distinction between these two harmonies may pass unnoticed.

[127] Adorno, *The Culture Industry*, p. 51.

To some extent the marginalizing of subsidiary voices is a legacy of jazz notation and the use of lead sheets, which specify only the melodic line and the chord sequence below it. Unlike the traditional figured bass, the lead sheet only rarely specifies intervals from the bass-line, relying on the instincts of the musician to choose between the various inversions. Those instincts are integral to the successful performance of jazz, and it is the loss of them that has led to the all-encumbering stodginess of pop harmony.

Recent pop has come in for criticism on account of its lyrics, which often dwell on violence, sex and rebellion in ways that romanticize the kind of conduct of which fathers used to disapprove, in the days when disapproval was permitted and fathers stayed around long enough to exercise it. (Consider 'Anarchy', by the Sex Pistols, 'Breaking the Law', by Judas Priest, the video of which is a dramatized encomium of crime, or The Prodigy in 'Slap My Bitch Up'.) But these criticisms do not, I think, get to the heart of the matter. Even if every pop song consisted of a setting of Christ's beatitudes (and there have been born-again groups in America – 16 Horsepower, for example – that have specialized in such things), it would make little or no difference to the effect, which is communicated through the notes, regardless of what is sung to them. The only thing that is really wrong with the usual lyrics is what is really right about them – namely, that they successfully capture what the music means. And this identity of meaning is invariably emphasized by the video.

In fact the externality of the movement is precisely what suits the music for its social role. The kind of music that I am describing might be called 'music from elsewhere'. It is music without a foreground. However loudly it is sounded, it lies in the background, something to be overheard, as though supporting an unseen music video. It is the background to a drama, and that drama consists in the 'real presence' of the singer. Externalization therefore represents something deeper and more tribal than the 'wishing well of masculinity' described by Ruth Padel.

The relation between the performer and the fan begins in a musical experience but goes far beyond any exercise in taste. Like the football team, the pop group recruits its fans, and the CD often contains instructions as to where to write for further information, with a help line and support service, in the form of posters, diary items and bulletins, like the circulars and briefings offered to its congregation by an activist church. The group offers membership. It is therefore imperative for the fans – or at least for a certain kind of fan – to choose *their* group, and to exalt it above any rivals. The choice is, in the end, arbitrary – or, at least, not guided by any criterion of musical merit. But it is a choice that must be made. (This aspect of the sociology of popular music has been well documented by Simon Frith, who notes the ease with which the fan receives any insult to his group as an insult to himself.[128])

The phenomenon can be most interestingly witnessed in the cult of Nirvana, the grunge musicians whose lead guitarist, Kurt Cobain, specialized in a systematic negation of life, supposedly captured in the Buddhist concept which the group adopted as its name. When Cobain committed suicide, thousands of young people entered a state of crisis, comparable to the crisis that attends the deaths of monarchs or religious leaders. Many of the fans needed intense and prolonged counselling; not a few committed suicide themselves. A whole tribe entered a state of wandering and mourning, unable to believe that their totem had died. In natural totemic societies it is normal for the totem to die – but since the totem is not, in these societies, an individual but a species, incarnate in the sacrificial victim but also surviving it, the death of the totem is also a rebirth, in which the life of the community is renewed.[129] The fan is not so lucky, since his emotions focus on a real and vulnerable human being. Death, in these circumstances, is a major social catastrophe.

---

[128] S. Frith, 'Towards an Aesthetic of Popular Music', in Richard Leppert and Susan McClary, eds, *Music and Society: The Politics of Composition, Performance and Reception* (Cambridge, 1987).
[129] The discussion of totemism and its meaning has moved on since Sir James Frazer's *Totem and Exogamy* (London, 1910) and Freud's contentious *Totem and Taboo* (Berlin, 1913). More important in current thinking is the element of animal sacrifice, as discussed by Walter Burkert, *Homo Necans* (Oxford, 1972), and René Girard, *Violence and the Sacred* (Paris, 1972). This is the aspect represented by the Nirvana cult.

The external movement of modern pop connects with an important fact of modern life. Modern adolescents find themselves in a
world that has been set in motion; they are beset by noise, by external
pressures and by forces that they cannot control. The pop star is displayed in the same condition, high up on electric wires, the currents
of modern life zinging through him, but miraculously unharmed. He
is the guarantee of safety, the living symbol that you can live like this
for ever. His death or decay is simply inconceivable, like the death
of Elvis.[130] To die, after all, you must first pass through the long sad
corridor of adulthood: and that corridor is one on which the music
closes a door.

Pop songs are not improvised as jazz is improvised, and do not
as a rule owe their appeal to the kind of spectacular musicianship
that we witness in Art Tatum, Charlie Parker or Thelonious Monk.
They are meticulously put together, often by artificial means, so as to
be indelibly stamped with the trademark of the group. Lead singers
project *themselves* and not the melody, emphasizing their particular
tone, sentiment and gesture. The melodic paucity is partly explained
by this. By subtracting the melody, or reducing it to stock phrases
that can be reapplied in any context, the singer draws attention to the
song's one distinguishing feature, namely himself. The singer stands
revealed exactly where the music should be. (Contrast here the
American Songbook, in which singers are the servants of the music,
hiding behind the notes that they produce.)

The harmony may be surrendered to a process of distortion,
involving much mixing and editing. It is therefore often impossible
to reproduce it by any means normally available. The music is simultaneously ephemeralized and eternally transfixed. It is an unrepeat-
able moment in the life of the great machine, which, by means of the
machine, can be repeated for ever. It is almost impossible to sing for
yourself the tunes and words of the more aggressive kind of Rock,
such as the 'songs' of AC/DC or the barked out verses of metal groups
like Meshuggah – your performance in the shower will be a kind of

---

[130] See Grail Marcus, *Dead Elvis* (New York, 1991).

subdued shouting. Even if with the comparative melodious Indie idiom, actually to *perform* the music you must impersonate the idol during Karaoke Night at the local, when you have the benefit of full instrumental backing, amplification and audience, and can briefly fit yourself into the groove from which the sacred presence has been lifted. This intense and cathartic experience once over, you must step down from the stage and reassume the burden of silence.

In effect, we witness a reversal of the old order of performance. Instead of the performer being the means to present the music, which exists independently in the tradition of song, the music has become the means to present the performer. The music is part of the process whereby a human individual or group is iconized. In consequence it has a tendency to lose musical character. For music, properly constructed, has a life of its own, and is always more interesting than the person who performs it. Much as we may love Louis Armstrong, Ella Fitzgerald or Cole Porter, we love them for their music – not their music for them. And this is music we can perform for ourselves.

In much recent pop music, therefore, singers, groups or lead performers are not constrained by musical standards. But they are constrained by their totemic role. Often they refuse to answer to a normal human name, since to do so would compromise their totemic status. R.E.M., Nirvana, The Who, AC/DC, U2 are like the species names assumed by tribal groups, icons of the membership that they promise.

The idolization of the pop star is assisted by the music video. The video sublimates the star, recycles him as image, more effectively than any painted icon of a saint. It is expressly designed for home consumption, and brings the sacred presence into the living room. And it completes the demotion of music, which now becomes background, with the pop star, transfigured into the divine status of the TV advert, occupying the foreground. The idol has entered the condition familiar from the other forms of youth art. Like Damien Hirst and 'YBA', he has become the advert that advertises itself. To give credit to Adorno, he presciently understood, in the very earliest days of the pop phenomenon, that the destiny of popular music and that of advertising would henceforth be entwined.

The societies studied by the Victorian anthropologists were organic communities, bound by kinship, which sustained themselves through myths and rituals devoted to the idea of the tribe. In such communities, the dead and the unborn were present among the living. Rituals, ceremonies, gods and stories were the private property of the tribe, designed to enhance and fortify the experience of membership. Birth, marriage and death were collective and not merely individual experiences, while the crucial process of acculturation – the transition from raw human material to a responsible adult member of the community – was marked by rites of passage, trials and ordeals, through which the adolescent cast off his childish wilfulness and took on the task of social reproduction.[131]

In the society of the Victorians themselves there existed a common store of myths, rituals and ceremonies which created a comparable sense of the divine origin of society and its absolute right to sacrifice. Adolescents were instructed in the ancestral religion, and made to respect its rites. Crucial human experiences such as birth, marriage and death were still collective experiences, in which individuals passed from one state of membership to another. Erotic feelings were regarded as the preparations for marriage. They were duly sublimated – which means, not idealized only, but also *ordealized*, hemmed in by interdictions. Marriage was (as it has always been) the principal instrument of social reproduction. But all the institutions of society played their part, and all contained their ceremonies of initiation. The transition from adolescent to adult was marked by complex forms of induction, which reinforced the view that all stages of existence prior to the adult state were but preparations for it. In exploring primitive societies, the Victorians were delighted to discover simpler and more transparent versions of an experience which lay at the heart of their own civilization – the experience of membership, enhanced by a common religion, and by the rites

[131] See Arnold van Gennep, *Les Rites de passage* (Paris, 1901).

of passage which led to the full adult state, in which the burden of social reproduction is assumed.

None of that is true of modern adolescents, who have neither the tribal nor the modern urban experience of membership. They exist in a world protected from external and internal threat, and are therefore rescued from the elementary experiences – in particular the experience of war – which renew the bond of social member-ship. Sex has broken free from the process of social reproduction, to become readily available in all its forms, as an intrinsically adoles-cent experience. The rite of passage from the virgin to the married state has disappeared, and with it the 'lyrical' experience of sex, as a yearning for another and higher state of membership, to which the hard-won consent of society is a necessary precondition. All other rites of passage have similarly withered away, since no social institu-tion demands them – or, if it does demand them, it will be avoided as judgemental, hierarchical or in some way oppressive. The result is an adolescent community that suffers from an accumulating deficit in the experience of membership, while resolutely turning its back on the adult world – the world in which the burden of social reproduc-tion must be finally assumed.

At the same time, modern adolescents have money to spend, and they spend it on entertaining themselves, so as to enjoy the condition of adolescence and to make it into something permanent. From this arise the new forms of entertainment, through which youth isolates itself from the world of adults, and by means of which the refusal of youth to assume the ancestral burden is recast as a kind of virtue.

Now human beings, whatever their condition, are social animals, and can live with themselves only if they also live with others. There is implanted in us the need to join things, to be a part of some larger and justifying enterprise, which will ennoble our small endeavours and protect us from the sense that we are ultimately alone. The deficit of membership must therefore be made good, but in another way – without the rite of passage to a higher or more responsible condition. Hence new forms of 'joining in' arise. Unlike armies, schools, scout troops, churches and charities, these new forms of joining in need not involve participation – unless of a rough and undemanding kind that imposes no discipline on those who opt for them. They centre on spectacles rather than activities.

Hence the emergence of professional sport as a central drama in popular culture. Football, for example, has lost its original character as a form of recreation and become instead a spectacle, through which the fans rehearse their social identity and achieve a kind of substitute form of membership, not as active participants in a real community but as passive respondents to the virtual community of fans. The fan is, in some sense, a part of the group, in just the way that the football supporter is a part of his team, bound to it by a mystical bond of membership.

Of course, the old tribal feelings are there just below the surface, waiting to be activated, and erupting every now and then with their usual tributes to the god of war. In a sense, the membership offered to the fan – in which a mesmerized passivity neutralizes the desire for action – is the greatest safeguard we have that modern societies will not fragment into tribal sub-groups. And we should therefore be grateful for professional football, and for all the other ways in which an icon of membership is offered to those who might otherwise chase after some adolescent version of the real thing. For when tribal groups emerge in modern conditions, they take the form of teenage gangs, whose initiation ceremonies forbid the transition to the adult world and are designed to arrest their members in a stage of rebellion. The first concern of such a gang is to establish a right to territory, by violently suppressing all rival claims – and hence the cult of graffiti, which deny the reality of public space and erase all claims to ownership save those announced by the gang.

The teenage gang is a natural response to a world in which the rites of passage into adulthood are no longer offered or respected. I do not say that such a world is a healthy one. But it is our world, and we have to make the best of it. Pop culture is an attempt to make the best of it – to make oneself at home in a world that is not, in any real sense, a home, since it has ceased to dedicate itself, as a home must dedicate itself, to the task of social reproduction. Home, after all, is the place where parents are. The world displayed in the culture of youth is a world from which the parents have absconded – as these days they generally do.[132] This culture aims to present youth as the goal and fulfilment of human life, rather than a transitional phase that must be cast off as an impediment once the business of social reproduction calls. It promotes experiences that can be obtained without undertaking the burdens of responsibility, work, child-rearing and marriage. When the adult world is mentioned, it is in order to pour scorn on it as a delusive fiction or a source of tyrannical constraints.

Now there is an academic industry devoted to representing youth culture in general, and pop in particular, as genuinely subversive, a response to oppression, a voice through which freedom, life and revolutionary fervour cry from the catacombs of bourgeois culture.[133] If the authorities of 'media studies' and 'cultural studies' are to be believed, youth finds itself hemmed in at every point by an 'official culture' dedicated to denying the validity of its experience. On this view the profane and anarchic messages of pop are a sign of uncontaminated virtue – gestures of protest against a life-denying social order.

In fact, however, the culture of youth is the official culture of Western democracies. Every public space is filled by pop, politicians of all persuasions seek endorsement from those who produce and market it, and dissidents who seek the few pockets of silence are an endangered species. The culture of youth seeks and finds legitimacy with the very transgressive gestures that deny there is any such thing. Hence groups who sing of their sufferings under the oppressive yoke of the grown-up society become millionaires, are fêted by the establishment and retire to country houses with their bodyguards.

In any age, the exuberance of youth finds expression in loud noise and violent dancing: Plato's celebrated attack on the corybants, and

---

[132] In the 1980s a group of concerned parents set up a 'Parents' Music Resource Center' in California, with the aim of censoring the anti-parent messages contained in pop lyrics. Frank Zappa spearheaded a campaign to counteract the Center's influence.

[133] See especially George Lipsitz, *Dangerous Crossroads: Popular Music, Postmodernism and the Poetics of Place* (London, 1994).

his desire to include only the stately and dignified modes in his ideal republic, testify to the suspicion with which the music of youth has always been regarded. But there has gradually emerged in our time a wholly new kind of music, serving a wholly new kind of dance, which serves to isolate youth in a world of its own and to neutralize the need for social continuity.

One significant result of this is that pop music has, to a great extent, lost the ability to develop. It remains fixed for ever in the stage of adolescent solidarity, unable to evolve, stylistically or philosophically, to a more adult form of itself. When ageing pop stars return to the scene, it is to perform, like the Rolling Stones, the songs for which they were famous when young. If they develop, then it is often by leaving the pop scene altogether and trying their hand, like Paul McCartney, at the old classical forms. Indeed, it is the urge to develop which lifts people, as a rule, out of the world of Rock on to the plateau where old and young still meet, mixing pop and classical in the manner of Michael Nyman or returning to the Songbook and the acoustic guitar, like Eric Clapton in 'Tears in Heaven'. In other words, they develop by *escaping* from Rock. To remain in that idiom is to remain in adolescence. Seriously talented musicians, such as the late Jimi Hendrix or Metallica, constantly increase their technical competence, without ever moving into new emotional or stylistic regions. And the Rock scene remains today what it has been for the past 20 years – a wilderness of repetition, in which nothing new is harvested because nothing new is sown.

BIBLIOGRAPHY

Abels, Birfit, ed., *Embracing Restlessness: Cultural Musicology*, Hildesheim, 2017

Adorno, Theodor, *The Philosophy of Modern Music*, tr. A. G. Mitchell and W. V. Bloomster, New York, 1973

Adorno, Theodor, *An Introduction to the Philosophy of Music*, tr. E. B. Ashton, New York, 1976

Adorno, Theodor, *The Culture Industry*, ed. J. M. Bernstein, London, 1991

Adorno, Theodor, 'The Musical Fetish and the Regression of Listening', in Andrew Arato and Eike Gephardt, eds, *The Essential Frankfurt School Reader*, New York, 1997

Adorno, Theodor, *In Search of Wagner*, tr. Rodney Livingstone, London, 2004

Adorno, Theodor, *Night Music: Essays in Music 1928-1962*, ed. Rolf Tiedermann, tr. Wieland Hoban, London and New York, 2009

Bloch, Ernst, *Essays on the Philosophy of Music*, tr. P. Palmer, intro. D. Drew, Cambridge, 1985

Burkert, Walter, *Homo necans*, Oxford, 1972

Collingwood, R. G., *The Principles of Art*, Oxford, 1938

Cross, Ian, 'Music, Cognition, Culture and Evolution', in Isabelle Peretz and Robert Zatorre, eds, *The Cognitive Neuroscience of Music*, Oxford, 2003

Currie, Gregory, *Arts and Minds*, Oxford, 2004

Dahlhaus, Carl, *The Idea of Absolute Music*, tr. Roger Lustig, Chicago, 1989

Danto, Arthur, 'The End of Art: A Philosophical Defense', *History and Theory*, vol. 37 no. 4, 1998, pp. 127–43

Deutsch, D., and Feroe, J., 'The Internal Representation of Pitch Sequences in Tonal Music', *Psychological Review*, vol. 88, 1981, pp. 503–22.

Diderot, Denis, *Le neveu de Rameau*, published in German 1805, in French in 1821, now best consulted in one or other Internet version

Dodds, E. R. *The Greeks and the Irrational*, Cambridge, 1951

Duteurtre, Benoît, *Requiem pour une avant-garde*, Paris, 1995

Eisler, Hanns, 'Musik und Politik', in *Schriften 1924–1948*, Leipzig, 1973

Feuerbach, Ludwig, *Principles of the Philosophy of the Future [1843]*, tr. Zawar Hanfi, London, 1972

Fodor, Jerry, *The Modularity of Mind*, Cambridge, MA, 1983

Forte, Allen, *The Structure of Atonal Music*, Oxford, 1973

Frazer, Sir James, *Totem and Exogamy*, London, 1910

Freud, Sigmund, *Totem and Taboo*, London, 1918

Frith, Simon, 'Towards an Aesthetic of Popular Music', in Richard Leppert and Susan McClary, eds, *Music and Society: The Politics of Composition, Performance and Reception*, Cambridge, 1987

Gelfand, S. A., *Hearing: An Introduction to Psychological and Physiological Acoustics*, 3rd edn, New York, 1998

Girard, René, *La Violence et le sacré*, Paris, 1972

Girard, René, *Des Choses cachées depuis la fondation du monde*, Paris, 1978

Gombrich, Ernst, *Art and Illusion*, London, 1960

Goodman, Nelson, *Languages of Art: An Approach to a Theory of Symbols*, Oxford, 1969

Gustin, Molly, *Tonality*, New York, 1969

Hanslick, Eduard, *On the Beautiful in Music*, tr. and ed. G. Payzant, Indianapolis, 1986

Hegel, G. W. F., *Aesthetics: Lectures on Fine Art*, tr. Sir Malcolm Knox, 2 vols, Oxford, 1975

Hegel, G. W. F. *The Phenomenology of Spirit*, tr. A. V. Miller, Oxford, 1977

Hodges, Wilfrid, 'The Geometry of Music', in John Fauvel, Raymond Flood and Robin Wilson, eds, *Music and Mathematics: From Pythagoras to Fractals*, Oxford, 2003

Holloway, Robin, *On Music: Essays and Diversions, 1963–2003*, Brinkworth, 2003

Hueffer, Francis, *Richard Wagner and the Music of the Future*, London, 1874

Hume, David, *A Treatise of Human Nature*, 1738, ed. L. A. Selby-Bigge, Oxford, 1896

Kant, Immanuel, *The Critique of Pure Reason*, tr. Norman Kemp-Smith, London, 1958

Kassabian, Anahid, *Ubiquitous Listening: Affect, Attention and Distributed Subjectivity*, Berkeley, CA, 2015

Kitcher, Philip, *Deaths in Venice: The Cases of Gustav von Aschenbach*, New York, 2013

Kivy, Peter, *The Corded Shell: Reflections on Musical Expression*, Princeton 1980

Köhler, Joachim, *Nietzsche and Wagner: A Lesson in Subjugation*, tr. Ronald Taylor, New Haven, CT, 1998

Langer, Susanne, *Feeling and Form*, New York, 1953

Lanza, Joseph, *Elevator Music*, New York, 1995

Lerdahl, Fred, and Jackendoff, Ray, *A Generative Theory of Tonal Music*, Cambridge, MA, 1983

Lerdahl, Fred, 'Cognitive Constraints on Compositional Systems', in Sloboda, *Generative Processes in Music*

Lerdahl, Fred, *Tonal Pitch Space*, Oxford, 2001

Levinas, Emmanuel, *Humanism of the Other*, tr. Nidra Poller, Chicago, 2003

Liébert, Georges, *Nietzsche and Music*, tr. David Pellauer and Graham Parkes, Chicago, 2004

Lipsitz, George, *Dangerous Crossroads: Popular Music, Postmodernism and the Politics of Place*, London, 1994

Longuet-Higgins, Christopher, *Mental Processes: Studies in Cognitive Science*, Cambridge, MA, 1987

Marcus, Grail, *Dead Elvis*, New York, 1991

Matthews, David, 'The Flaying of Marsyas', *Salisbury Review*, vol. 12, no. 3, March 1994, pp. 12–14

Meyer, Leonard B., *Emotion and Meaning in Music*, Chicago, 1956

Miller, Geoffrey, 'Evolution of Human Music through Sexual Selection', in Nils L. Wallin, Björn Merker and Steven Brown, eds, *The Origins of Music*, Cambridge, MA, 2000

Narmour, Eugene, *The Analysis and Cognition of Basic Melodic Structures*, Chicago, 1990

Nietzsche, Friedrich, *The Portable Nietzsche*, ed. Walter Kaufmann, New York, 1954

Nietzsche, Friedrich, *The Birth of Tragedy* and *The Case of Wagner*, tr. Walter Kaufmann, New York, 1967

Nordau, Max, *Degeneration*, London, 1895

Nussbaum, Charles, *The Musical Representation*, Cambridge, MA, 2007

Otto, Rudolf, *The Idea of the Holy*, Oxford, 1923

Padel, Ruth, *I Am a Man: Sex, Gods and Rock 'n' Roll*, London, 2000

Patel, Aniruddh D., *Music, Language and the Brain*, Oxford, 2008

Pinker, Steven, *How the Mind Works*, New York, 1997

Raffman, Diana, *Language, Music and Mind*, Cambridge, MA, 1993

Rameau, Jean-Philippe, *A Treatise on Harmony*, tr. Philip Gossett, Mineola, NY, 1971

Reilly, Robert R., *Surprised by Beauty: A Listener's Guide to the Recovery of Modern Music*, San Francisco, 2017

Riemann, Hugo, *Harmony Simplified, or the Theory of the Tonal Functions of Chords*, London and New York, 1893

Riemann, Hugo, *System der musikalischen Rhythmik und Metrik*, Leipzig, 1903

Ross, Alex, *The Rest is Noise: Listening to the Twentieth Century*, New York, 2007

Rousseau, Jean-Jacques, *A Complete Dictionary of Music*, London, 1779

Ruskin, John, 'Fiction, Fair and Foul', in *Works.*, ed. E. T. Cook and A. Wedderburn, London, 1909

Schelling, Friedrich Wilhelm Joseph von, *Schriften zur Philosophie der Kunst und zur Freiheitslehre* [1802/3], in *Schellings sämmtliche Werke*, ed. Karl Friedrich August Schelling, 14 vols, Stuttgart, 1856–61

Schenker, Heinrich, *Free Composition*, tr. Ernst Oster, London, 1979

Schoenberg, Arnold, *Harmonielehre*, 3rd edn, Vienna, 1922

Schoenberg, Arnold, *Style and Idea: Selected Writings of Arnold Schoenberg*, ed. Leonard Stein, tr. Leo Black, London, 1975

Schopenhauer, Arthur, *The World as Will and Representation*, tr. E. F. J. Payne, Indian Hills, 1958

Schuller, Gunther, *Early Jazz: Its Roots and Musical Development*, Oxford, 1968

Scruton, Roger, *Art and Imagination*, London, 1974

Scruton, Roger, *Perictione in Colophon*, South Bend, 2002

Scruton, Roger, *The Aesthetics of Music*, Oxford, 1997

Scruton, Roger, Review of Andy Hamilton: *Aesthetics and Music*, in *Mind*, vol. 117, 2008

Scruton, Roger, *Understanding Music: Philosophy and Interpretation*, London, 2009

Scruton, Roger, *The Face of God*, London, 2012

Scruton, Roger, *The Soul of the World*, Princeton, 2014

Searle, John R., *Speech Acts: An Essay in the Philosophy of Language*, Cambridge, 1969

Searle, John R., *Intentionality: An Essay in the Philosophy of Mind*, Cambridge, 1983

Sellars, Wilfrid, *Science, Perception and Reality*, Austin, TX, 1963

Siegel, Linda, 'Wackenroder's Musical Essays in "Phantasien über die Kunst"', *Journal of Aesthetics and Art Criticism*, vol. 30, 1972, pp. 351–8

Sloboda, John A., ed., *Generative Processes in Music*, Oxford, 1988

Stone-Davis, Férdia, 'Music and Liminality: Becoming Sensitized', in Abels, *Embracing Restlessness*

Tallis, Raymond, *Summers of Discontent: The Purposes of the Arts Today*, London, 2014

Teachout, Terry, 'The Great American Songbook', *Commentary*, summer 1999–spring 2002

Temperley, David, *The Cognition of Basic Musical Structures*, Cambridge, MA, 2001

Temperley, David, *Music and Probability*, Cambridge, MA, 2007

Tymoczko, Dmitri, *A Geometry of Music: Harmony and Counterpoint in the Extended Common Practice*, Oxford, 2011

Valberg, J. J., *Dream, Death and the Self*, Princeton, 2007

van Gennep, Arnold, *Les Rites de Passage*, Paris, 1901

Wagner, Richard, *The Artwork of the Future*, 1849, tr. William Ashton Ellis, London, 1895

Wittgenstein, Ludwig, *Philosophical Investigations*, ed. and tr. Elizabeth Anscombe et al., Oxford, 1952

Wittgenstein, Ludwig, *The Blue and Brown Books*, Oxford, 1958

Young, Julian, *Nietzsche's Philosophy of Art*, Cambridge, 1992

ACKNOWLEDGEMENTS

Chapter 2. An earlier version of this chapter appeared in *Philosophy*, vol. 75, October 2014, pp. 231–247.

Chapter 4. This is a revised version of an essay of the same title published in Férdia J. Stone-Davis, ed., *Music and Transcendence*, Farnham, Ashgate, 2015.

Chapter 6. An earlier version of this chapter appeared in Nicholas Boyle, Christoph Jamme and Ian Cooper, eds., *The Impact of Idealism: The Legacy of Post-Kantian German Thought*, vol. III, Aesthetics and Literature, Cambridge, Cambridge University Press, 2013.

Chapter 10. An earlier version of this chapter was published in Thomas Hyde, ed., *David Matthews: Essays, Tributes and Criticism*, London, Plumbago Press, 2013.

Chapter 11. An earlier version of this chapter was published in an edition of the Spanish journal *Teorema* from 2016, edited by Luis Valdes-Villanueva, and devoted to Philip Kitcher's book *Deaths in Venice*.

Chapter 15. This chapter first appeared in Daniel Came, ed., *Nietzsche on Art and Life*, Oxford, Oxford University Press, 2014.

Chapter 16. This chapter is adapted from a lecture delivered at the Donaueschingen Musiktage in 2016.

Chapter 17. This chapter began life as the Lesley Stephen Memorial Lecture in the University of Cambridge, 1997.

INDEX

A NOTE ON THE AUTHOR

Roger Scruton has written widely on the philosophy of music. His collection of essays, *Understanding Music*, was published by Bloomsbury in 2009, and his seminal treatise, *The Aesthetics of Music*, was published in 1997 by Oxford University Press. His acclaimed novel *The Disappeared*, which tells (among other things) of the fortunes and misfortunes of a Heavy Metal fan, was issued by Bloomsbury Reader in 2015. His opera *Violet* was premiered by the Guildhall School of Music in 2005. He currently teaches for the Humanities Research Institute of the University of Buckingham.

A NOTE ON THE TYPE

The text of this book is set in Minion, a digital typeface designed by Robert Slimbach in 1990 for Adobe Systems. The name comes from the traditional naming system for type sizes, in which minion is between nonpareil and brevier. It is inspired by late Renaissance-era type.